Ten Thousand Missouri Taxpayers

Sherida K. Eddlemon

Heritage Books, Inc.

Copyright 1996 by Sherida K. Eddlemon

Other Heritage Books from Sherida K. Eddlemon:

Missouri Genealogical Records and Abstracts, Volumes 1-5
Genealogical Abstracts from Tennessee Newspapers, Volumes 1-3
Callaway County, Missouri Marriage Records, 1821-1871
Dickson County, Tennessee Marriage Records, 1817-1879
Lewis County, Missouri Index to Circuit Court Records, Vols 1 and 2, 1833-1851
Morgan County, Missouri, Marriage Records 1833-1893
Ralls County, Missouri, Settlement Records 1832-1853
Records of Randolph County, Missouri 1833-1964
Missouri Genealogical Gleanings, 1840 and Beyond, Volumes 1 and 2
Genealogical Abstracts of the Cumberland Presbyterian Church, Vol. 1
Genealogical Abstracts from Missouri Church Records, Vol. 1
Missouri Birth and Death Records, Vol. 1

Published 1996 by HERITAGE BOOKS, INC.
1540E Pointer Ridge Place, Bowie, Maryland 20716
1-800-398-7709

ISBN 0-7884-0518-7

A Complete Catalog Listing Hundreds of Titles
On History, Genealogy, and Americana
Available Free Upon Request

PREFACE

Tax records can help fill the census gap. They can put an ancestor in a geographic location and time reference point.

Using tax records to their fullest extent can be time consuming, but worth the effort. Originals of the tax records can be found at the Missouri State Archives either in the county records or in the Capitol Fire Documents. In addition to personal property and real estate, individuals had to pay fees to have deeds recorded, purchase business licenses, and even to have writs and marriages filed. Most of these recorded additional fees only survive at the state level. Unfortunately the Capitol fire of 1911 destroyed most of those records.

Good luck in your search for your ancestor. Hopefully he is listed within these pages.

ACKNOWLEDGMENT

I appreciate the continued encouragement of my parents, Amelia and P. Nelson Eddlemon.

Dedication

This book is dedicated to the memory of my elusive French ancestor, Achilles Godin (Gaudin), who died between 1812 and 1818. He left his widow, Maugerite James, and children living near the mouth of the Arkansas River and the Mississippi several miles below Arkansas Post; but not a footstep to show whence he came.

DATES TO REMEMBER

1821	Missouri became the 24th state.
1835	Samuel K. Clemens or Mark Twain was born.
1837	Missouri gained six northwestern counties with the Platte Purchase.
1846	Mexican War
1848	California Gold Rush
1849	St. Louis Cholera Epidemic
1854	Kansas Territory was created.
1855	So many Missourians moved to Kansas that it was voted in as a slave state.
1857	Dred Scott Decision
1858	Colorado Gold Rush
1858	Butterfield Stage Line ran from St. Louis, MO to San Francisco, CA.
1860 - 1861	Pony Express mailrun from St. Joseph, MO to Sacramento, CA.
1863	Some State registration of births and deaths began, but very scattered.
1861 - 1865	Civil War
1865	New Missouri constitution was created with a "Test Oath" clause denying southern sympathizers the right to vote.
1865	Wm. C. Quantrill, guerilla raider, was killed.
1870	Great Mississippi steamboat race between the "Robert E. Lee" and the "Natchez" from St. Louis to New Orleans.
1870 - 1872	Missouri-Kansas-Texas Railroad in operation.
1875	Sixty-eight men were elected to draft a new Missouri constitution.

1883 - 1893	County Clerks were required to register births and deaths, but not enforced.
1889 & 1893	Oklahoma Land Rush
1896 - 1897	Gold Rush to the Klondike District of the Yukon.
1911	Full compliance for the State registration of births and deaths.

COUNTY ABBREVIATIONS

County Name		Abbreviation
Arkansas		Ark
Audrain		Audr
Barry		Barr
Benton		Bent
Callaway		Call
Cape Girardeau		CGir
Carroll		Carr
Cass		Cass
Chariton		Char
Clay		Clay
Cole		Cole
Cooper		Coop
Crawford		Craw
Howard		How
Jackson		Jack
Johnson		John
Jefferson		Jeff
Lawrence		Lawr
Lewis		Lew
Lincoln		Linc
Marion		Mari
Miller		Mill
New Madrid		NMad
Perry		Perr
Pettis		Pett
Platte		Plat
Ray		Ray
Ripley		Ripl
Reynolds		Reyn
Saline		Sali
St. Charles		StC
Ste. Genevieve		Steg
St. Louis		StL
Washington		Wash
Wayne		Wayn

TAX LIST TYPES

Type		Abbreviation
Personal Property	....	Prop
Patentee of record on Tax List	....	PropPt
Delinquent	....	DTL
Real Estate	....	Real
Poll	....	Poll
Certificate	....	Ct
Certificate Security	....	CtS
Public Monies Recieved by County	....	PM
County License Fees	....	Lisc
Assessment List	....	Ass
Military Roster	....	Mil
Spanish	....	Span

Last Name	First Name	Int	Year	County	Type
Abare	Julien		1836	StC	Prop
Abbott	John		1867	Reyn	DTL
Abbott	Cate		1867	Reyn	DTL
Abbott	George		1836	Char	DTL
Abbott	Spencer		1831	Craw	DTL
Abel	Ezekial		1805	Steg	Prop
Abernathy	Alarkin		1836	Perr	Poll
Abernathy	Alonzo		1836	Perr	Poll
Abernathy	Harley	D	1836	Perr	Poll
Abernathy	James	D	1836	Perr	Poll
Abernathy	Lott		1836	Perr	Poll
Abington	Henry		1836	StC	Prop
Abington	Samuel		1836	StC	Prop
Abington	Lea		1836	StC	Prop
Abington	John		1836	StC	Prop
Ableny	Sarah		1829	NMad	DTL
Abrams	R	R	1867	Reyn	DTL
Abrams	James		1867	Reyn	DTL
Acklin	John		1843	Char	DTL
Aclare	William		1836	StC	Prop
Acre	W	L	1840	Call	Poll
Adair	Andrew		1840	Call	Poll
Adair	John		1840	Call	Poll
Adair	Joseph		1840	Call	Poll
Adair, Jr	Joseph		1840	Call	Poll
Adams	J		1843	Audr	Prop
Adams	John		1826	Coop	DTL
Adams	Wm		1826	Coop	DTL
Adams	Thomas		1839	Plat	Prop
Adams	John		1836	Perr	Poll
Adams	Thomas		1836	Carr	Prop
Adams	David		1836	Carr	Prop
Adams	Thomas		1836	Carr	PrpPt
Adams	David		1836	Carr	PrpPt
Adams	William		1840	Call	Poll
Adams	Benjamin		1840	Call	Poll
Adams	William	M	1830	Coop	Ct
Adams	William	H	1830	Coop	CtS
Adams	John		1836	StC	Prop
Adams	Joshua		1821	Ray	Prop
Adams	Martin		1821	Ray	Prop
Adams	Richard		1821	Ray	Prop

Last Name	First Name	Int	Year	County	Type
Adams	William		1821	Ray	Prop
Adams	Pleasant		1821	Ray	Prop
Adams	Charles		1810	Ark	Prop
Adams	John	A	1838	Audr	DTL
Adams	Sally		1820	StL	Prop
Adams	John		1826	Coop	DTL
Adams	William		1826	Coop	DTL
Adams	John		1817	How	Prop
Adams	Thomas		1817	How	Prop
Adams	James		1839	Lew	DTL
Adams	Joshua		1822	Clay	Poll
Adams	Pleasant		1822	Clay	Poll
Adams	William		1834	Call	DTL
Adams, Sr	John		1834	Craw	DTL
Adamson	Samuel		1839	Plat	Prop
Adamson	Levi		1839	Plat	Prop
Adamson	Jacob		1839	Plat	Prop
Adcock	Joel	J	1840	Call	Poll
Adderton	J	A	1845	Sali	Lisc
Aderson	John		1867	Reyn	DTL
Adkins	William		1821	Ray	Prop
Adkins	William		1839	Lew	DTL
Adkins, Jr	Wiatt		1821	Ray	Prop
Adkins, Sr	William		1821	Ray	Prop
Agee	Ransom		1840	Call	Poll
Agee	Jacob		1843	Char	DTL
Agnes	William		1836	Carr	PrpPt
Agnew	William		1836	Carr	PrpPt
Agnew	William		1830	Ray	Prop
Ahart	Ferdinand		1836	StC	Prop
Ahart	Peter		1836	StC	Prop
Aigler	George		1836	Carr	Prop
Aigler	George		1836	Carr	PrpPt
Aikmon	William	E	1817	How	Prop
Aisquicks	E	M	1837	Boon	PM
Aisquicks	C	W	1837	Boon	PM
Akin	William		1839	Lew	DTL
Aklemauct	Adolphus		1836	StC	Prop
Akman	William	E	1829	Sali	DTL
Alavares	Wid Josephte		1820	StL	Prop
Alavares	Manuel		1820	StL	Prop
Albright	Joel		1839	Plat	Prop

2

Last Name	First Name	Int	Year	County	Type
Alcorn	James		1830	Howa	DTL
Alderson	Jonathan		1840	Call	Poll
Alderson	Michael		1840	Call	Poll
Aldman	W	B	1839	Plat	Prop
Aldridge	Samuel		1836	StC	Prop
Aldridge's Heirs	John		1836	Carr	Prop
Aldridge's Heirs	John		1836	Carr	PrpPt
Alexander	J		1827	Coop	DTL
Alexander	Jesse		1836	Carr	Prop
Alexander	Charles		1836	Carr	Prop
Alexander	Jesse		1836	Carr	PrpPt
Alexander	Charles		1836	Carr	PrpPt
Alexander	Willis	T	1840	Call	Poll
Alexander	William		1840	Call	Poll
Alexander	James		1810	Ark	Prop
Alexander	Abraham		1838	Audr	DTL
Alexander	J		1827	Coop	DTL
Alexander	James		1817	How	Prop
Alexander's Heirs	Jas	H	1836	StC	Prop
Alexis alias Pecard	Peter		1829	Sali	DTL
Alford	George	G	1822	NMad	Lisc
Alfry	Joseph		1839	Plat	Prop
Alkin	Mikul		1840	Call	Poll
Alkin	Samuel		1840	Call	Poll
Alkin	William		1840	Call	Poll
Alkins	Michael		1844	Osag	Real
Alkinson	Benjamin		1830	Ray	Prop
Alkire	Solomon		1836	StC	Prop
Alkire	Jesse		1836	StC	Prop
Allard	Lange		1818	StL	Real
Allard	Lange		1820	StL	Prop
Allcorn	James		1817	How	Prop
Allen	Solomon		1839	Plat	Prop
Allen	David		1839	Plat	Prop
Allen	Isaac		1839	Plat	Prop
Allen	Robert		1839	Plat	Prop
Allen	John		1839	Plat	Prop
Allen	Samuel		1839	Plat	Prop
Allen	Jesse	R	1839	Plat	Prop
Allen	Thomas		1839	Plat	Prop
Allen	Bethel		1839	Plat	Prop
Allen	Moses		1839	Plat	Prop

Last Name	First Name	Int	Year	County	Type
Allen	John		1839	Plat	Prop
Allen	Berryman		1859	Reyn	DTL
Allen	Campbell		1836	Carr	Prop
Allen	Campbell		1836	Carr	PrpPt
Allen	E		1828	Boon	Lisc
Allen	Walker		1840	Call	Poll
Allen	Appleton		1840	Call	Poll
Allen	Joseph		1840	Call	Poll
Allen	Arch		1840	Call	Poll
Allen	Hugh		1840	Call	Poll
Allen	Jas		1840	Call	Poll
Allen	Jesse	R	1840	Call	Poll
Allen	Frances		1821	StC	Ct
Allen	Beischell		1821	StC	CtS
Allen	Bethell		1834	Pett	Prop
Allen	G	W	1867	Reyn	DTL
Allen	John		1836	StC	Prop
Allen	Joseph	J	1836	StC	Prop
Allen	Robert	B	1836	StC	Prop
Allen	Robert	L	1836	StC	Prop
Allen	Rachel		1836	StC	Prop
Allen	Lucy	A	1836	StC	Prop
Allen	Susan	M	1836	StC	Prop
Allen	William	S	1836	StC	Prop
Allen	Moses		1823	Call	NRP
Allen	Isaac		1821	Ray	Prop
Allen	Abraham		1821	Ray	Prop
Allen	John		1821	Ray	Prop
Allen	Thornton	V	1821	Ray	Prop
Allen	Martin		1810	Ark	Prop
Allen	John		1838	Audr	DTL
Allen	????		1818	StL	Real
Allen	William		1817	How	Prop
Allen	John		1817	How	Prop
Allen	James		1830	Ray	Prop
Allen	Thomas		1830	Ray	Prop
Allen	Fred		1830	Ray	Prop
Allen	James	L	1839	Lew	DTL
Allen	Billings		1839	Lew	DTL
Allen	James	P	1822	Clay	Poll
Allen	Shubael		1822	Clay	Poll
Allen	William		1838	Ripl	DTL

4

Last Name	First Name	Int	Year	County	Type
Allen	Samuel		1838	Ripl	DTL
Allen	John		1834	Call	DTL
Allen	William		1834	Call	DTL
Allen	Moses		1834	Lew	DTL
Allen	Samuel		1829	NMad	DTL
Alley	Walter		1838	Ripl	DTL
Allington	William		1837	Lew	DTL
Allison	John		1810	Ark	Prop
Allman	William	B	1839	Plat	Prop
Allred	Jno	W	1863	Jeff	Ass
Alrembe	Ephraim		1838	Ripl	DTL
Alusns	William		1836	Carr	Prop
Alusns	William		1836	Carr	PrpPt
Alvares	Augustin		1820	StL	Prop
Alvarez	Eugenio		1791	StL	Span
Alvarez	Francois		1818	StL	Real
Alverice	Wid		1818	StL	Real
Alverice	Augustin		1818	StL	Real
Alverice	Manuel		1818	StL	Real
Alxander	James		1830	Coop	Ct
Amanerman	Phillip	H	1844	Osag	Real
Ambroin	Wid Batte		1810	Ark	Prop
Ambrose	Louis		1818	StL	Real
Ammons	Andrea		1836	Carr	PrpPt
Amoreau	Michael		1819	Steg	Lic
Amos	Thomas		1836	StC	Prop
Amoureux	????		1820	StL	Prop
Anderson	J	A S	1843	Audr	Prop
Anderson	Robt		1839	Plat	Prop
Anderson	Jacob		1839	Plat	Prop
Anderson	Wm		1839	Plat	Prop
Anderson	David		1839	Plat	Prop
Anderson	James		1839	Plat	Prop
Anderson	George	W	1839	Plat	Prop
Anderson	John		1836	Bent	DTL
Anderson	David	M	1836	Perr	Poll
Anderson	James		1836	Carr	Prop
Anderson	Solomon		1836	Carr	Prop
Anderson	Samuel		1836	Carr	Prop
Anderson	James		1836	Carr	PrpPt
Anderson	Solomon		1836	Carr	PrpPt
Anderson	Samuel		1836	Carr	PrpPt

Last Name	First Name	Int	Year	County	Type
Anderson	C	G	1840	Call	Poll
Anderson	William		1834	Pett	Prop
Anderson	Middleton		1834	Pett	Prop
Anderson	Andrew		1834	Pett	Prop
Anderson	James		1834	Pett	Prop
Anderson	Robert		1834	Pett	PrpPt
Anderson	Ambrose		1834	Pett	PrpPt
Anderson	James		1834	Pett	PrpPt
Anderson	Middleton		1834	Pett	PrpPt
Anderson	William		1834	Pett	PrpPt
Anderson	William	L	1836	StC	Prop
Anderson	Thomas		1818	StL	Real
Anderson	Othe		1837	Lew	DTL
Anderson	Kemp		1837	Lew	DTL
Anderson	Paul		1820	StL	Prop
Anderson	William		1820	StL	Prop
Anderson	William	S	1829	Mari	DTL
Anderson	Middleton		1817	How	Prop
Anderson	James		1817	How	Prop
Anderson	Samuel		1830	Ray	Prop
Anderson	Thomas		1844	Osag	Real
Anderson	Samuel		1836	Char	DTL
Andrew	Joseph		1839	John	DTL
Ange	Jesse		1844	Osag	Real
Ange	William	O	1844	Osag	Real
Angell	William		1828	Boon	Lisc
Angell	Willis	H	1828	Boon	Lisc
Anglin	Aaron		1836	Carr	Prop
Anglin	Aaron		1836	Carr	PrpPt
Anglin	Aaron		1836	Carr	PrtPt
Anson	Franklin		1867	Reyn	DTL
Anthony	James	A	1839	Plat	Prop
Anthony	Christopher		1810	Ark	Prop
Anthony	Christopher		1815	Ark	Prop
Anthony	Philip		1834	Call	DTL
Aoulard	Antoine		1818	StL	Real
Apling	William		1823	Call	NRP
Apperson	Jacob		1830	Call	DTL
Appleton	Joseph		1836	StC	Prop
Archambra	Charles		1805	Steg	Prop
Archer	Isaac		1839	Plat	Prop
Armin	James	A	1838	Ripl	DTL

6

Last Name	First Name	Int	Year	County	Type
Armsby	J	M	1867	Reyn	DTL
Armstead	George		1810	Ark	Prop
Armstead	Francois		1838	Audr	DTL
Armstead	George		1815	Ark	Prop
Armstrong	William		1840	Call	Poll
Armstrong	Henry		1867	Reyn	DTL
Armstrong	Andrew		1823	Call	NRP
Armstrong	Andrew		1830	Call	DTL
Armstrong	Thomas		1827	Mari	Prop
Armstrong	Thomas		1838	Ripl	DTL
Arnauld	Bartholemy		1820	StL	Prop
Arnold	Price		1816	How	Lic
Arnold	Lindsay		1836	Carr	Prop
Arnold	Lindsay		1836	Carr	PrpPt
Arnold	Barthelmy		1818	StL	Real
Arnold	James		1820	StL	Prop
Arnold	Price		1817	How	Prop
Arnold	Mark		1839	Lew	DTL
Arnold	Rueben		1839	Plat	Prop
Arrick	Alfred		1867	Reyn	DTL
Arter	James		1839	Plat	Prop
Arterberry	Isreal		1823	How	DTL
Artman	John		1839	Plat	Prop
Ashabranner	E		1867	Reyn	DTL
Ashabranner	J		1867	Reyn	DTL
Ashbrook	William		1836	Carr	Prop
Ashbrook	William		1836	Carr	PrpPt
Ashby	Cromwell		1839	Plat	Prop
Ashby	Daniel		1836	Carr	Prop
Ashecraft	Amos		1817	How	Prop
Ashecraft	Jesse		1817	How	Prop
Asher	William		1839	Plat	Prop
Ashley	James		1836	StC	Prop
Ashley	Daniel		1829	Char	DTL
Ashley	William		1830	Call	DTL
Ashley	William	H	1820	StL	Prop
Ashley	????		1820	StL	Prop
Ashly	George		1836	Perr	Poll
Ashly	William	H	1823	Call	NRP
Ashworth	Sterling		1839	Plat	Prop
Ashworth	David	D	1839	Plat	Prop
Ater	William		1837	Bent	DTL

7

Last Name	First Name	Int	Year	County	Type
Athen	John		1835	Barr	DTL
Atkins	Jeremiah		1839	Plat	Prop
Atkins	Joseph		1839	Plat	Prop
Atkinson	Benjamin		1836	Carr	Prop
Atkinson	Benjamin		1836	Carr	PrpPt
Atkinson	Henry		1840	Call	Poll
Atkinson	James		1840	Call	Poll
Atterberry	William		1840	Call	Poll
Atterberry	Samuel		1840	Call	Poll
Atterberry	Michael		1817	How	Prop
Atterbury	Williamson		1839	Plat	Prop
Atterbury	James		1839	Plat	Prop
Atterbury	Thomas		1839	Plat	Prop
Aubuchon	Adilaide		1818	StL	Real
Aubucohn's Heirs	???		1818	StL	Real
Aubury	Joseph		1836	StC	Prop
Aud	Joseph		1844	Osag	Real
Audrain	Samuel		1836	StC	Prop
Audrain	Peter	G	1836	StC	Prop
Audrain	James	H	1836	StC	Prop
Audrain	Peter	F	1836	StC	Prop
Aug	Tilman		1844	Osag	Real
Aug	Mathew		1844	Osag	Real
Aug	Samuel	D	1844	Osag	Real
August	Francis		1831	Jack	DTL
Aull	Thomas	M	1839	Plat	Prop
Ausborne	J	J	1840	Call	Poll
Austin	Moses		1805	Steg	Prop
Austin	Samuel		1839	Plat	Prop
Austin	Samuel		1859	Reyn	DTL
Austin	Peter		1827	Boon	Lisc
Austin	Absalom		1840	Call	Poll
Austin	Robert		1817	How	Prop
Austin	Joseph		1817	How	Prop
Austin	Peter		1817	How	Prop
Austin	John		1840	Call	Poll
Averett	Howard		1821	Ray	Prop
Ayres	Ebenezer		1821	StC	Ct
Ayres	E	D	1821	StC	CtS
Babaer	Jordan		1839	Plat	Prop
Babcock	Squire		1839	Plat	Prop
Baber	Isham		1839	Plat	Prop

8

Last Name	First Name	Int	Year	County	Type
Baber	Hiram	H	1821	StC	Ct
Baber	Hiram	H	1821	StC	CtS
Bachar	Josef		1791	StL	Span
Bachar	Antonio		1791	StL	Span
Bachar	Wid Madam		1791	StL	Span
Bachman	Uldrich		1836	Carr	Prop
Bachman	Uldrich		1836	Carr	PrpPt
Backers	Sandford		1844	Osag	Real
Backlin	Thomas		1844	Osag	Real
Bacon	William		1822	NMad	Lisc
Bacon	Ludwell		1823	Call	NRP
Bacon	Rueben		1823	Call	NRP
Bacon	Lancston		1823	Call	NRP
Baden	John		1829	Char	DTL
Baforta	Nathan	P	1810	Ark	Prop
Bagby	Daniel	W	1840	Call	Poll
Bagby	James	W	1840	Call	Poll
Bagby	Richard		1840	Call	Poll
Bagby	Samuel		1840	Call	Poll
Bagby	Waddy	C	1840	Call	Poll
Bage	Saml		1863	Jeff	Ass
Bagwell	William		1823	How	DTL
Baile	Henry		1863	Jeff	Ass
Bailey	Kindred		1840	Call	Poll
Bailey	Benj		1840	Call	Poll
Bailey	Charles		1840	Call	Poll
Bailey	W	A	1840	Call	Poll
Bailey	David		1821	StC	Ct
Bailey	Samuel		1821	StC	Ct
Bailey	Samuel		1821	StC	CtS
Bailey	David		1821	StC	CtS
Bailey	Robert		1818	StL	Real
Bailey	Munson		1843	Char	DTL
Bailey	Rueben	I	1834	Craw	DTL
Bailie	James		1863	Jeff	Ass
Bails	David		1836	Perr	Poll
Baily	Alexander		1836	Perr	Poll
Baily	Henry		1840	Call	Poll
Baily	Thomas		1810	Ark	Prop
Baily	????		1818	StL	Real
Bainbrick	Fred		1830	Howa	DTL
Baitman	John		1821	Ray	Prop

Last Name	First Name	Int	Year	County	Type
Baits	Nancy		1839	Plat	Prop
Baits	Jackson		1839	Plat	Prop
Baker	Austin		1830	Wash	DTL
Baker	Joseph		1839	Plat	Prop
Baker	Wesley		1839	Plat	Prop
Baker	John		1839	Plat	Prop
Baker	Lossen		1839	Plat	Prop
Baker	Randal		1839	Plat	Prop
Baker	Andrew		1839	Plat	Prop
Baker	Henry		1859	Reyn	DTL
Baker	I	H	1828	Boon	Lisc
Baker	Edmund	W	1840	Call	Poll
Baker	James	W	1840	Call	Poll
Baker	Robert	C	1840	Call	Poll
Baker	Thomas	H	1840	Call	Poll
Baker	Jas	A	1840	Call	Poll
Baker	Isaac		1840	Call	Poll
Baker	Benj		1840	Call	Poll
Baker	Thomas		1840	Call	Poll
Baker	William	F	1840	Call	Poll
Baker	William	M	1840	Call	Poll
Baker	A	J	1840	Call	Poll
Baker	Floyd		1840	Call	Poll
Baker	Thomas	F	1840	Call	Poll
Baker	John		1840	Call	Poll
Baker	Thos	H	1840	Call	Poll
Baker	John		1840	Call	Poll
Baker	M	E	1867	Reyn	DTL
Baker	John	W	1867	Reyn	DTL
Baker	Phillip		1836	StC	Prop
Baker	Love		1829	Char	DTL
Baker	John		1810	Ark	Prop
Baker	Henry		1810	Ark	Prop
Baker	Love		1830	Ray	Prop
Baker	Elisha	P	1838	Ripl	DTL
Baker	Adam		1837	Mill	DTL
Bakerly	William		1867	Reyn	DTL
Baldon	Bane		1839	Plat	Prop
Baldridge	James		1836	StC	Prop
Baldridge	William	H	1836	StC	Prop
Baldridge	Melkia		1836	StC	Prop
Baldridge	John		1836	StC	Prop

Last Name	First Name	Int	Year	County	Type
Baldridge	Daniel		1836	StC	Prop
Baldridge	Wilson		1836	StC	Prop
Baldridge	Robert		1836	StC	Prop
Baldridge	Alexander		1836	StC	Prop
Baldridge	Evin		1836	StC	Prop
Baldridge, Sr	Daniel		1836	StC	Prop
Baldridge, Sr	Jon		1836	StC	Prop
Baldridge, Sr	John		1836	StC	Prop
Baldwin	William		1836	Carr	Prop
Baldwin	William		1836	Carr	PrpPt
Baldwin	Benjamin		1836	StC	Prop
Baldwin	Moses		1820	StL	Prop
Bales	Perry		1839	Plat	Prop
Bales	Moses	D	1827	Mari	Prop
Baley	William		1839	Plat	Prop
Baley	Caleb		1839	Plat	Prop
Baley	Carr		1839	Plat	Prop
Baley	John		1867	Reyn	DTL
Ball	Josia		1836	StC	Prop
Ballard	Moses		1840	Call	Poll
Balle	Carlos		1780	StL	Mil
Balle	Alexandro		1780	StL	Mil
Ballinger	Frederick		1836	Perr	Poll
Bancroft	Elias		1836	Carr	Prop
Bancroft	Timothy		1821	Ray	Prop
Bane	William		1839	Plat	Prop
Bane	John		1839	Plat	Prop
Bangs	Henry		1836	StC	Prop
Banheson	Danl		1828	Sali	DTL
Banheson	Jas		1828	Sali	DTL
Bankard	James	M	1867	Reyn	DTL
Bankman	Jacob		1810	Ark	Prop
Banks	Nancy		1836	StC	Prop
Banta	William		1839	Plat	Prop
Barackman	A	W	1867	Reyn	DTL
Barada	Luis		1791	StL	Span
Barada	Louis		1836	StC	Prop
Baradie	Silvest		1836	StC	Prop
Baradie	Antwine		1836	StC	Prop
Baradie	????		1836	StC	Prop
Barbard	Harman		1867	Reyn	DTL
Barbee	Braxon	B	1843	Audr	Prop

Last Name	First Name	Int	Year	County	Type
Barbee	Ira		1830	Howa	DTL
Barber	Elias		1836	Perr	Poll
Barber	Samuel		1836	Perr	Poll
Barbrand	Joseph		1836	Carr	Prop
Barbrand	Joseph		1836	Carr	PrpPt
Barce	Henry		1829	NMad	DTL
Barclay	Robert		1817	How	Prop
Barcus	William		1859	Reyn	DTL
Bard	Abraham		1829	NMad	DTL
Barden	Edward		1867	Reyn	DTL
Bardon	David		1840	Call	Poll
Barge	John		1839	Plat	Prop
Barhouse	William		1829	Mari	DTL
Bark	Henry	F	1839	Plat	Prop
Barker	Henry		1839	Plat	Prop
Barker	Elias		1839	Plat	Prop
Barker	John		1839	Plat	Prop
Barker	Edward		1844	Osag	Real
Barker	Elias		1831	Craw	DTL
Barkerbread	Dert		1836	StC	Prop
Barkman	A	W	1867	Reyn	DTL
Barkman	Jacob		1810	Ark	Prop
Barlow	Thomas		1830	Coop	Ct
Barnes	John	W	1843	Audr	Prop
Barnes	Abraham		1826	Coop	DTL
Barnes	Abraham		1827	Coop	DTL
Barnes	Cyrus		1839	Plat	Prop
Barnes	Green	H	1839	Plat	Prop
Barnes	Henry		1839	Plat	Prop
Barnes	Isaac		1839	Plat	Prop
Barnes	William		1859	Reyn	DTL
Barnes	Edward		1859	Reyn	DTL
Barnes	William		1831	Jack	DTL
Barnes	Redman		1836	Carr	Prop
Barnes	Redman		1836	Carr	PrpPt
Barnes	Christain		1836	StC	Prop
Barnes	Abraham		1829	Char	DTL
Barnes	Miller	M	1838	Audr	DTL
Barnes	Jabez		1837	Lew	DTL
Barnes	Abraham		1827	Coop	DTL
Barnes	Abraham		1826	Coop	DTL
Barnes	Aquilla		1817	How	Prop

Last Name	First Name	Int	Year	County	Type
Barnes	John		1817	How	Prop
Barnes	Shadrick		1817	How	Prop
Barnes	Abraham		1817	How	Prop
Barnes	Thomas		1834	Call	DTL
Barnes (1)	James		1817	How	Prop
Barnes (2)	James		1817	How	Prop
Barnett	Elias		1837	Cass	DTL
Barnett	John	W	1827	Boon	Lisc
Barnett	John	W	1838	Audr	DTL
Barnett	Thomas	M	1838	Audr	DTL
Barnett	John		1839	John	DTL
Barnett	David		1817	How	Prop
Barnett, Jr	David		1817	How	Prop
Barney	Timthy		1843	Audr	Prop
Barnsback	Maria Louisa		1815	Ark	Prop
Barr	Tobias		1867	Reyn	DTL
Barra	Detreck		1836	StC	Prop
Barra	Augustus		1836	StC	Prop
Barrera	Francisco		1780	StL	Mil
Barrera	Franco		1791	StL	Span
Barret	John		1837	Lew	DTL
Barribeau	Pierre		1818	StL	Real
Barriebau	Pierre		1820	StL	Prop
Barriebeau	Pierre		1818	StL	Real
Barrier	Peter		1836	StC	Prop
Barringer	Mathias		1837	Perr	Lisc
Barringer	Mathias		1837	Perr	Adv
Barringer	Mathias		1838	Perr	Lisc
Barringer	Mathias		1838	Perr	Adv
Barringer	Mathias		1836	Perr	Poll
Barrow	Alfred		1840	Call	Poll
Barry	Barney	S	1836	Carr	Prop
Barry	Barney		1836	Carr	PrpPt
Bartholomew	Joseph		1815	Ark	Prop
Bartleson	John	A	1821	Ray	Prop
Bartleson	John		1822	Clay	Poll
Bartlett	Abraham		1836	Carr	Prop
Bartlett	Abraham		1836	Carr	PrpPt
Bartlett	John		1836	Carr	Prop
Bartlett	John		1836	Carr	PrpPt
Bartlett	Thomas		1822	NMad	Lisc
Bartlett	George		1840	Call	Poll

Last Name	First Name	Int	Year	County	Type
Bartlett	John		1840	Call	Poll
Bartlett	Henry		1818	StL	Real
Bartlett	Robert		1820	StL	Prop
Bartlett	Benjamin		1829	NMad	DTL
Bartley	John		1823	Call	NRP
Bartley	John		1831	Craw	DTL
Barton	David		1827	Coop	DTL
Barton	Abram		1839	Plat	Prop
Barton	Emily	A	1859	Reyn	DTL
Barton	Hiram		1836	Carr	Prop
Barton	Hiram		1836	Carr	PrpPt
Barton	Aaron		1836	Carr	Prop
Barton	Aaron		1836	Carr	PrpPt
Barton	Dods		1867	Reyn	DTL
Barton	Joshua		1820	StL	Prop
Barton	Taylor		1829	Mari	DTL
Barton	David		1827	Coop	DTL
Barton	Joshua		1817	How	Prop
Barton	Aaron		1830	Ray	Prop
Barton's Heirs	John	S	1836	Carr	Prop
Barton's Heirs	John		1836	Carr	PrpPt
Bartrim	S	M	1867	Reyn	DTL
Barwell	Zachariah		1836	Carr	Prop
Barwell	Zachariah		1836	Carr	PrpPt
Basedonio	Lorenzo		1780	StL	Mil
Basford	James		1836	Carr	PrpPt
Basford	James		1830	Ray	Prop
Basher	William		1836	Carr	Prop
Basher	William		1836	Carr	PrpPt
Basket	Thomas		1831	Craw	DTL
Baskin	John		1838	Cass	DTL
Baskin	James	H	1840	Call	Poll
Baskin	John	C	1840	Call	Poll
Basmekman	Jacob		1815	Ark	Prop
Basor	Bastilio		1780	StL	Mil
Basor	Joseph		1780	StL	Mil
Bass	Lawrence		1828	Boon	Lisc
Bass	William	T	1840	Call	Poll
Bass	Dabney		1836	StC	Prop
Bass	Peter		1823	Call	NRP
Bass	Lawrence		1823	Call	NRP
Bass	Mithelred		1837	Mill	DTL

14

Last Name	First Name	Int	Year	County	Type
Bass	Andrew		1831	Craw	DTL
Bassite	William		1810	Ark	Prop
Bates	Nicholas		1836	Carr	Prop
Bates	Nicholas		1836	Carr	PrpPt
Bates	William	D	1867	Reyn	DTL
Bates	Edward		1836	StC	Prop
Bates	Edward		1820	StL	Prop
Bates	John		1844	Osag	Real
Batiot	Lewis		1831	Jack	DTL
Bato	James		1818	Lawr	DTL
Batson	John	S	1834	Craw	DTL
Batson	Joseph		1834	Craw	DTL
Batt	Thomas	C	1836	StC	Prop
Battut	Henry		1820	StL	Prop
Baugh	James	F	1836	StC	Prop
Baugh	Joseph		1836	StC	Prop
Baugh	Benjamin		1836	StC	Prop
Bawn	Sarchel	C	1839	Plat	Prop
Baxen	Modest		1836	StC	Prop
Baxter	William		1867	Reyn	DTL
Baxter	Stephen		1821	Ray	Prop
Baxter	Jesse		1829	Mari	DTL
Baxter	William		1817	How	Prop
Baxter	Elijah		1827	Mari	Prop
Bay	Peter		1867	Reyn	DTL
Bay	Peter		1867	Reyn	DTL
Bay	Ira		1867	Reyn	DTL
Bayarth	Abner		1839	Plat	Prop
Bayley	James	G	1836	StC	Prop
Bayley	John	M	1836	StC	Prop
Bayley	Robert		1836	StC	Prop
Bayley's Heirs	Carr		1836	StC	Prop
Baynes	William		1859	Reyn	DTL
Baynham	Charles	H	1840	Call	Poll
Bays	Joseph		1817	How	Prop
Bays	Elijah		1831	Craw	DTL
Baysinger	John		1840	Call	Poll
Beadie	Samuel		1828	Boon	Lisc
Beaman	James	W	1834	Pett	Prop
Bean	James		1836	Carr	PrpPt
Beancur	Joseph		1780	StL	Mil
Beard	Preston		1863	Jeff	Ass

Last Name	First Name	Int	Year	County	Type
Beasley	James		1836	Perr	Poll
Beatie	Samuel		1830	Howa	DTL
Beatie	James		1823	Call	NRP
Beatty	John	B	1867	Reyn	DTL
Beatty	Edward		1838	Audr	DTL
Beaty	Edward		1843	Audr	Prop
Beaty	Joseph		1843	Audr	Prop
Beaty	Jas		1843	Audr	Prop
Beaty	Robert		1834	Pett	Prop
Beaty	William		1821	Ray	Prop
Beauchamp	D	G	1839	Plat	Prop
Beauchamp	R ·	P	1839	Plat	Prop
Beauchamp	Stephen		1839	Plat	Prop
Beaufils	Jean		1820	StL	Prop
Beaugnenon	Vital		1820	StL	Prop
Beauman	Vital		1805	Steg	Prop
Beauonouis	L'Guierme		1805	Steg	Prop
Beauvais	Barthw		1805	Steg	Prop
Beauval	Vital St James		1805	Steg	Prop
Beauviere	Jos	V	1838	Perr	Lisc
Beauviere	Jos		1838	Perr	Adv
Beauvoire	Jos	V	1837	Perr	Lisc
Beauvoire	Jos		1837	Perr	Adv
Beaver	????		1834	Call	DTL
Beavin	Theodore		1840	Call	Poll
Beavin	Zadock		1840	Call	Poll
Beckel	Joseph		1805	Steg	Prop
Becket, Sr	Baptist		1805	Steg	Prop
Beddow	Leonard		1836	StC	Prop
Bedell	Hazen		1830	Ray	Prop
Bedford	Edwin		1839	Plat	Prop
Bedler	David		1836	StC	Prop
Bedwell	Stephen		1839	Plat	Prop
Beebe	Elisha		1820	StL	Prop
Beegle	Thomas		1839	Plat	Prop
Beegle	James		1839	Plat	Prop
Beegle	Wm		1839	Plat	Prop
Beevers	Samuel	H	1840	Call	Poll
Belamy	John		1840	Call	Poll
Belamy	James		1840	Call	Poll
Belamy	Rueben		1840	Call	Poll
Belcher	Alexander		1838	Cass	DTL

16

Last Name	First Name	Int	Year	County	Type
Beldon	G	H	1843	Char	DTL
Belerle	Mortiz		1838	Perr	Lisc
Belerle	Mortiz		1838	Perr	Adv
Beletre	Luis		1791	StL	Span
Belfort	Baptiste		1818	StL	Real
Belfort	Baptiste		1820	StL	Prop
Belhumor	Pedro		1780	StL	Mil
Beliener	James		1839	Plat	Prop
Beliener	Micajah		1839	Plat	Prop
Beliener, Sr	John		1839	Plat	Prop
Belissime	Alexander		1820	StL	Prop
Bell	Arnold		1816	How	Lic
Bell	William		1839	Plat	Prop
Bell	Lewis	W	1839	Plat	Prop
Bell	David		1839	Plat	Prop
Bell	William		1838	Steg	DTL
Bell	James		1840	Call	Poll
Bell	Andrew	K	1840	Call	Poll
Bell	John		1823	Call	NRP
Bell	Philip		1823	Call	NRP
Bell	J	M	1829	Char	DTL
Bell	Jabish		1830	Linc	DTL
Bell	Jno		1820	StL	Prop
Bellas	George		1817	How	Prop
Bellecourt	Louis Jos		1820	StL	Prop
Bellfort	J	B	1818	StL	Real
Bellond	Michael		1836	StC	Prop
Bellows	John		1840	Call	Poll
Bellville	Pierre		1818	StL	Real
Belotte	Edmund		1836	Carr	PrpPt
Belpecher	Ant		1780	StL	Mil
Belsha	Ferdiand		1836	Perr	Poll
Belville	Pierre		1818	StL	Real
Belzar	Mantle		1867	Reyn	DTL
Benadict	Albert		1836	StC	Prop
Benard	Joseph		1867	Reyn	DTL
Bender	Henry		1836	StC	Prop
Benedict	Chauncey		1836	Carr	Prop
Benedict	Chauncey		1836	Carr	PrpPt
Benedict	Jonathan		1817	How	Prop
Benick	Henry		1836	StC	Prop
Benner	John		1836	StC	Prop

17

Last Name	First Name	Int	Year	County	Type
Bennet	William		1820	StL	Prop
Bennett	Chiles		1839	Plat	Prop
Bennett	William		1839	Plat	Prop
Bennett	Joel	A	1840	Call	Poll
Bennett	Joseph		1840	Call	Poll
Bennett	Milton		1840	Call	Poll
Bennett	Moses		1840	Call	Poll
Bennett	A	G	1840	Call	Poll
Bennett	George		1830	Coop	CtS
Bennett	Thomas		1867	Reyn	DTL
Bennett	Thomas	W	1867	Reyn	DTL
Bennett	William		1818	StL	Real
Bennette	Wid Colin		1815	Ark	Prop
Bennette	Peter	H	1815	Ark	Prop
Bennom	Robert		1817	How	Prop
Beno	Luis		1780	StL	Mil
Benoist, dec	M		1820	StL	Prop
Benoit	Toussaint		1818	StL	Real
Benoit	Francois		1818	StL	Real
Benoit	Toussaint		1820	StL	Prop
Benson	James	H	1828	Boon	Lisc
Benson	Jefferson	B	1840	Call	Poll
Benson	Eden		1840	Call	Poll
Benson	Zachariah		1834	Pett	PrpPt
Benson	Zachariah		1834	Pett	PrpPt
Benson	James	H	1823	Call	NRP
Benson	James		1817	How	Prop
Bent	Silas		1818	StL	Real
Bentley	Thomas		1830	Ray	Prop
Benton	Williard		1836	Carr	Prop
Benton	Williard		1836	Carr	PrpPt
Benton	John		1836	Carr	Prop
Benton	John		1836	Carr	PrpPt
Benton	Thomas	H	1840	Call	Poll
Benton	Thomas	H	1823	Call	NRP
Benton	Thomas	H	1820	StL	Prop
Benton	James		1836	Char	DTL
Benton's Heirs	Jno	S	1836	Carr	PrpPt
Bequet	Juan Bapt		1791	StL	Span
Bequete	Pedro		1780	StL	Mil
Bequete	Gabriel		1780	StL	Mil
Bequett	D		1839	Wash	Lisc

Last Name	First Name	Int	Year	County	Type
Berchard	Rufus	E	1840	Call	Poll
Berge	Joseph		1780	StL	Mil
Bermington	John		1867	Reyn	DTL
Bernard	Thomas		1840	Call	Poll
Bernard	Joseph		1867	Reyn	DTL
Bernard	Isidore		1836	StC	Prop
Bernard	Hypolite		1836	StC	Prop
Bernard	Patterson		1836	StC	Prop
Bernard	John		1836	StC	Prop
Bernard	James		1836	StC	Prop
Bernard's Heirs	Ettienne		1836	StC	Prop
Bernie	Pedro		1780	StL	Mil
Bernie	Francisco		1780	StL	Mil
Bernum	Thomas		1836	StC	Prop
Beron	Esteban		1780	StL	Mil
Berry	Elizabeth		1843	Audr	Prop
Berry	Henry		1843	Audr	Prop
Berry	William	I	1843	Audr	Prop
Berry	Taylor		1827	Coop	DTL
Berry	Martin	T	1839	Plat	Prop
Berry	James	H	1839	Plat	Prop
Berry	T	G	1828	Boon	Lisc
Berry	Ben	F	1840	Call	Poll
Berry	Edward		1840	Call	Poll
Berry	Thomas		1840	Call	Poll
Berry	Charles	R	1830	Coop	Ct
Berry	James		1830	Coop	CtS
Berry	Finis	E	1834	Pett	PrpPt
Berry	Finis	E	1834	Pett	PrpPt
Berry	Jas	W	1863	Jeff	Ass
Berry	Terry		1823	Call	NRP
Berry	John		1810	Ark	Prop
Berry	Taylor		1827	Coop	DTL
Berry	Taylor		1817	How	Prop
Berry	John		1817	How	Prop
Berry	William		1817	How	Prop
Berry	John		1844	Osag	Real
Berry's Heirs	????		1830	Ray	Prop
Berthand	Michel		1818	StL	Real
Berthol	Joseph		1836	StC	Prop
Berthold	????		1820	StL	Prop
Berthold	Bartholmew		1820	StL	Prop

Last Name	First Name	Int	Year	County	Type
Bertrand	Michel		1818	StL	Real
Bertrand	Michael		1820	StL	Prop
Bess	John		1836	Perr	Poll
Bess	Joshua		1836	Perr	Poll
Bessan	Peter		1844	Osag	Real
Bessonet	Ambrose		1818	StL	Real
Best	Mary		1836	StC	Prop
Best	Stephen		1836	StC	Prop
Best	Humphrey		1821	Ray	Prop
Best	Humphrey		1817	How	Prop
Bethias	Christian		1844	Osag	Real
Bethill	Samuel		1840	Call	Poll
Betteche	James		1863	Jeff	Ass
Beurbon	Frederick		1836	StC	Prop
Beurbon	Henry		1836	StC	Prop
Bevaman	Acan		1836	StC	Prop
Beverley	John		1836	StC	Prop
Bevier	Edward		1859	Reyn	DTL
Bevin	Joseph		1837	Cass	DTL
Bevins	John		1836	Carr	Prop
Bevins	Thomas		1836	Carr	Prop
Bevins	John		1836	Carr	PrpPt
Bevins	Thomas		1836	Carr	PrpPt
Bevins	James		1836	Carr	PrtPt
Bevious	William		1836	Carr	PrtPt
Biba	Martilus		1843	Audr	Prop
Bibb	R		1828	Boon	Lisc
Bibran	Bapt		1780	StL	Mil
Bichenou	Nicolas		1791	StL	Span
Bickerstall	Richard		1839	Plat	Prop
Bickles	Robert		1840	Call	Poll
Bicknell	William		1817	How	Prop
Bienvenue	Eugen		1820	StL	Prop
Bigalow	Moses		1836	StC	Prop
Bigg's Heirs	Randolph		1836	StC	Prop
Biggers	James		1833	Wayn	DTL
Bigham	John		1839	Plat	Prop
Bigham	James	W	1839	Plat	Prop
Bilings	A	W	1859	Reyn	DTL
Billingsley	John		1810	Ark	Prop
Billingsley	James		1810	Ark	Prop
Billon	Charles		1820	StL	Prop

Last Name	First Name	Int	Year	County	Type
Bills	Royal		1810	Ark	Prop
Bingham	Bartlett		1837	Cass	DTL
Birch	Albert		1823	Steg	Lisc
Birch	Daniel		1836	Carr	Prop
Birch	Daniel		1836	Carr	PrpPt
Birchard	Rufus	E	1844	Osag	Real
Bird	James		1839	Plat	Prop
Bird	Michael		1839	Plat	Prop
Bird	William		1839	Plat	Prop
Bird	Marshal		1836	StC	Prop
Bird	Thompson		1818	StL	Real
Bird	Abraham		1827	Mari	Prop
Birdsong	William		1831	Cole	DTL
Birk	Pleasant	T	1844	Osag	Real
Bishop, Sr	George		1844	Osag	Real
Bisonet	Juana		1791	StL	Span
Bisonete	Wid. Maria		1791	StL	Span
Bissonet	Ambrose		1820	StL	Prop
Biter	Nicholas		1836	Carr	PrpPt
Bittick	Thos		1863	Jeff	Ass
Bitticks	J	L	1863	Jeff	Ass
Biuat	Lewis		1805	Steg	Prop
Biveon	William		1839	Lew	DTL
Black	Isaac		1843	Audr	Prop
Black	J		1843	Audr	Prop
Black	Robert		1837	Perr	Lisc
Black	H		1836	Perr	Poll
Black	Robert		1836	Perr	Poll
Black	William	A	1836	Perr	Poll
Black	Thomas		1836	StC	Prop
Black	Simon		1823	Call	NRP
Black	James	W	1821	Ray	Prop
Black	William	L	1821	Ray	Prop
Black	William		1821	Ray	Prop
Black	Isaac		1838	Audr	DTL
Black	William		1838	Ripl	DTL
Black, Jr	John		1836	StC	Prop
Blackburn	John		1840	Call	Poll
Blackburn	John		1840	Call	Poll
Blackburn	Robert		1840	Call	Poll
Blackburn	William		1840	Call	Poll
Blackenburg	Phillip		1840	Call	Poll

Last Name	First Name	Int	Year	County	Type
Blackforth	Hermon		1836	StC	Prop
Blackman	Adolph		1836	StC	Prop
Blackwell	John	W	1840	Call	Poll
Blackwell	Joab		1835	Barr	DTL
Bladwin	Martin		1839	Plat	Prop
Blair	Thompson		1840	Call	Poll
Blake	William		1836	Carr	PrtPt
Blakely	William		1810	Ark	Prop
Blakey	William		1827	Mari	Prop
Blamore	Isaac		1818	Lawr	DTL
Blanchard	????		1820	StL	Prop
Blankenship	Morton		1843	Audr	Prop
Blankenship	Thomas		1839	Plat	Prop
Blankenship	Sylvester		1839	Plat	Prop
Blanton	Isaac		1839	Plat	Prop
Blanton	Ezekiel		1839	Plat	Prop
Blanton	Joel		1839	Plat	Prop
Blattenburg	Jacob		1834	Call	DTL
Blaylock	Lewis		1810	Ark	Prop
Blaze	Lewis		1836	Perr	Poll
Bleamer	Charles		1836	StC	Prop
Bledsoe	Willis		1839	Plat	Prop
Bledsoe	Sampson		1837	Cass	DTL
Bledsoe	Isaac		1838	Cass	DTL
Bledsoe	Sampson		1838	Cass	DTL
Bledsoe	Alexander		1831	Jack	DTL
Bledsoe	A		1840	Call	Poll
Blevins	Daniel		1830	Ray	Prop
Block	Levi		1837	Perr	Lisc
Block	H		1837	Perr	Lisc
Block	Herman		1837	Perr	Lisc
Block	Hyman		1837	Perr	Lisc
Block	Hyman		1837	Perr	Adv
Block	Levi		1838	Perr	Lisc
Block	Morris		1838	Perr	Lisc
Block	Hyman		1838	Perr	Lisc
Block	Levi		1838	Perr	Adv
Block	Morris		1838	Perr	Adv
Block	Hyman		1838	Perr	Adv
Block	M		1825	CGir	Lisc
Block	Z		1825	CGir	Lisc
Block	Simon		1820	StL	Prop

Last Name	First Name	Int	Year	County	Type
Block	Eliazar		1820	StL	Prop
Block, Sr	Simon		1819	Steg	Lic
Blocker	Austin		1817	How	Prop
Blough	Jough		1829	NMad	DTL
Blount	John	W	1840	Call	Poll
Blount	Samuel		1840	Call	Poll
Blount	Peter		1821	StC	Ct
Blucher	John	P	1836	StC	Prop
Blue	Neal		1843	Audr	Prop
Blue	John		1843	Audr	Prop
Blue	Ducan	G	1843	Audr	Prop
Blue	Neal		1838	Audr	DTL
Blue	Duncan		1838	Audr	DTL
Blumencarian	Gerard		1844	Osag	Real
Bluster	Elisha		1836	StC	Prop
Blythe	John		1840	Call	Poll
Bobb	John		1820	StL	Prop
Bobbinrath	Sebastian		1836	StC	Prop
Bockman	Frederick		1836	Carr	Prop
Boduen	Juan		1780	StL	Mil
Boduen	Luis		1780	StL	Mil
Boduen	Josef		1791	StL	Span
Boduen (1)	Jose		1791	StL	Span
Boduen (2)	Jose		1791	StL	Span
Boencamp	August		1867	Reyn	DTL
Bofrer	Pedro		1780	StL	Mil
Bogart	Alexander		1821	Ray	Prop
Bogeneau	Nicolas		1780	StL	Mil
Bogg	James		1829	Char	DTL
Boggs	Lawrence		1843	Audr	Prop
Boggs	Tyre	R	1827	Boon	Lisc
Boggs	Liburn		1830	Call	DTL
Boggs	Geo	D	1837	Lew	DTL
Bogguss	Richard	H	1840	Call	Poll
Bogguss	Mathew	D	1840	Call	Poll
Boggy	Joseph		1823	Steg	Lisc
Bogy	Louis		1810	Ark	Prop
Bogy	Joseph		1810	Ark	Prop
Bogy	Charles		1810	Ark	Prop
Bogy	Joseph		1815	Ark	Prop
Bogy	Louis		1815	Ark	Prop
Bogy	Charles		1815	Ark	Prop

Last Name	First Name	Int	Year	County	Type
Bohannan	John		1843	Char	DTL
Boile	Michael		1836	StC	Prop
Boiles	John		1822	Clay	Poll
Boilston	Nathaniel		1839	Plat	Prop
Boilston	Thomas		1839	Plat	Prop
Boilston	Moses		1839	Plat	Prop
Boissy	Louis		1818	StL	Real
Boissy, dec	Louis		1820	StL	Prop
Boland	Delania		1839	Plat	Prop
Boland	William		1839	Plat	Prop
Boland	Benj		1839	Plat	Prop
Boland	William	D	1839	Plat	Prop
Boldene	Madame Ls		1805	Steg	Prop
Boldua	Squire		1805	Steg	Prop
Bolerle	Moritz		1837	Perr	Lisc
Boles	Franklin		1838	Steg	DTL
Bolotte	Edmund		1836	Carr	PrpPt
Bolten	Th	L	1844	Osag	Real
Bolton	Joseph	B	1820	StL	Prop
Bolvele	Mortiz		1836	Perr	Lisc
Bolwar	Philip		1839	Plat	Prop
Boly	Jacob		1863	Jeff	Ass
Boly	John		1863	Jeff	Ass
Bomer	George		1838	Audr	DTL
Bommes	Michell		1815	Ark	Prop
Bompart	Louis		1820	StL	Prop
Bonami	Pierre		1818	StL	Real
Bonamie	Pierre		1820	StL	Prop
Bond	David		1840	Call	Poll
Bond	Edward		1840	Call	Poll
Bones	Silas		1838	John	DTL
Bones	Enos		1839	John	DTL
Bonnet	Stacey		1844	Osag	Real
Boody	Bayou	K	1836	Carr	PrpPt
Booker	Edward		1840	Call	Poll
Boom	Saml		1840	Call	Poll
Boom	Joshua	M	1840	Call	Poll
Boon	M	M	1843	Audr	Prop
Boon	W	C	1843	Audr	Prop
Boon	Nathan		1836	StC	Prop
Boon	Squire		1836	StC	Prop
Boon	Sydner	S	1836	StC	Prop

Last Name	First Name	Int	Year	County	Type
Boon	Haden		1836	StC	Prop
Boon	Jonathan		1844	Osag	Real
Boon	Israel		1844	Osag	Real
Boone	V	D	1840	Call	Poll
Boone	Nathan		1823	Call	NRP
Booth	William		1840	Call	Poll
Boother	W	R	1829	Char	DTL
Boqua	Andrew	D	1837	Mill	DTL
Borden	David		1839	Plat	Prop
Borden	William		1839	Plat	Prop
Boren	William		1863	Jeff	Ass
Boren	F	M	1863	Jeff	Ass
Boris	Luis		1791	StL	Span
Bork	John		1805	Steg	Prop
Borrosie	Francisco		1780	StL	Mil
Borrosier	Franco		1791	StL	Span
Bosah	Jacob		1836	StC	Prop
Bosen	Henry		1844	Osag	Real
Bosern	Charles		1820	StL	Prop
Boshett	David		1836	StC	Prop
Boshett	John		1836	StC	Prop
Boshett's Heirs	Harmon		1836	StC	Prop
Boshick	John		1820	StL	Prop
Boshma	Louis		1836	StC	Prop
Boshman	Andrew		1836	StC	Prop
Boss	Daniel	C	1820	StL	Prop
Bossin	Jean Bte		1823	Steg	Lisc
Boswell	George		1836	StC	Prop
Bosworth	Isaac		1836	Carr	Prop
Bosworth	Isaac		1836	Carr	PrpPt
Boteler	Enrique		1791	StL	Span
Botts	James	F	1838	Audr	DTL
Botts	Set		1817	How	Prop
Boucher	Francois		1820	StL	Prop
Bough	E	E	1867	Reyn	DTL
Bouis	Wid Vincent		1820	StL	Prop
Boujin	Joseph		1820	StL	Prop
Boujn	Joseph		1818	StL	Real
Boulward	Barney		1844	Osag	Real
Boulware	Daniel		1840	Call	Poll
Boulware	Stephen	C	1840	Call	Poll
Boulware	Theodrick		1840	Call	Poll

Last Name	First Name	Int	Year	County	Type
Boulware	Willis		1827	Mari	Prop
Boulware	Mordecai		1827	Mari	Prop
Boulware	George		1844	Osag	Real
Boulware	Anthony		1844	Osag	Real
Bound	G	W	1867	Reyn	DTL
Bounds	John	B	1839	Plat	Prop
Bourne, Sr	William		1827	Mari	Prop
Bouvet	Jean Baptist		1820	StL	Prop
Bovauschecter	Anton		1836	StC	Prop
Bowen	Henry		1844	Osag	Real
Bowes	Boswell	B	1867	Reyn	DTL
Bowles	William		1867	Reyn	DTL
Bowles	Walter		1836	StC	Prop
Bowles	Leao		1836	StC	Prop
Bowles	James		1836	StC	Prop
Bowles	Stephen		1839	Lew	DTL
Bowlin	Joseph		1843	Char	DTL
Bowls	Benjamin		1827	Mari	Prop
Bowlwar	John		1839	Plat	Prop
Bowman	Jesse	B	1867	Reyn	DTL
Bowman	Jesse	B	1867	Reyn	DTL
Bowman	Jesse	B	1867	Reyn	DTL
Bowman	John		1844	Osag	Real
Box	Aike		1831	Jack	DTL
Box	Muke		1823	How	DTL
Boyce	Rober		1840	Call	Poll
Boyce	Robert	C	1834	Call	DTL
Boyd	John		1840	Call	Poll
Boyd	Micajah		1840	Call	Poll
Boyd	Robert		1840	Call	Poll
Boyd	Robert		1830	Coop	Ct
Boyd	Robert		1830	Coop	CtS
Boyd	Hyram		1836	StC	Prop
Boyd	Ruthe		1836	StC	Prop
Boyd	Carry	A	1836	StC	Prop
Boyd	Christopher		1820	StL	Prop
Boyd, Sr	Thomas		1840	Call	Poll
Boydston	James	H	1834	Craw	DTL
Boyer	Antonie		1839	Wash	Lisc
Bozarth	Squire		1827	Mari	Prop
Bozarth, Sr	John		1827	Mari	Prop
Bozer	David		1817	How	Prop

26

Last Name	First Name	Int	Year	County	Type
Brabourn	Frank		1830	Howa	DTL
Brack	E	J	1867	Reyn	DTL
Bradbury	John		1818	Lawr	DTL
Bradford	E		1843	Audr	Prop
Bradford	George		1840	Call	Poll
Bradford	George		1840	Call	Poll
Bradford	Nathaniel		1840	Call	Poll
Bradley	Benjn		1824	Boon	Deed
Bradley	Thos.		1843	Audr	Prop
Bradley	John	J	1843	Audr	Prop
Bradley	Edward		1843	Audr	Prop
Bradley	Wm.		1843	Audr	Prop
Bradley	Henry		1839	Plat	Prop
Bradley	Thomas	P	1840	Call	Poll
Bradley	A	P	1840	Call	Poll
Bradley	F	B	1840	Call	Poll
Bradley	G	E	1840	Call	Poll
Bradley	John	T	1840	Call	Poll
Bradley	Edward		1830	Coop	CtS
Bradley	Hughes		1838	John	DTL
Bradley	Edward		1810	Ark	Prop
Bradley	John	T	1820	StL	Prop
Bradley	Joseph		1817	How	Prop
Bradley	Leon		1817	How	Prop
Bradley	Littlem		1827	Mari	Prop
Bradley	Daniel		1827	Mari	Prop
Bradshaw	Charles		1818	Lawr	DTL
Bradwell	Joseph		1836	Carr	Prop
Bradwell	Joseph		1836	Carr	PrpPt
Brady	Josia		1836	StC	Prop
Brady	Thomas		1820	StL	Prop
Brady	T		1820	StL	Prop
Bragg	Nathaniel		1867	Reyn	DTL
Bragg	John	B	1834	Call	DTL
Bragles	Goodlow	H	1867	Reyn	DTL
Brail	Henry		1839	Plat	Prop
Braily	G	W	1840	Call	Poll
Brainerd	J	A	1867	Reyn	DTL
Braks	John		1867	Reyn	DTL
Brand	John	C	1867	Reyn	DTL
Brandon	Smith	A	1840	Call	Poll
Brandon	Abner	H	1840	Call	Poll

27

Last Name	First Name	Int	Year	County	Type
Branham	Richard		1836	Carr	Prop
Branham	Richard		1836	Carr	PrpPt
Branham	H	M	1840	Call	Poll
Branham	Thomas	H	1840	Call	Poll
Brannon	James		1818	Lawr	DTL
Branson	Andrew		1844	Osag	Real
Branson	David		1844	Osag	Real
Branson's Heirs	N		1829	Char	DTL
Brant	Archibald		1827	Mari	Prop
Brantine	Charles		1836	StC	Prop
Brantram	Frank		1840	Call	Poll
Brasan	Andrew		1844	Osag	Real
Brasfield	James		1839	Plat	Prop
Brashear	Thomas		1843	Audr	Prop
Brashear	Benjamin		1840	Call	Poll
Brashear	Levi		1840	Call	Poll
Brashear	William		1840	Call	Poll
Brashear	Joseph		1834	Craw	DTL
Brashears	Solomon		1836	Carr	Prop
Brashears	Solomon		1836	Carr	PrpPt
Brasher	Joseph		1817	How	Prop
Brasher	Judson		1817	How	Prop
Braton	David		1839	Plat	Prop
Braus	????		1820	StL	Prop
Brawdy	Alexander		1829	Mari	DTL
Brawdy	Richard		1829	Mari	DTL
Brazeau	Luis		1791	StL	Span
Brazeau	Josef		1791	StL	Span
Brazeau	Wid Madam		1791	StL	Span
Brazeau	Louis		1830	Linc	DTL
Brazeau	Francois		1818	StL	Real
Brazeau	Auguste		1818	StL	Real
Brazeau	Nicolas		1818	StL	Real
Brazeau	Widow		1818	StL	Real
Brazeau	Louis Jos		1820	StL	Prop
Brazeau	Auguste		1820	StL	Prop
Brazeaux	Nicolas		1820	StL	Prop
Brazeaux	Wid Therese		1820	StL	Prop
Brazier	John		1820	StL	Prop
Brazier's Heirs	Thomas		1836	Carr	Prop
Brazier's Heirs	Thomas		1836	Carr	PrpPt
Breda	Luis		1780	StL	Mil

28

Last Name	First Name	Int	Year	County	Type
Breeding	Elijah		1844	Osag	Real
Breeding	James		1844	Osag	Real
Breene	William		1867	Reyn	DTL
Brent	Anthony		1805	Steg	Prop
Brete	John		1836	Perr	Poll
Brewer	Charles		1836	Perr	Poll
Brewer	John		1836	Perr	Poll
Brewer	Mark		1836	Perr	Poll
Brewer	Stephen		1821	Ray	Prop
Brewer	Thomas		1821	Ray	Prop
Brewer	Henry		1821	Ray	Prop
Brezeau	Nicolas Colas		1818	StL	Real
Brickey	John		1839	Wash	Lisc
Brickley	John		1867	Reyn	DTL
Bridges	Horey	H	1844	Osag	Real
Bridges, Sr	James		1844	Osag	Real
Briggins	Broomfield		1836	Carr	Prop
Briggins	Broomfield		1836	Carr	PrpPt
Brighana	M	F	1867	Reyn	DTL
Bright	David		1840	Call	Poll
Bright	Henry	T	1840	Call	Poll
Bright	????		1820	StL	Prop
Brigpohe	Ignacio		1780	StL	Mil
Briham	Benjamin		1838	John	DTL
Brimbal	Wid Raphael		1810	Ark	Prop
Brimshell	James Joseph		1838	Ripl	DTL
Brine	Pat	O	1859	Reyn	DTL
Bringh	Christian		1810	Ark	Prop
Brink	E		1843	Audr	Prop
Brink	John		1839	Plat	Prop
Brite	Wm	A	1840	Call	Poll
Britian	Joseph		1839	Plat	Prop
Broadly	N	G	1840	Call	Poll
Broadwater	William		1834	Craw	DTL
Broadwell	William		1840	Call	Poll
Brock	Perry	G	1834	Pett	PrpPt
Brock	William		1863	Jeff	Ass
Brock	James		1817	How	Prop
Brock	Perry		1817	How	Prop
Brocket	Sydney		1836	Carr	Prop
Brocket	Sydney		1836	Carr	PrpPt
Brocks	James		1840	Call	Poll

Last Name	First Name	Int	Year	County	Type
Brocks	Robert		1840	Call	Poll
Brocks	Thomas		1840	Call	Poll
Broght	Josiah		1820	StL	Prop
Broison	William		1820	StL	Prop
Brook	Ewill		1840	Call	Poll
Brookman	Harman		1844	Osag	Real
Brooks	Elias		1843	Audr	Prop
Brooks	Sidney		1839	Plat	Prop
Brooks	James		1839	Plat	Prop
Brooks	H		1859	Reyn	DTL
Brooks	Richard		1859	Reyn	DTL
Brooks	John		1859	Reyn	DTL
Brooks	John		1859	Reyn	DTL
Brooks	Pleasant	D	1840	Call	Poll
Brooks	W	C	1867	Reyn	DTL
Brooks	Ira	S	1838	Audr	DTL
Brooks	Gilbert		1839	Lew	DTL
Brookshire	William		1831	Cole	DTL
Broomer	John		1836	Carr	Prop
Broomer	John		1836	Carr	PrpPt
Broomfield	R	B	1836	StC	Prop
Browley	John		1817	How	Prop
Brown	Laben	T	1843	Audr	Prop
Brown	Coleburn		1843	Audr	Prop
Brown	William		1843	Audr	Prop
Brown	John		1843	Audr	Prop
Brown	Thos.		1843	Audr	Prop
Brown	Nancy		1843	Audr	Prop
Brown	Milton		1839	Plat	Prop
Brown	David		1839	Plat	Prop
Brown	Hugh		1839	Plat	Prop
Brown	Gotham		1839	Plat	Prop
Brown	B	C	1839	Plat	Prop
Brown	Elisha		1839	Plat	Prop
Brown	Micajah		1839	Plat	Prop
Brown	Samuel		1839	Plat	Prop
Brown	John	E	1839	Plat	Prop
Brown	Andrew		1839	Plat	Prop
Brown	L	F	1839	Plat	Prop
Brown	Archibald		1839	Plat	Prop
Brown	B	C	1839	Plat	Prop
Brown	Adam		1839	Plat	Prop

Last Name	First Name	Int	Year	County	Type
Brown	Gray	B	1839	Plat	Prop
Brown	Robert	T	1838	Perr	Lisc
Brown	Robert		1838	Perr	Adv
Brown	Thomas	R	1859	Reyn	DTL
Brown	W	H	1859	Reyn	DTL
Brown	Robert	T	1836	Perr	Poll
Brown	Thomas		1836	Perr	Poll
Brown	Vimzod		1836	Perr	Poll
Brown	Mathias		1836	Carr	Prop
Brown	Christian		1836	Carr	Prop
Brown	Joseph		1836	Carr	Prop
Brown	Mathias		1836	Carr	PrpPt
Brown	Christian		1836	Carr	PrpPt
Brown	Joseph		1836	Carr	PrpPt
Brown	Bazel		1828	Boon	Lisc
Brown	Hiram		1840	Call	Poll
Brown	Charles	K	1840	Call	Poll
Brown	Mosley		1840	Call	Poll
Brown	John		1840	Call	Poll
Brown	James		1840	Call	Poll
Brown	Griffith		1821	StC	Ct
Brown	James		1830	Coop	Ct
Brown	Samuel		1830	Coop	Ct
Brown	Thomas		1863	Jeff	Ass
Brown	George		1867	Reyn	DTL
Brown	James		1867	Reyn	DTL
Brown	William		1867	Reyn	DTL
Brown	Jane		1836	StC	Prop
Brown	Josephus		1836	StC	Prop
Brown	Sophara		1836	StC	Prop
Brown	John		1823	Call	NRP
Brown	H		1829	Char	DTL
Brown	William		1830	Linc	DTL
Brown	Hugh		1821	Ray	Prop
Brown	James		1821	Ray	Prop
Brown	Joseph		1821	Ray	Prop
Brown	James		1810	Ark	Prop
Brown	Joseph		1838	Audr	DTL
Brown	William		1818	StL	Real
Brown	James		1829	Mari	DTL
Brown	Robert		1817	How	Prop
Brown	Samuel		1817	How	Prop

Last Name	First Name	Int	Year	County	Type
Brown	James		1817	How	Prop
Brown	William	B	1827	Mari	Prop
Brown	Jacob		1830	Ray	Prop
Brown	Colburn		1839	Lew	DTL
Brown	Lewis		1839	Lew	DTL
Brown (1)	William		1817	How	Prop
Brown (2)	William		1817	How	Prop
Brown's Heirs	James		1836	Carr	Prop
Brown's Heirs	James		1836	Carr	PrpPt
Brown's Heirs	James		1830	Ray	Prop
Brown, Jr	William		1839	Plat	Prop
Brown, Sr	William		1839	Plat	Prop
Browning	D	F G	1836	StC	Prop
Broy	Eilas		1839	Lew	DTL
Broy	Washington		1839	Lew	DTL
Bruce	Jacob		1843	Audr	Prop
Bruce	Ruefus		1843	Audr	Prop
Bruce	John		1867	Reyn	DTL
Bruce	Carl	C	1867	Reyn	DTL
Bruce	Jacob		1838	Audr	DTL
Bruce	Richard		1827	Mari	Prop
Brucieras	Juan Bapt		1780	StL	Mil
Brud	John	C	1867	Reyn	DTL
Bruer	Richard		1827	Mari	Prop
Bruffee	James		1830	Coop	Ct
Bruffee	James		1830	Coop	CtS
Bruin	Timothy		1836	StC	Prop
Bruin	John		1836	StC	Prop
Bruin	Even		1836	StC	Prop
Brunell	Tuscint		1836	StC	Prop
Bruner	Jacob		1828	Boon	Lisc
Bruner	Manuel		1791	StL	Span
Bruner	Barnhart		1844	Osag	Real
Brunet	Noel		1780	StL	Mil
Brunet	Luis		1780	StL	Mil
Brunet	Antonio		1780	StL	Mil
Brunett	G	W	1839	Plat	Prop
Brusier	Baptist		1836	StC	Prop
Brusier	Charles		1836	StC	Prop
Bruton	Addison		1839	Plat	Prop
Bryan	M		1839	Plat	Prop
Bryan	Thomas	L	1827	Boon	Lisc

Last Name	First Name	Int	Year	County	Type
Bryan	Joseph	T	1840	Call	Poll
Bryan	James		1836	StC	Prop
Bryan	Jonathan		1836	StC	Prop
Bryant	John		1839	Plat	Prop
Bryant	Joshua		1836	Carr	Prop
Bryant	Joshua		1836	Carr	PrpPt
Bryant	Felix		1840	Call	Poll
Bryant	James		1836	StC	Prop
Bryant	Washington		1836	StC	Prop
Bryant	Weston		1836	StC	Prop
Bryant	Elija		1836	StC	Prop
Bryant	Jonathan		1823	Call	NRP
Bryant	William		1830	Call	DTL
Bryant	David		1817	How	Prop
Bryant	Henry		1834	Call	DTL
Bryns	William		1838	Audr	DTL
Buch	John		1844	Osag	Real
Buchanan	William	R	1867	Reyn	DTL
Buchanan	James		1821	Ray	Prop
Buchanan	Mary		1818	StL	Real
Buchanan	Mary		1820	StL	Prop
Buckers	John		1844	Osag	Real
Buckley	John		1836	StC	Prop
Buckner	Thomas		1834	Craw	DTL
Buckrays	Jas		1822	Clay	Poll
Buckridge	James		1821	Ray	Prop
Buddle	Harim		1836	Carr	Prop
Buddle	Harim		1836	Carr	PrpPt
Buefe	Frank	W	1859	Reyn	DTL
Buefe	J	W	1859	Reyn	DTL
Buell	John	M	1867	Reyn	DTL
Buff	Martin		1839	Plat	Prop
Buffington	William	H	1843	Char	DTL
Buffrey	Femer		1836	StC	Prop
Buford	Abraham		1867	Reyn	DTL
Buges	Alexander		1838	Steg	DTL
Buich	Ami		1805	Steg	Prop
Buirry	Luis		1780	StL	Mil
Bull	William	A	1836	Perr	Poll
Bullard	Nathaniel		1822	NMad	Lisc
Bullard	Richard		1840	Call	Poll
Bullinger	Adam	J	1836	Perr	Poll

33

Last Name	First Name	Int	Year	County	Type
Bumby, Jr	James		1867	Reyn	DTL
Bumpass	William		1844	Osag	Real
Bunch	William	T	1828	Boon	Lisc
Bunch	Pleasant		1840	Call	Poll
Bunch	Samuel		1840	Call	Poll
Bunch	Elijah		1810	Ark	Prop
Bunch	Elijah		1815	Ark	Prop
Bunch	Henry		1844	Osag	Real
Bunhett	John		1840	Call	Poll
Bunt	Andrew		1867	Reyn	DTL
Burbank	David		1844	Osag	Real
Burbank	Ludwick		1844	Osag	Real
Burbank	Peter		1844	Osag	Real
Burch	Thomas	C	1831	Cole	DTL
Burchard	George	W	1844	Osag	Real
Burchsill	M	H	1859	Reyn	DTL
Burdit	John		1840	Call	Poll
Burdo	Baptist		1836	StC	Prop
Burdyne	Amos		1836	StC	Prop
Burdyne	William		1836	StC	Prop
Burdyne	James		1836	StC	Prop
Burdyne, Jr	Amos		1836	StC	Prop
Buren	Jno	W	1863	Jeff	Ass
Burg	James		1867	Reyn	DTL
Burgan	Isaac		1863	Jeff	Ass
Burgee	Joab		1836	Perr	Poll
Burgen	William		1831	Jack	DTL
Burgess	Thomas		1859	Reyn	DTL
Burgett	John	E	1836	Perr	Poll
Burgin	Thomas		1830	Coop	Ct
Burk	William		1867	Reyn	DTL
Burk	Peter		1867	Reyn	DTL
Burk	William		1867	Reyn	DTL
Burke	William		1823	How	DTL
Burkenmaster	Jacob		1836	StC	Prop
Burleson	James		1817	How	Prop
Burlison	John		1834	Craw	DTL
Burnes	Lewis		1839	Plat	Prop
Burnett	James	M	1825	CGir	Lisc
Burnett	Aquilla		1840	Call	Poll
Burnett	John	D S	1840	Call	Poll
Burnett	Samuel		1840	Call	Poll

34

Last Name	First Name	Int	Year	County	Type
Burnett	G		1826	Coop	DTL
Burney	William		1815	Ark	Prop
Burnnett	G		1826	Coop	DTL
Burns	Henry	R	1859	Reyn	DTL
Burns	James		1836	Perr	Poll
Burns	Michael		1836	Perr	Poll
Burns	Benjamin	F	1831	Jack	DTL
Burns	Jeremiah		1821	Ray	Prop
Burnsides	David		1836	Carr	PrpPt
Burrell	Mansfield		1836	Carr	PrpPt
Burrice	Francois		1805	Steg	Prop
Burris	Arthut		1830	Linc	DTL
Burris	Thomas		1817	How	Prop
Burris	Walter		1817	How	Prop
Burris	William		1831	Cole	DTL
Burrow	John		1836	Carr	PrpPt
Burrow's Heirs	William		1830	Ray	Prop
Burrows	John		1830	Ray	Prop
Burrs	William		1836	Perr	Poll
Burt	Franklin		1840	Call	Poll
Burt	Holman	M	1829	Mari	DTL
Buser	J	H	1867	Reyn	DTL
Bush	Felix	G	1839	Plat	Prop
Bush	Jordan		1840	Call	Poll
Bush	Frederick		1836	StC	Prop
Bush	Jacob		1836	StC	Prop
Bush	Jeremiah		1834	Call	DTL
Butcher	Icim		1836	StC	Prop
Butcher	Jane		1836	StC	Prop
Butcher's Heirs	Bazil		1836	StC	Prop
Butler	Tobias		1805	Steg	Prop
Butler	Sampson		1839	Plat	Prop
Butler	James		1839	Plat	Prop
Butler	William		1839	Plat	Prop
Butler	William		1837	Cass	DTL
Butler	Henry		1836	Carr	Prop
Butler	Henry		1836	Carr	PrpPt
Butler	Upton	C	1822	NMad	Lisc
Butler	Hiram		1867	Reyn	DTL
Butter	A	J	1867	Reyn	DTL
Butts	Jackson		1839	Plat	Prop
Butts	Henry		1839	Plat	Prop

Last Name	First Name	Int	Year	County	Type
Byers	Preston		1840	Call	Poll
Bynum	Gray		1817	How	Prop
Byran	Richard		1838	Audr	DTL
Byran	Elija	M	1838	Audr	DTL
Byrd	G	W	1863	Jeff	Ass
Byren	M		1859	Reyn	DTL
Byrne	Wm		1863	Jeff	Ass
Byrnie	Patrick		1863	Jeff	Ass
Byrns	William		1843	Audr	Prop
Byrns	Richard		1843	Audr	Prop
Byrns	Thos		1863	Jeff	Ass
Byrns	????		1867	Reyn	DTL
Cabana	Denis		1791	StL	Span
Cabanne	Jean	P	1820	StL	Prop
Cabble	Edward		1827	Sali	DTL
Cader	Joseph		1836	StC	Prop
Cader	Michael		1836	StC	Prop
Cadle	Benjamin		1836	Carr	Prop
Cadle	Benjamin		1836	Carr	PrtPt
Caffey	J	R	1867	Reyn	DTL
Caida	Francisco		1780	StL	Mil
Caillow	Louis		1820	StL	Prop
Caine	James		1823	How	DTL
Calahan	John		1867	Reyn	DTL
Calaway	Boon		1836	StC	Prop
Calaway	Therese		1836	StC	Prop
Calaway	Thomas		1836	StC	Prop
Calaway	William	B	1836	StC	Prop
Calaway's Heirs	John	B	1836	StC	Prop
Calbraith	J	H	1840	Call	Poll
Caldwell	Cornelius		1840	Call	Poll
Caldwell	Robert	A	1840	Call	Poll
Caldwell	Thomas		1840	Call	Poll
Caldwell	Thomas	H	1840	Call	Poll
Caldwell	Samuel		1821	StC	Ct
Caldwell	Saml	K	1821	StC	Ct
Caldwell	Robert		1867	Reyn	DTL
Caldwell	Mary	J	1867	Reyn	DTL
Caldwell	Archibald		1836	StC	Prop
Caldwell	James		1833	Wayn	DTL
Cale	Joseph		1780	StL	Mil
Caley	Williams		1867	Reyn	DTL

Last Name	First Name	Int	Year	County	Type
Calfield	John		1859	Reyn	DTL
Calhoun	Robert		1843	Audr	Prop
Call, Jr	Rufus		1836	Carr	Prop
Call, Jr	Rufus		1836	Carr	PrpPt
Callagher	John		1867	Reyn	DTL
Callaway	Thomas		1840	Call	Poll
Callaway	Joseph	P	1840	Call	Poll
Callerson	Robert		1836	StC	Prop
Callerson	James		1836	StC	Prop
Callerson	Ann		1836	StC	Prop
Callerson's Heirs	Absolem		1836	StC	Prop
Callicotte	William		1840	Call	Poll
Calliot	Antoine		1830	Jeff	DTL
Callison	Cyrus		1834	Call	DTL
Callon	Louis		1818	StL	Real
Calve	Jose		1791	StL	Span
Calvert	William		1817	How	Prop
Calvert	George		1827	Mari	Prop
Calvin	David	P	1840	Call	Poll
Cambas	Juan Bapt		1780	StL	Mil
Cambel	????		1836	StC	Prop
Cameron	Jonathan		1822	Clay	Poll
Cameron	Elisha		1822	Clay	Poll
Cammel	Samuel		1838	Audr	DTL
Camp	????		1867	Reyn	DTL
Camp	Benedict		1839	Lew	DTL
Campbel	Widow		1791	StL	Span
Campbel	????		1818	StL	Real
Campbell	Saml.		1843	Audr	Prop
Campbell	John		1843	Audr	Prop
Campbell	Wm	N	1843	Audr	Prop
Campbell	Andrew		1839	Plat	Prop
Campbell	Archibald		1839	Plat	Prop
Campbell	Washington		1839	Plat	Prop
Campbell	John		1859	Reyn	DTL
Campbell	Thomas		1840	Call	Poll
Campbell	William		1840	Call	Poll
Campbell	James	D	1830	Coop	Ct
Campbell	Joseph		1838	John	DTL
Campbell	William	M	1836	StC	Prop
Campbell	Robert	A	1836	StC	Prop
Campbell	Alex	B	1836	StC	Prop

Last Name	First Name	Int	Year	County	Type
Campbell	James		1836	StC	Prop
Campbell	Charles	G	1836	StC	Prop
Campbell	Thomas		1821	Ray	Prop
Campbell	James		1837	Lew	DTL
Campbell	Jno	B	1837	Lew	DTL
Campbell	Joseph		1839	John	DTL
Campbell	William		1817	How	Prop
Campbell	Samuel		1829	NMad	DTL
Campfield	Zebedee		1829	Mari	DTL
Camplin	Edward		1828	Boon	Lisc
Camplin	E		1828	Boon	Lisc
Camplin	Edward		1828	Boon	Lisc
Camron	Elisha		1821	Ray	Prop
Camron	Jonathan		1821	Ray	Prop
Canady	H		1843	Audr	Prop
Canahan	John		1810	Ark	Prop
Cane	Mathew		1867	Reyn	DTL
Canegy	John		1839	Lew	DTL
Canell's Heirs	Acan		1836	StC	Prop
Canerty	Thos		1859	Reyn	DTL
Cannell	Dennis		1867	Reyn	DTL
Cannon	George	W	1839	Plat	Prop
Cannon	Joseph	I	1839	Plat	Prop
Cannon	Samuel		1839	Plat	Prop
Cannon	????		1867	Reyn	DTL
Cannon	Joseph		1836	StC	Prop
Cannon	Phillip		1836	StC	Prop
Cannon	James		1839	Lew	DTL
Canny	Barrett		1830	Ray	Prop
Canory	Cornelius		1867	Reyn	DTL
Canote	????		1826	Coop	DTL
Canote	????		1826	Coop	DTL
Canpo	Pablo		1780	StL	Mil
Cansey	Bartlett		1836	Carr	PrpPt
Cantara	Baptista		1780	StL	Mil
Canter	James		1839	Plat	Prop
Canterberry	John	C	1843	Audr	Prop
Canterberry	Benjamin		1843	Audr	Prop
Canterberry	Lawrence		1843	Audr	Prop
Canterbury	Rueben	M	1843	Audr	Prop
Canterbury	Franklin	P	1843	Audr	Prop
Canterbury	B		1843	Audr	Prop

Last Name	First Name	Int	Year	County	Type
Canterbury	Benjamin		1838	Audr	DTL
Canterbury	Franklin	P	1838	Audr	DTL
Canterbury	Rueben		1838	Audr	DTL
Canwell	Jacob		1844	Osag	Real
Canwell	Nancy		1844	Osag	Real
Capehart	George		1833	Wayn	DTL
Capten	Baptist		1840	Call	Poll
Carathers	Edith		1836	StC	Prop
Cardinal	C		1831	Jack	DTL
Cardwell	Geo	W	1843	Audr	Prop
Cardwell	Wm		1843	Audr	Prop
Cardwell	Wyatt		1838	Audr	DTL
Carell	John		1821	Ray	Prop
Carell	James		1821	Ray	Prop
Carey	Edward		1827	Mari	Prop
Carl	William	H	1835	Barr	DTL
Carllow	James		1836	Carr	Prop
Carllow	James		1836	Carr	PrtPt
Carlocker	William		1867	Reyn	DTL
Carmen	Samuel		1818	StL	Real
Carmody's Heirs	John		1836	Carr	Prop
Carmody's Heirs	John		1836	Carr	PrpPt
Carmody's Heirs	John		1830	Ray	Prop
Carnes	John		1844	Osag	Real
Carney	John		1839	John	DTL
Carpenter	Peter		1818	Lawr	DTL
Carpenter	Beaufort		1839	Plat	Prop
Carpenter	Jonathan		1839	Plat	Prop
Carr	Joseph		1840	Call	Poll
Carr	James		1836	StC	Prop
Carr	William	C	1818	StL	Real
Carr	William	C	1820	StL	Prop
Carrington	William		1840	Call	Poll
Carrol's Heirs	James		1836	StC	Prop
Carroll	Henry		1836	Carr	Prop
Carroll	Henry		1836	Carr	PrtPt
Carroll	Hamilton		1836	Carr	PrpPt
Carroll	Henry		1830	Ray	Prop
Carroll	James		1822	Clay	Poll
Carroll	John		1822	Clay	Poll
Carrot	Louis		1805	Steg	Prop
Carson	George		1817	How	Prop

Last Name	First Name	Int	Year	County	Type
Carson	Lindsay		1817	How	Prop
Carson	William		1817	How	Prop
Carson	William		1827	Mari	Prop
Carson's Heirs	William		1836	Carr	Prop
Carson's Heirs	William		1836	Carr	PrpPt
Carter	Chas	H	1843	Audr	Prop
Carter	W	M	1839	Plat	Prop
Carter	Lacy		1839	Plat	Prop
Carter	Creed	C	1840	Call	Poll
Carter	Robert		1840	Call	Poll
Carter	William	H H	1836	StC	Prop
Carter	William		1836	StC	Prop
Carter	Cyrus		1836	StC	Prop
Carter	Christopher		1836	StC	Prop
Carter	James		1836	StC	Prop
Carter	Edmund		1817	How	Prop
Carter	James		1817	How	Prop
Carter	Garnett	J	1839	Lew	DTL
Cartmill	Wid Maria		1820	StL	Prop
Cartner	????		1867	Reyn	DTL
Cartwill	????		1818	StL	Real
Cartwright	Willis		1839	Plat	Prop
Cartwright	James		1839	Plat	Prop
Cartwright	Isaac		1839	Plat	Prop
Carty	James		1867	Reyn	DTL
Carutherathers	A	H	1836	StC	Prop
Carver	M	C	1836	Perr	Poll
Carwood	Berry		1839	Plat	Prop
Cary	Kemp		1821	Ray	Prop
Cary	Jefferson		1821	Ray	Prop
Cary	Nathaniel		1821	Ray	Prop
Cary	John		1844	Osag	Real
Casa Noba	Juan		1780	StL	Mil
Casbourn	John		1867	Reyn	DTL
Casey	Eli		1839	Plat	Prop
Casey	Thomas		1836	Carr	Prop
Casey	Thomas		1836	Carr	PrpPt
Casey	John	H	1839	Wash	Lisc
Casey	Daniel		1839	Wash	Lisc
Casey	John		1839	Wash	Lisc
Casey	James		1867	Reyn	DTL
Casey	Thomas		1830	Ray	Prop

Last Name	First Name	Int	Year	County	Type
Casey, Jr	John		1839	Wash	Lisc
Cash	John		1867	Reyn	DTL
Casidy	John	C	1843	Audr	Prop
Casner	Jonas		1821	Ray	Prop
Casner	George		1818	StL	Real
Cassidy	Patrick		1810	Ark	Prop
Cassidy	Patrick		1815	Ark	Prop
Cassidy	Henry		1815	Ark	Prop
Cassonget	Charles		1828	Sali	DTL
Cassott	Francis		1815	Ark	Prop
Casteel	Joseph		1823	How	DTL
Caster	Daniel		1820	StL	Prop
Castilio	J	H	1836	StC	Prop
Castleman	John		1830	Linc	DTL
Castlio	John	H	1836	StC	Prop
Castor	Alexander		1818	StL	Real
Catching	William	W	1839	John	DTL
Catherwood	????		1820	StL	Prop
Cathey	George		1817	How	Prop
Caton	William	S	1837	Cass	DTL
Caton	William		1817	How	Prop
Caton	William		1837	Cass	DTL
Cauchrun	George		1836	StC	Prop
Caussott	Pierre		1815	Ark	Prop
Cauthorn	Alfred		1843	Audr	Prop
Cauthorn	Allen		1843	Audr	Prop
Cauthorn	James	M	1843	Audr	Prop
Cauthorn	James		1843	Audr	Prop
Cauthorn	Carter		1843	Audr	Prop
Cauthorn	Paul		1843	Audr	Prop
Cauthorn	Silas		1843	Audr	Prop
Cauthorn	Peter		1843	Audr	Prop
Cauthorn	David		1843	Audr	Prop
Cauthorn	Carter		1843	Audr	Prop
Cay	John		1859	Reyn	DTL
Cayey	Pleasant		1836	StC	Prop
Cayou	Francis		1818	StL	Real
Cayou	Francois		1820	StL	Prop
Cayson	William		1840	Call	Poll
Cayson	Benjamin		1840	Call	Poll
Cayson	Hawkin		1840	Call	Poll
Cayson	Larkin		1840	Call	Poll

Last Name	First Name	Int	Year	County	Type
Caze	Joseph		1780	StL	Mil
Cean	Bernard		1863	Jeff	Ass
Cenaway	Lewis		1838	Ripl	DTL
Cenaway	Charles		1838	Ripl	DTL
Cerre	Gabriel		1791	StL	Span
Cerre	P Leon		1818	StL	Real
Cerre	Paseal Leon		1820	StL	Prop
Cewinth	James		1837	Mill	DTL
Chace	Elisha		1840	Call	Poll
Chairmuer	Jos		1836	StC	Prop
Chairmuer	John		1836	StC	Prop
Chamberlain	Gilbert		1836	Carr	Prop
Chamberlain	Gilbert		1836	Carr	PrpPt
Chambers	John		1859	Reyn	DTL
Chambers	Benjamin		1830	Coop	Ct
Chambers	Alexander		1836	StC	Prop
Chambers	William		1818	StL	Real
Chambers	William		1820	StL	Prop
Chambers	William		1817	How	Prop
Chambers	George		1839	Lew	DTL
Champaign	Mary		1836	StC	Prop
Chance	William		1839	Plat	Prop
Chance	Henry		1836	Carr	Prop
Chance	Henry		1836	Carr	PrpPt
Chanchillar's Heirs	Louis		1836	StC	Prop
Chanchillar, Jr	Louis		1836	StC	Prop
Chandler	David		1838	Cass	DTL
Chandler's Heirs	Jacob		1836	Carr	PrtPt
Chaney	Benoni		1827	Boon	Lisc
Chaney	Rubin		1840	Call	Poll
Chaney	Parke	I	1840	Call	Poll
Channcey	Viets		1867	Reyn	DTL
Chanrrion	Carlos		1780	StL	Mil
Chaplin	Peyer		1829	NMad	DTL
Chapman	R	D	1867	Reyn	DTL
Chapman	John		1822	Clay	Poll
Chapman	Thomas		1843	Char	DTL
Charless	Joseph		1820	StL	Prop
Charless	Edward		1820	StL	Prop
Charleswort	Walter	M	1836	StC	Prop
Charleville	Franco		1791	StL	Span
Charleville	Wid C		1818	StL	Real

42

Last Name	First Name	Int	Year	County	Type
Charleville	Joseph		1818	StL	Real
Charleville	Joseph		1818	StL	Real
Charleville	Wid Francoin		1820	StL	Prop
Charlton	John		1843	Audr	Prop
Charlton	John	H	1843	Audr	Prop
Charlton	Thomas		1836	Carr	Prop
Charlton	Thomas		1836	Carr	PrpPt
Charton	Hieronymus		1834	Pett	Prop
Chartran	Joseph		1780	StL	Mil
Chase	Joseph		1839	Lew	DTL
Chaspering	J	F	1867	Reyn	DTL
Chatelero	Luis		1780	StL	Mil
Chauncey	Cowls		1836	Carr	Prop
Chauncey	Cowls		1836	Carr	PrpPt
Chauvin	Santiago		1791	StL	Span
Chauvin	Devins		1818	StL	Real
Chavalie	Luis		1780	StL	Mil
Cheaney	John	L	1840	Call	Poll
Cheatham	David		1840	Call	Poll
Cheatham	Claiborn		1840	Call	Poll
Cheatham	David	L	1840	Call	Poll
Cheatham	Harrison	L	1840	Call	Poll
Cheatham	Leonard		1840	Call	Poll
Cheatham	Lewis		1840	Call	Poll
Cheatham	Luther		1840	Call	Poll
Cheatham	Turley		1840	Call	Poll
Cheatham	William		1838	Ripl	DTL
Cheeley	Joseph		1836	StC	Prop
Cheely	Charles		1836	StC	Prop
Cheely	Robert		1836	StC	Prop
Chevalier	Luis		1791	StL	Span
Chick	Joseph		1840	Call	Poll
Chil	Luis		1780	StL	Mil
Child	Susan	S	1867	Reyn	DTL
Childers	Abram		1840	Call	Poll
Childs	John	H	1840	Call	Poll
Chillere	Luis		1791	StL	Span
Chinn	Thomas		1836	StC	Prop
Chisholm	Ignatius		1815	Ark	Prop
Chisum	Jacob		1827	Coop	DTL
Chisum	Jacob		1827	Coop	DTL
Chole	Francisco		1780	StL	Mil

Last Name	First Name	Int	Year	County	Type
Chornete	Pedro		1791	StL	Span
Chorret	Nicolas		1780	StL	Mil
Chorrete	Jose		1791	StL	Span
Choteau	Augustus		1830	Linc	DTL
Chouteau	August		1780	StL	Mil
Chouteau	Pedro		1780	StL	Mil
Chouteau	Augustin		1791	StL	Span
Chouteau	Wid. Maria		1791	StL	Span
Chouteau	Pedro		1791	StL	Span
Chouteau	Pierre		1823	Call	NRP
Chouteau	Paul		1830	Linc	DTL
Chouteau	Pierre		1830	Linc	DTL
Chouteau	????		1820	StL	Prop
Chouteau	Auguste	P	1820	StL	Prop
Chouteau	Auguste		1820	StL	Prop
Chouteau	Peter		1817	How	Prop
Chouteau, Jr	Peter		1818	StL	Real
Chouteau, Jr	Pierre		1820	StL	Prop
Chouteau, Sr	Pierre		1820	StL	Prop
Chouvin	Frs Devins		1820	StL	Prop
Christian	William		1839	Lew	DTL
Christopher	John	D	1815	Ark	Prop
Christy	S	P	1836	StC	Prop
Christy	William	M	1836	StC	Prop
Christy, Jr	William		1836	StC	Prop
Church	R		1839	Plat	Prop
Cimins	Francis		1805	Steg	Prop
Cissell	John	R	1836	Perr	Poll
Citerly	Samuel		1840	Call	Poll
Clack	Dickson		1821	Ray	Prop
Clanton	James	H	1840	Call	Poll
Claren	William		1844	Osag	Real
Clarenbaugh	Peter	F	1844	Osag	Real
Clark	Wm	N	1843	Audr	Prop
Clark	Isaac		1843	Audr	Prop
Clark	John	P	1843	Audr	Prop
Clark	Tilman		1825	Clay	DTL
Clark	Gabriel		1839	Plat	Prop
Clark	Francis		1836	Perr	Poll
Clark	Charles		1836	Carr	Prop
Clark	Andrew		1836	Carr	Prop
Clark	Charles		1836	Carr	PrpPt

44

Last Name	First Name	Int	Year	County	Type
Clark	Andrew		1836	Carr	PrpPt
Clark	William		1836	Carr	Prop
Clark	William		1836	Carr	PrtPt
Clark	B	P	1827	Boon	Lisc
Clark	Isaac		1830	Coop	Ct
Clark	Robert	P	1830	Coop	Ct
Clark	Robert	P	1830	Coop	CtS
Clark	John	B	1830	Howa	DTL
Clark	J		1867	Reyn	DTL
Clark	Milton		1867	Reyn	DTL
Clark	John		1867	Reyn	DTL
Clark	Samuel		1836	StC	Prop
Clark	John		1823	Call	NRP
Clark	Isaac		1823	Call	NRP
Clark	Amos		1823	Call	NRP
Clark	Rensselser		1821	Ray	Prop
Clark	Gov William	C	1820	StL	Prop
Clark	Isaac		1817	How	Prop
Clark	David		1827	Mari	Prop
Clark	Benjamin		1831	Cole	DTL
Clark	Parsons		1830	Ray	Prop
Clark	Malakiah	W	1844	Osag	Real
Clark	Benjamin		1838	Ripl	DTL
Clarmo	Louis		1836	StC	Prop
Clarmo	Francis		1836	StC	Prop
Clary	Daniel		1839	Plat	Prop
Clary	Robert		1815	Ark	Prop
Clatterbuck	James		1840	Call	Poll
Clatterbuck	Cazeby		1840	Call	Poll
Clatterbuck	John		1840	Call	Poll
Clatterbuck	John	C	1840	Call	Poll
Clatterbuck	Richard		1840	Call	Poll
Clatterbuck	William		1840	Call	Poll
Clay	William		1839	Plat	Prop
Clay	Johnson		1839	Plat	Prop
Clay	Nancy	H	1836	StC	Prop
Clay	Nancy		1836	StC	Prop
Clay's Heirs	Eley		1836	StC	Prop
Clayton	John		1818	Lawr	DTL
Clayton	John	P	1839	Lew	DTL
Clayton	John	W	1834	Craw	DTL
Clemens, Jr	James		1820	StL	Prop

Last Name	First Name	Int	Year	County	Type
Clement	Francois		1820	StL	Prop
Clemmons	Thomas		1828	Sali	DTL
Clemons	Hanibal		1837	Lew	DTL
Clemont	Francis		1818	StL	Real
Clemorgan	Santiago		1791	StL	Span
Clemson	Eli	S	1823	Call	NRP
Clendennen	James		1831	Cole	DTL
Clendennen	Mathew		1831	Cole	DTL
Clendenon	Thadius		1843	Audr	Prop
Clendenon	T		1843	Audr	Prop
Cleton	William		1817	How	Prop
Cleveland	Yarrow		1836	Carr	Prop
Cleveland	Martin		1836	Carr	PrpPt
Cleveland	Warren		1836	Carr	PrpPt
Cleveland	Milton		1840	Call	Poll
Cleveland	Milton		1823	Call	NRP
Cleveland	Warren		1830	Ray	Prop
Clevenger	Pharis		1821	Ray	Prop
Clevenger	John		1821	Ray	Prop
Clevenger	Richard		1821	Ray	Prop
Clevenger	Samuel		1821	Ray	Prop
Clevenger	Zacahariah		1821	Ray	Prop
Clifton	Franklin		1836	Perr	Poll
Clifton	Jacob		1836	Perr	Poll
Clifton	Samuel		1836	Perr	Poll
Clifton	William	W	1833	Lew	DTL
Cline	Daniel		1836	Perr	Poll
Clinger	Fanny		1818	StL	Real
Clinger	Fanny		1820	StL	Prop
Clingsmith	Adam		1825	CGir	Lisc
Clinton	J	A	1867	Reyn	DTL
Clipper's Heirs	George		1830	Ray	Prop
Clogar	Leanzo		1867	Reyn	DTL
Clopton	John	D	1836	StC	Prop
Clough	William		1836	StC	Prop
Clyman	John	S	1835	Barr	DTL
Coalter	B	T	1836	StC	Prop
Coalter	John	D	1836	StC	Prop
Coats	Hiram		1840	Call	Poll
Coats	Lemuel	B	1840	Call	Poll
Coats	Mashall	S	1840	Call	Poll
Coats	William		1840	Call	Poll

Last Name	First Name	Int	Year	County	Type
Cob	Daniel		1834	Craw	DTL
Cobb	Joseph		1836	Carr	Prop
Cobb	Joseph		1836	Carr	PrtPt
Cobb	John		1831	Craw	DTL
Cobbs	Samuel	M	1836	Perr	Poll
Cocheran	John		1867	Reyn	DTL
Cochran	Thomas		1838	Perr	Lisc
Cochran	Thomas		1838	Perr	Adv
Cochran	James		1830	Linc	DTL
Cochran's Heirs	Jesse		1836	Carr	Prop
Cochran's Heirs	Jesse		1836	Carr	PrpPt
Cockburn	George		1859	Reyn	DTL
Cockrell	Thomas	N	1836	Carr	Prop
Cockrell	James		1830	Jeff	DTL
Cockrell	James		1817	How	Prop
Codwaleder	Eli		1867	Reyn	DTL
Cofer	M		1838	Steg	DTL
Coffell	Enoch		1844	Osag	Real
Coffelt	James		1844	Osag	Real
Coffer	Richard		1844	Osag	Real
Coffin	Banrabas		1867	Reyn	DTL
Coffman	Jacob		1838	John	DTL
Cogdale	William		1823	How	DTL
Cohagen	John		1840	Call	Poll
Coil	John		1843	Audr	Prop
Coil	John	C	1867	Reyn	DTL
Coks	Wakefield		1839	Plat	Prop
Coks	W		1839	Plat	Prop
Coks	Rev James	W	1839	Plat	Prop
Cole	N		1816	How	Lic
Cole	Mark		1840	Call	Poll
Cole	Stephen		1840	Call	Poll
Cole	Stephen		1830	Coop	Ct
Cole	Samuel		1836	StC	Prop
Cole	Hiram		1836	StC	Prop
Cole	Hannah		1817	How	Prop
Cole	James		1817	How	Prop
Cole's Heirs	Luther		1836	StC	Prop
Cole's Heirs	Ann		1836	StC	Prop
Cole, Sr	Stephen		1817	How	Prop
Coleman	James		1839	Plat	Prop
Coleman	Fisher		1830	Howa	DTL

Last Name	First Name	Int	Year	County	Type
Coleman	J		1829	Char	DTL
Coleman	Oliver	H P	1839	Lew	DTL
Coleman	Thomas		1843	Char	DTL
Colett	R		1818	StL	Real
Colgan, Sr	Daniel		1821	StC	CtS
Colgan, Sr	Daniel		1821	StC	CtS
Colirs	James		1830	Coop	CtS
Collard	E		1821	StC	CtS
Collard	E		1830	Linc	DTL
Collard	Joseph		1830	Linc	DTL
Collet	Ventura		1791	StL	Span
Collet	Robert		1820	StL	Prop
Collet	Thomas		1820	StL	Prop
Collet	????		1818	StL	Real
Collett	Abraham		1839	Plat	Prop
Collier	William		1828	Boon	Lisc
Collier	G		1828	Boon	Lisc
Collier	G		1836	StC	Prop
Collier	John		1821	Ray	Prop
Collier	Martin		1810	Ark	Prop
Collin	John		1810	Ark	Prop
Collin's Heirs	John		1836	Carr	Prop
Collin's Heirs	John		1836	Carr	PrpPt
Collins	Charley		1859	Reyn	DTL
Collins	Henry		1836	Carr	PrpPt
Collins	Brice	D	1840	Call	Poll
Collins	James	S	1830	Coop	Ct
Collins	David		1867	Reyn	DTL
Collins	William		1836	StC	Prop
Collins	James		1821	Ray	Prop
Collins	Henry		1830	Ray	Prop
Collins	James		1822	Clay	Poll
Collins	William		1822	Clay	Poll
Collins (1)	James		1836	Char	DTL
Collins (2)	James		1836	Char	DTL
Collis	David		1836	Carr	Prop
Collis	David		1836	Carr	PrtPt
Colson	James		1834	Craw	DTL
Colter	????		1867	Reyn	DTL
Colter	David		1820	StL	Prop
Colton	Leroy	C	1840	Call	Poll
Combs	John		1840	Call	Poll

Last Name	First Name	Int	Year	County	Type
Combs	William		1837	Bent	DTL
Comegy	John		1837	Lew	DTL
Comegys	Jacob		1836	StC	Prop
Comegys	James		1836	StC	Prop
Comegys	Benjamin		1836	StC	Prop
Comer	John	A	1840	Call	Poll
Comins	Christopher		1867	Reyn	DTL
Concaid	John	P	1839	Plat	Prop
Conger	Thomas	D	1840	Call	Poll
Conger	John		1840	Call	Poll
Conger	Stephen	D	1840	Call	Poll
Conklin	James		1820	StL	Prop
Conly	John		1828	Boon	Lisc
Connell	Daniel	O	1859	Reyn	DTL
Connell	Jeremiah		1836	Carr	Prop
Connell	Jeremiah		1836	Carr	PrpPt
Connelly	???heal		1859	Reyn	DTL
Connelly	M	C	1867	Reyn	DTL
Connelly	Michael		1867	Reyn	DTL
Conner	William	W	1867	Reyn	DTL
Conner	Pat		1867	Reyn	DTL
Conner	Jeremiah		1820	StL	Prop
Connor	John	O	1867	Reyn	DTL
Conory	Corneales		1859	Reyn	DTL
Conrad	Jacob		1836	Perr	Poll
Conrad	Peter		1836	Perr	Poll
Convine	Geo		1867	Reyn	DTL
Conway	Simon		1859	Reyn	DTL
Conway	Mary		1827	Mari	Prop
Conway	Samuel		1827	Mari	Prop
Cook	James		1843	Audr	Prop
Cook	John		1836	Carr	Prop
Cook	Willis		1836	Carr	Prop
Cook	Peter		1836	Carr	Prop
Cook	John		1836	Carr	PrpPt
Cook	Willis		1836	Carr	PrpPt
Cook	Peter		1836	Carr	PrpPt
Cook	Austin		1836	Carr	PrtPt
Cook	Joel	B	1840	Call	Poll
Cook	Joel		1840	Call	Poll
Cook	Lorenzo		1840	Call	Poll
Cook	John	H	1840	Call	Poll

Last Name	First Name	Int	Year	County	Type
Cook	J	P	1867	Reyn	DTL
Cook	Thomas	W	1867	Reyn	DTL
Cook	B		1818	StL	Real
Cook	John		1830	Ray	Prop
Cook	Henry		1830	Ray	Prop
Cook's Heirs	Paul		1836	Carr	Prop
Cook's Heirs	Paul		1836	Carr	PrpPt
Cooke	John		1818	Lawr	DTL
Cooke	John		1867	Reyn	DTL
Cooksey	Samuel		1836	Carr	PrpPt
Cooley	Perrin		1830	Howa	DTL
Cooley	Joseph		1817	How	Prop
Cooley	Perrin		1817	How	Prop
Coonce	Abraham		1840	Call	Poll
Cooner	Frederick		1830	Coop	CtS
Coons	Henry		1840	Call	Poll
Coons	Joseph		1840	Call	Poll
Coons	James		1840	Call	Poll
Coons	Mary		1836	StC	Prop
Coons	Rebecca		1836	StC	Prop
Coons	William		1836	StC	Prop
Coons	Felix		1836	StC	Prop
Coons	Nicholas		1836	StC	Prop
Coons' Heirs	Nicholas		1836	StC	Prop
Cooper	John		1839	Plat	Prop
Cooper	James		1839	Plat	Prop
Cooper	Nelson	H	1859	Reyn	DTL
Cooper	Moses		1836	Carr	Prop
Cooper	Moses		1836	Carr	PrpPt
Cooper	William		1840	Call	Poll
Cooper	Joseph		1830	Howa	DTL
Cooper	Eli	N	1867	Reyn	DTL
Cooper	F	W	1867	Reyn	DTL
Cooper	H		1867	Reyn	DTL
Cooper	H	J	1867	Reyn	DTL
Cooper	Eliza	N	1867	Reyn	DTL
Cooper	B	C	1829	Char	DTL
Cooper	????		1810	Ark	Prop
Cooper	Benjamin		1817	How	Prop
Cooper	Robert		1817	How	Prop
Cooper	Ruth		1817	How	Prop
Cooper	George		1817	How	Prop

Last Name	First Name	Int	Year	County	Type
Cooper's Heirs	Janny		1830	Howa	DTL
Cooper, dec	Braxton		1817	How	Prop
Cooper, Jr	Benjamin		1817	How	Prop
Cootes	Peter		1836	Carr	PrpPt
Coots	Abraham		1821	Ray	Prop
Copeland	J	E	1867	Reyn	DTL
Copeland	John		1817	How	Prop
Copeland	William		1844	Osag	Real
Copes	T	P	1827	Coop	DTL
Copes	Thomas	P	1836	StC	Prop
Copes	T	P	1827	Coop	DTL
Coppedge	George	W	1834	Craw	DTL
Cora	John	H	1840	Call	Poll
Cora	Joseph	H	1840	Call	Poll
Corbet	James	W	1836	Carr	PrpPt
Corbono	Louis		1836	StC	Prop
Corckett	Hugh		1838	Audr	DTL
Corden	George		1867	Reyn	DTL
Cordon	George		1867	Reyn	DTL
Cordwell	Madison		1837	Lew	DTL
Corlemus	Absalom		1822	Clay	Poll
Corlew	John		1824	Boon	Deed
Corley	George		1836	StC	Prop
Cormick	E	L	1859	Reyn	DTL
Cormick	E	S	1867	Reyn	DTL
Cormick	E	L	1867	Reyn	DTL
Cornan	Girdin		1859	Reyn	DTL
Cornelius	Benjamin		1821	Ray	Prop
Cornelius	W		1837	Boon	PM
Cornelius	John		1822	Clay	Poll
Cornell	Lewis		1867	Reyn	DTL
Cornelous	John		1821	Ray	Prop
Cornet	Nathaniel		1843	Audr	Prop
Cornett	A	B	1867	Reyn	DTL
Corno	Francisco		1780	StL	Mil
Cornoirer	Pier		1836	StC	Prop
Coshow	William		1836	StC	Prop
Cota	Baptista		1836	StC	Prop
Cote	Joseph		1780	StL	Mil
Cotland	????		1820	StL	Prop
Cotoe	Alexandre		1780	StL	Mil
Cott	Joshua		1867	Reyn	DTL

Last Name	First Name	Int	Year	County	Type
Cotter	Garrett		1867	Reyn	DTL
Cotter	J	H	1867	Reyn	DTL
Cotterman's Heirs	David		1836	Carr	Prop
Cotterman's Heirs	David		1836	Carr	PrpPt
Cottle	Oliver		1821	StC	CtS
Cottle	Alecta		1836	StC	Prop
Cottle	Lorenzo		1836	StC	Prop
Cottle	Alonzo		1836	StC	Prop
Cottle's Heirs	Warren		1836	StC	Prop
Cottle's Heirs	Sulvenis		1836	StC	Prop
Cotton	John	I	1828	Boon	Lisc
Cotts	Abram		1822	Clay	Poll
Couch	Thos		1843	Audr	Prop
Couder	Pedro		1791	StL	Span
Coulter's Heors	D		1829	Char	DTL
Couns	Juan		1791	StL	Span
Coursalt	E		1829	Char	DTL
Courtermach	Andrew		1836	StC	Prop
Courtney's Heirs	Samuel		1836	StC	Prop
Coutler	John		1818	StL	Real
Covert	J	L	1867	Reyn	DTL
Covert	James	L	1867	Reyn	DTL
Cowan	John		1859	Reyn	DTL
Cowan	William		1836	Carr	Prop
Cowan	William		1836	Carr	PrtPt
Cowan	Ephraim		1836	Carr	PrpPt
Cowbes	William		1836	Bent	DTL
Cox	Jester		1818	Lawr	DTL
Cox	William		1839	Plat	Prop
Cox	James		1839	Plat	Prop
Cox	Jacob		1839	Plat	Prop
Cox	William		1836	Perr	Poll
Cox	Jesse		1836	StC	Prop
Cox	Henry		1836	StC	Prop
Cox	Joseph		1821	Ray	Prop
Cox	Caleb		1820	StL	Prop
Cox	William		1844	Osag	Real
Cox	Rheuben		1844	Osag	Real
Cox	Samuel		1834	Lew	DTL
Coy	John		1829	Char	DTL
Coy	Simon		1823	How	DTL
Coyier	Henry		1867	Reyn	DTL

Last Name	First Name	Int	Year	County	Type
Coyle	Noah		1843	Audr	Prop
Coyle	James		1834	Craw	DTL
Cozine	Marcelous		1867	Reyn	DTL
Crabtree	Abraham		1831	Cole	DTL
Crabtree	John		1835	Barr	DTL
Crabtree	William		1835	Barr	DTL
Crabtree	James		1835	Barr	DTL
Craft	George	D	1836	Carr	Prop
Craft	George		1836	Carr	PrpPt
Cragg	Jacob		1818	Lawr	DTL
Craig	Carter	T	1840	Call	Poll
Craig	William		1840	Call	Poll
Craig	J	T	1840	Call	Poll
Craig	Larkin		1840	Call	Poll
Craig	Isaih		1840	Call	Poll
Craig	S	B	1830	Howa	DTL
Craig	John	T	1830	Howa	DTL
Craig	Jonathan		1836	StC	Prop
Craig	Isaac		1836	StC	Prop
Craig	James		1823	Call	NRP
Craig	George		1829	Char	DTL
Craig	Hiram		1817	How	Prop
Craig, Jr	William		1836	StC	Prop
Craig, Sr	William		1836	StC	Prop
Craige	Jesse	P	1840	Call	Poll
Craighead	Isaih	W	1840	Call	Poll
Craighead	J	W	1840	Call	Poll
Craighead	J	R	1840	Call	Poll
Craighead	James	L	1840	Call	Poll
Craighead	John		1840	Call	Poll
Craighead	Robert		1840	Call	Poll
Craighead	Solomon		1840	Call	Poll
Craighead	Stephen		1840	Call	Poll
Craighead	W	A B	1840	Call	Poll
Craighead	William		1840	Call	Poll
Crain	Thomas		1831	Craw	DTL
Crandell	Aaron		1836	Carr	PrpPt
Crank	Dabney	H	1840	Call	Poll
Crank	Henry		1840	Call	Poll
Crank	Nathaniel	H	1840	Call	Poll
Crasy	Jacob		1836	Carr	Prop
Crasy	Jacob		1836	Carr	PrtPt

Last Name	First Name	Int	Year	County	Type
Crawford	John		1820	StL	Prop
Creach	Simon		1830	Linc	DTL
Creacy	William		1838	Audr	DTL
Creacy	John		1838	Audr	DTL
Creason	Oran		1831	Jack	DTL
Creason	William		1821	Ray	Prop
Creason	James		1817	How	Prop
Creasy	John		1843	Audr	Prop
Creasy	Peter		1843	Audr	Prop
Creasy	James		1834	Lew	DTL
Creed	Augustin		1843	Audr	Prop
Creed	John		1843	Audr	Prop
Creed	Jas	M	1843	Audr	Prop
Creek	Beery		1839	Plat	Prop
Creek	Abraham		1821	Ray	Prop
Crely	Francis		1818	StL	Real
Crenshaw	Thomas		1837	Bent	DTL
Crepo	Luis		1780	StL	Mil
Creswell	George		1839	Wash	Lisc
Crevier	Antoine		1818	StL	Real
Crevier	F Xavier		1818	StL	Real
Crevier	Francois		1820	StL	Prop
Crews	William		1840	Call	Poll
Crews	Samuel		1840	Call	Poll
Crews	Thomas	P	1840	Call	Poll
Crickett	David		1822	Clay	Poll
Crimbo	J	R	1843	Char	DTL
Crisman	John		1844	Osag	Real
Crisman	John		1844	Osag	Real
Crisman	William		1844	Osag	Real
Crist	H	Y J	1867	Reyn	DTL
Cristison	Adam		1839	Plat	Prop
Criswell	William		1840	Call	Poll
Criswell	George		1840	Call	Poll
Criswell, Jr	James		1840	Call	Poll
Criswell, Sr	James		1840	Call	Poll
Crittendon	J	J	1829	Char	DTL
Crocket	Joseph		1843	Audr	Prop
Crocket	Wm		1843	Audr	Prop
Crocket	Hugh		1843	Audr	Prop
Crocket	David		1821	Ray	Prop
Crockett	James		1830	Coop	CtS

Last Name	First Name	Int	Year	County	Type
Crockett	Joseph		1821	Ray	Prop
Crockett	Joseph		1822	Clay	Poll
Crofford	John		1834	Lew	DTL
Cromwell	A	J	1863	Jeff	Ass
Cromwell	Oliver		1863	Jeff	Ass
Crook	John		1839	Plat	Prop
Crooks	John		1840	Call	Poll
Cropper	Levin		1817	How	Prop
Cross	Osborn		1836	Carr	PrpPt
Cross	H	C	1867	Reyn	DTL
Crosswhite	Joel		1843	Audr	Prop
Crosswhite	John	A	1843	Audr	Prop
Crosswhite	Jas		1843	Audr	Prop
Crosswhite	David		1843	Audr	Prop
Crosswhite	Wm		1843	Audr	Prop
Crosswhite	John		1840	Call	Poll
Crosswhite	John		1838	Audr	DTL
Crouch	John		1830	Linc	DTL
Crouch	Thomas		1838	Audr	DTL
Crouch	Pleasant		1844	Osag	Real
Crous	Adam		1838	John	DTL
Crow	Benjamin		1818	Lawr	DTL
Crow	Lewis		1836	StC	Prop
Crow	George		1836	StC	Prop
Crow	Jonathan		1836	StC	Prop
Crow	Daniel		1836	StC	Prop
Crow	Elizabeth		1836	StC	Prop
Crow	David		1836	StC	Prop
Crow	Joseph		1823	Call	NRP
Crowder	William	C	1836	Carr	Prop
Crowder	William		1836	Carr	PrpPt
Crowder	William		1838	Ripl	DTL
Crowley	John		1821	Ray	Prop
Crowley	Samuel		1821	Ray	Prop
Crowley	Thomas		1821	Ray	Prop
Crowley	James		1821	Ray	Prop
Crowley	John		1821	Ray	Prop
Crowley	Samuel		1821	Ray	Prop
Crowley	John		1821	Ray	Prop
Crowson	Jacob		1840	Call	Poll
Crowsyer	Michael		1830	Linc	DTL
Crud	John		1838	Audr	DTL

Last Name	First Name	Int	Year	County	Type
Crump	Willis		1827	Jack	DTL
Crump	Samuel	R	1840	Call	Poll
Crump	George		1817	How	Prop
Crump	Samuel	R	1835	Barr	DTL
Crunham	Thomas		1836	Bent	DTL
Cruse	George		1844	Osag	Real
Cruse	Nathan		1844	Osag	Real
Crutchlow	James		1836	Carr	PrtPt
Cruthers	Joseph		1836	Carr	PrpPt
Crutize	George		1844	Osag	Real
Crutsinger	Alfred		1818	StL	Real
Crutsinger	Alfred		1820	StL	Prop
Cryer	Morgan		1810	Ark	Prop
Cudorche	Pedro		1780	StL	Mil
Culbertson	Joseph		1827	Mari	Prop
Cullins	Tilman		1823	Call	NRP
Cully	John		1838	John	DTL
Culp	Nathan		1823	How	DTL
Culp	Jonatahn		1823	How	DTL
Cumins	James		1815	Ark	Prop
Cummas	James		1815	Ark	Prop
Cummesky	Pat		1863	Jeff	Ass
Cummings	Ephraim		1836	Carr	Prop
Cummings	Ephraim		1836	Carr	PrpPt
Cummings	Stewart		1830	Howa	DTL
Cummins	????		1836	StC	Prop
Cummins	James		1810	Ark	Prop
Cunningham	Jacob	F	1836	Carr	Prop
Cunningham	Jacob		1836	Carr	PrpPt
Cunningham	A	S	1867	Reyn	DTL
Cunningham	Thomas	M	1836	StC	Prop
Cunningham	Samuel		1836	StC	Prop
Cunningham	Thomas		1836	StC	Prop
Cunningham	William		1836	StC	Prop
Curle	Edwin		1836	StC	Prop
Curnutt	William		1834	Pett	Prop
Curray	Isaac		1867	Reyn	DTL
Currier's Heirs	Samuel		1836	Carr	Prop
Currier's Heirs	Samuel		1836	Carr	PrpPt
Currin	James		1810	Ark	Prop
Currin	Lemuel		1810	Ark	Prop
Curry	John		1840	Call	Poll

56

Last Name	First Name	Int	Year	County	Type
Curry	William		1840	Call	Poll
Curry	Isaac		1867	Reyn	DTL
Curry	C	H	1867	Reyn	DTL
Curtis	Henry		1836	Carr	PrtPt
Curtis	Williamson		1830	Coop	CtS
Curtis	William		1830	Coop	CtS
Curtsinger	Amelia		1844	Osag	Real
Custer	Hancy		1836	StC	Prop
Cutsinger	Aaron		1818	StL	Real
Cuyler	D	E	1829	Char	DTL
Cuzot	Simon		1780	StL	Mil
Cuzote	Pedro		1780	StL	Mil
Dabadia	Josef		1791	StL	Span
Dagguit	Peter		1819	Steg	Lic
Daggy	Michael		1867	Reyn	DTL
Dagley	John		1821	Ray	Prop
Dagley	James		1822	Clay	Poll
Daily	Michael		1836	Carr	Prop
Daily	Michael		1836	Carr	PrtPt
Daily	????		1818	StL	Real
Daley	Michael		1836	Perr	Poll
Daller	William		1859	Reyn	DTL
Dallins	William	T	1838	Audr	DTL
Dalremble	Antoine		1818	StL	Real
Dalrymple	Malone		1836	Carr	Prop
Dalrymple	Malone		1836	Carr	PrpPt
Dalton	James		1859	Reyn	DTL
Dalton	John	C	1838	Ripl	DTL
Dalton	Lewis		1838	Ripl	DTL
Daly	Thomas	S	1836	Carr	Prop
Daly	Thomas		1836	Carr	PrpPt
Dame	Daniel	M	1840	Call	Poll
Dame	Simon		1840	Call	Poll
Damsel	Elisha		1843	Audr	Prop
Dane	George		1840	Call	Poll
Danhorn	N		1825	CGir	Lisc
Daniel	Nicolas		1780	StL	Mil
Daniel	This		1859	Reyn	DTL
Daniel	William	R	1836	Carr	PrpPt
Daniel	Wright		1810	Ark	Prop
Daniel	Aaron		1818	StL	Real
Daniel	Arund		1820	StL	Prop

57

Last Name	First Name	Int	Year	County	Type
Daniel	Volentine		1839	John	DTL
Daniel	Wright		1815	Ark	Prop
Daniels	William	P	1836	Carr	Prop
Daniels	William		1836	Carr	PrtPt
Daniels	John	M	1867	Reyn	DTL
Daniels	Let???		1867	Reyn	DTL
Daniels	Letatia		1867	Reyn	DTL
Daniels	William	R	1830	Ray	Prop
Daniels	Elisha		1844	Osag	Real
Daniels	James		1844	Osag	Real
Daniels, Sr	Marmaduke		1844	Osag	Real
Danning	Patrick		1867	Reyn	DTL
Danny	William		1867	Reyn	DTL
Daquet	Peter		1823	Steg	Lisc
Darionne	Joseph		1815	Ark	Prop
Darionne	Baptiste		1815	Ark	Prop
Darst	David	H	1836	StC	Prop
Darst	Isaac		1836	StC	Prop
Datcherute	Isabelle		1818	StL	Real
Datcherute, dec	Elizabeth		1818	StL	Real
Datcherutte, dec	Elizabeth		1820	StL	Prop
Datchouiet	Francois		1818	StL	Real
Daugherty	James		1859	Reyn	DTL
Daugherty	Margarett		1818	StL	Real
Davenport	John		1828	Boon	Lisc
Davenport	George		1830	Ray	Prop
Daves	J	L	1863	Jeff	Ass
Daves	Joel		1836	Char	DTL
David	Eli		1836	Carr	Prop
David	William		1836	Carr	Prop
David	Eli		1836	Carr	PrtPt
David	William		1836	Carr	PrtPt
David	Archibald		1836	Carr	PrpPt
David	John		1838	Audr	DTL
David	William		1844	Osag	Real
David (free colored)	Afreu		1836	StC	Prop
Davidson	George		1843	Audr	Prop
Davidson	G		1843	Audr	Prop
Davidson	Andrew		1836	StC	Prop
Davidson's Heirs	Robert		1836	Carr	Prop
Davidson's Heirs	Robert		1836	Carr	PrpPt
Davis	Davis		1843	Audr	Prop

Last Name	First Name	Int	Year	County	Type
Davis	Spencer		1843	Audr	Prop
Davis	Simeon		1843	Audr	Prop
Davis	Elijah		1843	Audr	Prop
Davis	Jas		1843	Audr	Prop
Davis	M	L	1843	Audr	Prop
Davis	Harper	C	1816	How	Lic
Davis	Elias		1839	Plat	Prop
Davis	Wade		1839	Plat	Prop
Davis	Joseph		1839	Plat	Prop
Davis	James	M	1839	Plat	Prop
Davis	Allen		1839	Plat	Prop
Davis	Benjamin		1839	Plat	Prop
Davis	Robert		1839	Plat	Prop
Davis	C		1837	Sali	DTL
Davis	???niel	K	1859	Reyn	DTL
Davis	William		1836	Carr	PrpPt
Davis	Thomas		1836	Carr	PrpPt
Davis	Benjamin		1828	Boon	Lisc
Davis	John		1828	Boon	Lisc
Davis	John		1840	Call	Poll
Davis	Jonthan		1840	Call	Poll
Davis	Jos	G	1840	Call	Poll
Davis	Robert	L	1840	Call	Poll
Davis	John		1840	Call	Poll
Davis	Philip		1840	Call	Poll
Davis	Henry		1840	Call	Poll
Davis	James		1840	Call	Poll
Davis	Thomas	J	1840	Call	Poll
Davis	Barnabas	C	1840	Call	Poll
Davis	Robert		1840	Call	Poll
Davis	Thomas		1840	Call	Poll
Davis	M	V	1840	Call	Poll
Davis	George	W T	1840	Call	Poll
Davis	George		1840	Call	Poll
Davis	David	B	1840	Call	Poll
Davis	Gerrard		1840	Call	Poll
Davis	James	M	1840	Call	Poll
Davis	James		1840	Call	Poll
Davis	Mathew		1840	Call	Poll
Davis	John		1840	Call	Poll
Davis	John	B	1840	Call	Poll
Davis	Rufus		1840	Call	Poll

Last Name	First Name	Int	Year	County	Type
Davis	W	C	1840	Call	Poll
Davis	Cornelius		1830	Coop	Ct
Davis	Isaac		1830	Coop	Ct
Davis	Cornelius		1830	Coop	CtS
Davis	Thomas		1830	Coop	CtS
Davis	John		1867	Reyn	DTL
Davis	John		1867	Reyn	DTL
Davis	J	A	1867	Reyn	DTL
Davis	Henry		1867	Reyn	DTL
Davis	Therren	H	1836	StC	Prop
Davis	Isaac		1836	StC	Prop
Davis	Frederick		1836	StC	Prop
Davis	John		1836	StC	Prop
Davis	Norman		1821	Ray	Prop
Davis	William		1821	Ray	Prop
Davis	John		1821	Ray	Prop
Davis	Edward		1810	Ark	Prop
Davis	Zacahriah		1810	Ark	Prop
Davis	Mathew		1838	Audr	DTL
Davis	Ephriam		1838	Audr	DTL
Davis	Simon		1838	Audr	DTL
Davis	Ralph		1818	StL	Real
Davis	James		1837	Lew	DTL
Davis	John		1817	How	Prop
Davis	Abner		1817	How	Prop
Davis	Shadrick		1827	Mari	Prop
Davis	William		1830	Ray	Prop
Davis	Thomas		1830	Ray	Prop
Davis	Thomas		1830	Ray	Prop
Davis	John		1830	Ray	Prop
Davis	Flemming		1839	Lew	DTL
Davis	John		1839	Lew	DTL
Davis	James		1839	Lew	DTL
Davis	Isaac		1839	Lew	DTL
Davis	Jonatahn		1844	Osag	Real
Davis	Thomas		1844	Osag	Real
Davis	James		1834	Call	DTL
Davis	Joshua		1834	Craw	DTL
Davis	James		1837	Mill	DTL
Davis	Morris		1837	Mill	DTL
Davis (1)	James		1838	Audr	DTL
Davis (2)	James		1838	Audr	DTL

Last Name	First Name	Int	Year	County	Type
Davis (3)	James		1838	Audr	DTL
Davis' Heirs	Lewis		1836	Carr	Prop
Davis' Heirs	Lewis		1836	Carr	PrtPt
Davis' Heirs	Edmond		1836	StC	Prop
Davis, Jr	William		1822	Clay	Poll
Davis, Jr	John		1837	Mill	DTL
Davis, Sr	William		1822	Clay	Poll
Davison	Asa		1837	Lew	DTL
Daviss	Richard		1840	Call	Poll
Daviss	Ralph		1820	StL	Prop
Dawling	Peter		1836	Carr	Prop
Dawling	Peter		1836	Carr	PrpPt
Dawling	Peter		1836	Carr	PrpPt
Dawson	Benj		1840	Call	Poll
Dawson	Elijah		1840	Call	Poll
Dawson	George		1840	Call	Poll
Dawson	James	A	1840	Call	Poll
Dawson	Martin		1840	Call	Poll
Dawson	Robert		1840	Call	Poll
Dawson	Robert	D	1823	Call	NRP
Day	A		1843	Audr	
Day	Lewis		1843	Audr	Prop
Day	Truman		1843	Audr	Prop
Day	A		1843	Audr	Prop
Day	L		1843	Audr	Prop
Day	Truman		1839	Plat	Prop
Day	George		1836	Carr	Prop
Day	George		1836	Carr	PrtPt
Day	George		1836	Carr	PrpPt
Day	Ackly		1840	Call	Poll
Day	Charles	A	1840	Call	Poll
Day	Truman		1840	Call	Poll
Day	Ezekiel		1840	Call	Poll
Day	Samuel		1840	Call	Poll
Day	Solomon		1840	Call	Poll
Day	Thomas		1840	Call	Poll
Day	Daniel	T	1840	Call	Poll
Day	P	E	1840	Call	Poll
Day	W	T	1840	Call	Poll
Day	Nathaniel		1836	StC	Prop
Day	Nighton		1836	StC	Prop
Day	Lewis		1838	Audr	DTL

Last Name	First Name	Int	Year	County	Type
Dayal	Willey		1836	Carr	Prop
Dayal	Willey		1836	Carr	PrpPt
De Pre	Rene		1780	StL	Mil
De Rouen	Wid. Madam		1791	StL	Span
De Thier	????		1821	StC	Ct
De Vau	Pedro		1791	StL	Span
Dea	Patrick	O	1859	Reyn	DTL
Deakers	William		1820	StL	Prop
Dean	Abner		1839	Plat	Prop
Dean	Bartlett		1839	Plat	Prop
Dean	Francis		1839	Plat	Prop
Dean	Fred	J	1859	Reyn	DTL
Dean	S	M	1830	Linc	DTL
Dean	John		1821	Ray	Prop
Dean	Jesse		1810	Ark	Prop
Dean	Seth		1815	Ark	Prop
Dear	George		1836	StC	Prop
Deaster	George		1836	StC	Prop
Deaster	Christopher		1836	StC	Prop
Debeaugh	Cefrey		1836	StC	Prop
Debo	Pedro		1780	StL	Mil
Debo	John		1840	Call	Poll
Decamp	Stephen		1836	StC	Prop
Decari	Franco		1791	StL	Span
Dechene	Pedro		1780	StL	Mil
Dechneueday	Paschal		1839	Wash	Lisc
Decker	John		1823	Call	NRP
Decker	Luke		1838	Ripl	DTL
Deckers	Willia,		1818	StL	Real
Deeclos	Antoine		1839	Wash	Lisc
Deen	Henry		1836	Perr	Poll
Deen	Peter		1836	Perr	Poll
Deen	William		1836	Perr	Poll
Degraffenrua	John		1837	Mill	DTL
Degrew	William		1836	Carr	Prop
Degrew	William		1836	Carr	PrpPt
Dehart	John		1810	Ark	Prop
Dehault	Domitil		1833	Wayn	DTL
DeHaven	Isaac		1840	Call	Poll
Dehetre	Antonio		1791	StL	Span
Deirice	William	L	1836	StC	Prop
Dejaveret	Henry		1843	Audr	Prop

Last Name	First Name	Int	Year	County	Type
Dejerden	Peter		1818	StL	Real
Delamn	Thomas	R	1836	Carr	Prop
Delamn	Thomas		1836	Carr	PrpPt
Delaney	T	L	1843	Audr	Prop
Delaney	Joseph	S	1838	Audr	DTL
Delaney	Joseph	S	1838	Audr	DTL
Delano	John		1867	Reyn	DTL
Delany	John		1859	Reyn	DTL
Delany	Pat		1859	Reyn	DTL
Delany	David		1818	StL	Real
Delaroderie	A		1822	NMad	Lisc
Delassus	Charles		1818	StL	Real
Delauny	David		1820	StL	Prop
Delaurier	C	F	1818	StL	Real
Delaurier	Henry		1820	StL	Prop
Delba	Frances		1838	Steg	DTL
Delisla	Luis		1791	StL	Span
Delisle	Carlos		1791	StL	Span
Delorier	Francisco		1780	StL	Mil
Delorier	Lorenzo		1791	StL	Span
Deluquerre	Mos		1805	Steg	Prop
Demarre	Amable		1780	StL	Mil
Demasters	Anderson		1839	John	DTL
Dement	John		1867	Reyn	DTL
Dempsey	George		1867	Reyn	DTL
Dennis	Jas	M	1843	Audr	Prop
Dennis	William		1843	Audr	Prop
Dennis	Joseph		1836	Carr	Prop
Dennis	Joseph		1836	Carr	PrpPt
Dennis	Given		1867	Reyn	DTL
Dennis	John	H	1836	StC	Prop
Denny	Charles		1821	StC	CtS
Denny, Jr	Charles		1836	StC	Prop
Denny, Sr	Charles		1836	StC	Prop
Denoier	Francis		1840	Call	Poll
Denoye	Guiery		1780	StL	Mil
Densman	Thomas		1830	Coop	Ct
Denson	Jon		1831	Cole	DTL
Dent	Frederick		1820	StL	Prop
Denton	Jonatahn		1822	Clay	Poll
Denton	Tipton		1835	Barr	DTL
Deraway	Michael		1836	StC	Prop

Last Name	First Name	Int	Year	County	Type
Deraway	Joseph		1836	StC	Prop
Derick	Grase		1859	Reyn	DTL
Derland	James		1839	Plat	Prop
Dermon	David		1863	Jeff	Ass
Deroin	Bptiste		1818	StL	Real
Deroughy	St. Croix		1836	StC	Prop
Derouse	Francis		1830	Howa	DTL
Derroge	Lorenzo		1780	StL	Mil
Derruen	Juan Luis		1780	StL	Mil
Derruen	Juan Baptista		1780	StL	Mil
Derruen	Estevan		1780	StL	Mil
Deruisseaux	Jean Bte		1810	Ark	Prop
Dervins, Sr	Frances		1818	StL	Real
Desery	Louis		1818	StL	Real
Desotel	Josef		1791	StL	Span
Desusseaux	Francois		1810	Ark	Prop
Detrandbaratz	????		1820	StL	Prop
Deufau	Charles		1836	StC	Prop
Deveciant	John		1867	Reyn	DTL
Dever	Allen		1824	Boon	Deed
Dever	Henry	E	1824	Boon	Deed
Deverusseau	Joseph		1815	Ark	Prop
Deveusseau	John Bte		1815	Ark	Prop
Devieusseau	Francis		1815	Ark	Prop
Devilmont	Charles		1815	Ark	Prop
Devine	John		1867	Reyn	DTL
Devine	Michael		1867	Reyn	DTL
Devine	Michael		1867	Reyn	DTL
Devolsey	Pedro		1791	StL	Span
Devore	Uriah	S	1821	StC	Ct
Devore	James		1821	StC	Ct
Devore	Uriah	S	1821	StC	CtS
DeWitt	Walter		1830	Jeff	DTL
DeWitt	Henry		1830	Jeff	DTL
DeWitt	Thomas		1835	Barr	DTL
Deyer	David	P	1859	Reyn	DTL
Dianne	Madam		1810	Ark	Prop
Dianne	Widow		1815	Ark	Prop
Dickerson	Samuel	D	1840	Call	Poll
Dickerson	Adam		1840	Call	Poll
Dickerson	N		1845	Sali	Lisc
Dickerson	Josuah		1867	Reyn	DTL

Last Name	First Name	Int	Year	County	Type
Dickerson	Obediah		1827	Mari	Prop
Dickerson	Obadiah		1827	Mari	Prop
Dickerson	Silas		1838	Ripl	DTL
Dickhoust	Henry		1836	StC	Prop
Dickson	Lewis		1836	Perr	Poll
Dickson	Jessey		1836	Perr	Poll
Dickson	Wilson		1836	Carr	Prop
Dickson	Wilson		1836	Carr	PrpPt
Dickson	Hezekiah		1810	Ark	Prop
Dickson's Heirs	Thomas		1836	Carr	Prop
Dickson's Heirs	Thomas		1836	Carr	PrpPt
Dill's Heirs	Caleb		1836	Carr	Prop
Dill's Heirs	Caleb		1836	Carr	PrtPt
Dill's Heirs	Caleb		1830	Ray	Prop
Dillahunt	????		1867	Reyn	DTL
Dillin	Walter		1836	StC	Prop
Dillingham	M		1829	Char	DTL
Dillon	Washington		1843	Audr	Prop
Dillon	P	M	1818	StL	Real
Dillon	Hugh		1831	Cole	DTL
Dinelly	Joseph		1830	Jeff	DTL
Dingle	Carter		1843	Audr	Prop
Dingle	John		1843	Audr	Prop
Dingle	Saml		1843	Audr	Prop
Dingley	Daniel		1830	Ray	Prop
Dirkskill	James	H	1840	Call	Poll
Disard	Madison		1838	Audr	DTL
Dishon	James		1836	Carr	Prop
Dishon	James		1836	Carr	PrpPt
Divers	John		1834	Call	DTL
Divine	Nathaniel	J	1836	Perr	Poll
Dixon	Cyrus		1840	Call	Poll
Dixon	Widow		1815	Ark	Prop
Doan	H	I M	1843	Audr	Prop
Doan	H	I M	1843	Audr	Prop
Doan	Sanford		1843	Audr	Prop
Doan	H	J M	1838	Audr	DTL
Dobbins	Jonn	L	1867	Reyn	DTL
Doboy	John		1830	Ray	Prop
Dobson	John		1821	Ray	Prop
Dobson	Joseph		1839	Lew	DTL
Dodd	Abel		1840	Call	Poll

Last Name	First Name	Int	Year	County	Type
Dodd	Francis		1844	Osag	Real
Dodd	William		1844	Osag	Real
Dodd	Josephus		1844	Osag	Real
Dodd	John		1844	Osag	Real
Dodd	Joab		1844	Osag	Real
Dodds	John		1840	Call	Poll
Dodds	Williams	S	1840	Call	Poll
Dodge	Grael		1805	Steg	Prop
Dodge	Charles		1867	Reyn	DTL
Dodge	William		1839	Lew	DTL
Dodie	Gabriel		1780	StL	Mil
Dodie	Agustin		1780	StL	Mil
Dodier	Gabriel		1791	StL	Span
Dodier	Augustin		1791	StL	Span
Dodson	Samuel		1835	Barr	DTL
Doe	David		1836	Carr	Prop
Doe	David		1836	Carr	PrpPt
Doe	David		1830	Ray	Prop
Doggen	Thomas		1844	Osag	Real
Doiser	William		1823	How	DTL
Dolan	Michael		1818	StL	Real
Dolan	Edward		1818	StL	Real
Dolan	Edwrd		1820	StL	Prop
Dolkill	Hiram		1835	Barr	DTL
Dollins	William	T	1843	Audr	Prop
Dollins	Jas	D	1843	Audr	Prop
Dollins	Richard		1843	Audr	Prop
Dollins	Pheby		1843	Audr	Prop
Dollins	William		1843	Audr	Prop
Dollins	William		1843	Audr	Prop
Dolson	Steven		1836	Perr	Poll
Dolton	Joseph		1835	Barr	DTL
Domine	Baptiste		1818	StL	Real
Domine	Frances		1818	StL	Real
Donahoe	Rephin		1818	StL	Real
Donahoo	Stephen		1836	Carr	Prop
Donahoo	Samuel		1836	Carr	Prop
Donald	????		1845	Sali	Lisc
Donaldson	Williamson		1839	Plat	Prop
Donally	Gilfield		1836	Carr	Prop
Donally	Gilfield		1836	Carr	PrtPt
Donaway	Joseph		1836	Carr	Prop

Last Name	First Name	Int	Year	County	Type
Donaway	Joseph		1836	Carr	PrtPt
Donnan	John		1844	Osag	Real
Donohoe	William		1825	Char	DTL
Donohoe	Stephen		1825	Char	DTL
Dooley	Paul	H	1840	Call	Poll
Dooley	Thomas		1810	Ark	Prop
Doolin	Peter		1817	How	Prop
Dophine	Pattrice		1836	StC	Prop
Dophine	Alexa		1836	StC	Prop
Dority	Haw		1840	Call	Poll
Dority	Mathew		1840	Call	Poll
Dorlac	Franco		1791	StL	Span
Dorlac	August		1836	StC	Prop
Dorlac's Heirs	Baptiste		1836	StC	Prop
Dorrel	William		1836	Char	DTL
Dorsey	Lyada		1836	StC	Prop
Dorst's Heirs	Lyman		1836	Carr	Prop
Dorst's Heirs	Lyman		1836	Carr	PrpPt
Dosier	William		1840	Call	Poll
Dotson	William		1836	StC	Prop
Dotson's Heirs	Joshua		1836	StC	Prop
Doublenay	Jo		1805	Steg	Prop
Dougan	William		1830	Ray	Prop
Dougan	James		1837	Mill	DTL
Dougherty	James		1839	Plat	Prop
Dougherty	Charles		1840	Call	Poll
Dougherty	John		1867	Reyn	DTL
Dougherty	J	M	1867	Reyn	DTL
Dougherty	Stephen		1867	Reyn	DTL
Dougherty	James		1867	Reyn	DTL
Dougherty	John		1834	Call	DTL
Dougherty	Mathew		1834	Call	DTL
Douglas	????		1827	Coop	DTL
Douglas	James		1830	Howa	DTL
Douglas	John		1827	Coop	DTL
Douglass	William	B	1843	Audr	Prop
Douglass	William		1827	Boon	Lisc
Douglass	Thomas	L	1840	Call	Poll
Douglass	John		1840	Call	Poll
Douglass	A	T	1836	StC	Prop
Douglass	Edward	H	1838	Audr	DTL
Dousman	Michael		1829	Char	DTL

Last Name	First Name	Int	Year	County	Type
Dousman	Michael		1830	Ray	Prop
Dovovan	????chael		1859	Reyn	DTL
Dowling	Peter		1830	Ray	Prop
Dowling	Joseph		1830	Ray	Prop
Downing	John		1839	Plat	Prop
Downing	David		1829	Mari	DTL
Doxey	John		1817	How	Prop
Doyle	Mathew		1867	Reyn	DTL
Doyle	Mathew		1867	Reyn	DTL
Draice	Madison		1839	Plat	Prop
Drake	James	K	1836	Carr	Prop
Drake	James		1836	Carr	PrtPt
Drake	Jefferson		1836	StC	Prop
Drake	Isaac		1817	How	Prop
Draper	I	I	1839	Plat	Prop
Drennen	Rich		1863	Jeff	Ass
Drennen	Doc		1863	Jeff	Ass
Drennen	George		1863	Jeff	Ass
Drennen	Aquilla		1863	Jeff	Ass
Drew	Jesse		1843	Char	DTL
Dreyer	Dennis		1867	Reyn	DTL
Drinkard	Francis		1830	Howa	DTL
Drouin	Frances		1818	StL	Real
Drouin	John		1818	StL	Real
Drouin	Jean		1820	StL	Prop
Drummon's Heirs	Mellom		1836	StC	Prop
Drummonds	Samuel		1836	StC	Prop
Drummons	Flemmonds		1839	Plat	Prop
Drummons	Lott		1839	Plat	Prop
Drummons	James		1836	StC	Prop
Drummons	Harrison		1836	StC	Prop
Drury	James	W	1836	StC	Prop
Drusdale	Adam		1867	Reyn	DTL
Druvin, Jr	Frances		1818	StL	Real
Duane	David		1840	Call	Poll
Dubal	Benrardo		1780	StL	Mil
Dubaugh	Jacko		1836	StC	Prop
Dubaugh	Acan		1836	StC	Prop
Dubet	Frederick		1836	StC	Prop
Dubet	Henry		1836	StC	Prop
Dubey	John		1836	Carr	PrtPt
Dubois	Elisha		1836	Carr	Prop

Last Name	First Name	Int	Year	County	Type
Dubois	Elisha		1836	Carr	PrpPt
Dubremble	Antonie		1818	StL	Real
Dubreuil	Luis		1791	StL	Span
Dubreuil	Luis		1791	StL	Span
Dubreuil	Susanne Santores		1820	StL	Prop
Dubreuil	Antoine		1820	StL	Prop
Dubreville	Widow		1830	Linc	DTL
Dubroy	Luis		1780	StL	Mil
Duchene	Joseph		1780	StL	Mil
Duchequete	Francisco		1780	StL	Mil
Duchoquet	Francois		1818	StL	Real
Duchoquete	Enrique		1780	StL	Mil
Duchouquette	Bapt		1830	Call	DTL
Duchouquette	Baptiste		1818	StL	Real
Duckworth	John		1840	Call	Poll
Duckworth	William		1844	Osag	Real
Dudgen	Armstrong	C	1844	Osag	Real
Dudley	William		1836	Carr	Prop
Dudley	William		1836	Carr	PrpPt
Dudley	Wm		1840	Call	Poll
Dudley	Peyton	J	1840	Call	Poll
Dudley	Stephen		1840	Call	Poll
Dudley	John		1810	Ark	Prop
Dudley	William		1830	Ray	Prop
Dufaut	Juan Bapt		1791	StL	Span
Duffey	Garrett		1863	Jeff	Ass
Dugan	Daniel		1817	How	Prop
Dugan's Heirs	James		1836	Carr	PrtPt
Duggins	Samuel		1836	Carr	Prop
Duggins	Samuel		1836	Carr	PrpPt
Duggins	Samuel		1830	Ray	Prop
Dujo	Baptista		1780	StL	Mil
Duley	Thomas		1829	Char	DTL
Dulin	Thomas		1840	Call	Poll
Dulin	Thadeus	G	1836	StC	Prop
Dull	William		1839	Plat	Prop
Dumay	Joseph		1828	Sali	DTL
Dumme	Louis		1815	Ark	Prop
Dumolin	J	B	1818	StL	Real
Dumon	Louis		1810	Ark	Prop
Dumont	Pedro		1791	StL	Span
Dumore	Thomas		1836	StC	Prop

Last Name	First Name	Int	Year	County	Type
Dumoulin	Jean Bapt		1820	StL	Prop
Dunagan	D	L	1840	Call	Poll
Dunart	Edward		1867	Reyn	DTL
Dunbar	Sullivan		1836	Carr	Prop
Dunbar	Sullivan		1836	Carr	PrpPt
Duncan	James		1818	Lawr	DTL
Duncan	William		1818	Lawr	DTL
Duncan	Edward	P	1839	Plat	Prop
Duncan	William		1839	Plat	Prop
Duncan	Davis		1839	Plat	Prop
Duncan	Washington		1839	Plat	Prop
Duncan	Drury		1839	Plat	Prop
Duncan	James		1839	Plat	Prop
Duncan	Thos		1859	Reyn	DTL
Duncan	Fred	W	1840	Call	Poll
Duncan	Sally		1817	How	Prop
Duncan	William		1827	Mari	Prop
Duncan	Jepthah		1831	Cole	DTL
Duncan	Flemming		1839	Lew	DTL
Duncan	William	D	1834	Craw	DTL
Duncan, Jr	John		1840	Call	Poll
Duncanson	John		1840	Call	Poll
Dunham	Jabez		1836	Carr	Prop
Dunham	Jabez		1836	Carr	PrtPt
Dunham	Daniel		1840	Call	Poll
Dunham	Jonathan		1838	John	DTL
Dunham	Joseph	P	1844	Osag	Real
Dunigan	John		1839	Plat	Prop
Dunklin	S	T	1839	Wash	Lisc
Dunlap	John		1826	Coop	DTL
Dunlap	David	M	1840	Call	Poll
Dunlap	Robert		1840	Call	Poll
Dunlap	John		1826	Coop	DTL
Dunlap, Sr	David		1840	Call	Poll
Dunlay	Preston		1839	Plat	Prop
Dunn	John		1859	Reyn	DTL
Dunn	Dangerfield		1840	Call	Poll
Dunn	William	F	1840	Call	Poll
Dunn	James	L	1867	Reyn	DTL
Dunn	Jas	L	1867	Reyn	DTL
Dunn	Armand	C	1815	Ark	Prop
Dunnegan	Peter		1863	Jeff	Ass

Last Name	First Name	Int	Year	County	Type
Dunnica	W	F	1829	Char	DTL
Dunning	????		1859	Reyn	DTL
Dunning	Patrick		1867	Reyn	DTL
Dunning	Patrick		1867	Reyn	DTL
Duoby	John		1815	Ark	Prop
Dupuis	Wid Madam		1791	StL	Span
Dupuy	Andres		1780	StL	Mil
Duquette	Mary	L	1836	StC	Prop
Durben	Daniel		1817	How	Prop
Durbin	Daniel		1830	Howa	DTL
Durbin	Evematez		1839	Lew	DTL
Durbois	Pedro		1780	StL	Mil
Durfey	Ann	G	1836	StC	Prop
Duricay	Rock		1836	Carr	Prop
Duricay	Rock		1836	Carr	PrtPt
Durm	William		1810	Ark	Prop
Durminant	Walter		1836	Carr	Prop
Durminant	Walter		1836	Carr	PrtPt
Durochier	F Craig		1821	StC	Ct
Dusenberry	L	C	1859	Reyn	DTL
Dutcherut	Devins		1818	StL	Real
Dutcherute	Pierre		1818	StL	Real
Dutcherute	Adelaid		1818	StL	Real
Dutcherutte	Isabella		1820	StL	Prop
Dutcherutte	Pierre		1820	StL	Prop
Dutchimendy	Pasquale		1805	Steg	Prop
Dutramble	Antoine		1820	StL	Prop
Duvall	George	W	1840	Call	Poll
Duvall	John		1830	Linc	DTL
Duvual	Daniel		1821	Ray	Prop
Dyae	John		1840	Call	Poll
Dyas	Richard		1859	Reyn	DTL
Dye	Thomas		1839	Plat	Prop
Dyer	John		1839	Plat	Prop
Dyer	Washington		1839	Plat	Prop
Dyer	Samuel		1823	Call	NRP
Dyle	George		1839	Plat	Prop
Dyre	Jefferson		1836	StC	Prop
Dysart	Nicholas		1825	Char	DTL
Dysert	M		1843	Audr	Prop
Dyson	William		1840	Call	Poll
Eadford	James		1836	Carr	PrpPt

Last Name	First Name	Int	Year	County	Type
Eads	Jesse		1839	Plat	Prop
Eads	Solomon		1839	Plat	Prop
Eads	Moses		1839	Plat	Prop
Earl	James	D	1836	StC	Prop
Earl	Isaac		1825	Char	DTL
Early	Charles		1839	Plat	Prop
Earnes	Anton		1836	StC	Prop
Earsom	Simeon		1843	Audr	Prop
Earsom	Jas	M	1843	Audr	Prop
Earsom	Saml	H	1843	Audr	Prop
Earthman	Henry		1830	How	DTL
Earthman	Henry		1817	How	Prop
Earthman	John		1817	How	Prop
Eastin	Willia,		1827	Mari	Prop
Easton	Rufus		1821	StC	Ct
Easton	Reuben		1810	Ark	Prop
Easton's Heirs	Rufus		1836	StC	Prop
Eastus	William		1822	Clay	Poll
Eastwood	James		1859	Reyn	DTL
Eaton	John		1839	Plat	Prop
Eaton	Benjamin		1836	StC	Prop
Eaves	Edward	S	1836	StC	Prop
Ebau	Noil Saint		1836	StC	Prop
Echart	William		1836	StC	Prop
Eckert	William		1821	StC	Ct
Eckford	James		1836	Carr	Prop
Eckford	James		1836	Carr	PrpPt
Edds	Benjamin		1844	Osag	Real
Ede	Henry		1863	Jeff	Ass
Edens	Absalom		1810	Ark	Prop
Edgar	George		1830	Coop	Ct
Edgar	James		1830	Coop	Ct
Edgar	James		1830	Coop	Ct
Edge	James	W	1840	Call	Poll
Edington	Nicholas		1836	Carr	Prop
Edington	Nicholas		1836	Carr	PrpPt
Edling	Daniel		1836	StC	Prop
Edson	James		1859	Reyn	DTL
Edward's Heirs	Elisha		1836	Carr	Prop
Edward's Heirs	Elisha		1836	Carr	PrpPt
Edwards	Thomas		1839	Plat	Prop
Edwards	Elisha	J	1839	Plat	Prop

Last Name	First Name	Int	Year	County	Type
Edwards	Isaac	J	1839	Plat	Prop
Edwards	Perry		1836	Carr	PrpPt
Edwards	William		1867	Reyn	DTL
Edwards	William	O	1867	Reyn	DTL
Edwards	William	C	1836	StC	Prop
Edwards	Henry		1836	StC	Prop
Edwards	Thomas		1821	Ray	Prop
Edwards	John		1821	Ray	Prop
Edwards	Nicholas		1829	Sali	DTL
Edwards	Peter		1815	Ark	Prop
Edwinson	Wilson		1838	Ripl	DTL
Egg	Joseph		1810	Ark	Prop
Elam	James		1840	Call	Poll
Elclosh	William		1836	StC	Prop
Elder	Joseph		1839	Plat	Prop
Elder	R		1836	Perr	Poll
Elder	Jesse		1823	Call	NRP
Elias	Pedro		1780	StL	Mil
Elim	Elisha	C	1836	Carr	Prop
Elim	Elisha		1836	Carr	PrpPt
Eliot	William		1835	Barr	DTL
Elkins	Stephen		1839	John	DTL
Eller	Elius		1843	Audr	Prop
Eller	Peter		1836	Carr	Prop
Eller	Peter		1836	Carr	PrpPt
Ellett	Elisha		1836	StC	Prop
Ellington	John William		1839	Plat	Prop
Elliott	Archibald		1839	Plat	Prop
Elliott	John		1839	Plat	Prop
Elliott	John		1821	Ray	Prop
Elliott	John		1817	How	Prop
Ellis	Charles		1819	Steg	Lic
Ellis	Isaac	M C	1839	Plat	Prop
Ellis	Doctor		1839	Plat	Prop
Ellis	William	F	1838	Cass	DTL
Ellis	Peter		1828	Boon	Lisc
Ellis	Abrm		1840	Call	Poll
Ellis	Abram		1840	Call	Poll
Ellis	Peter		1823	Call	NRP
Ellis	Peter		1830	Call	DTL
Ellis	Levi		1831	Cole	DTL
Ellis	Abraham		1839	Lew	DTL

Last Name	First Name	Int	Year	County	Type
Ellison	John		1815	Ark	Prop
Ellston	Charlotte		1843	Audr	Prop
Elston	James		1867	Reyn	DTL
Elston	J		1829	Char	DTL
Elthred	William		1844	Osag	Real
Emarine	Martin		1836	StC	Prop
Embau	Joseph		1815	Ark	Prop
Embau	Francis		1815	Ark	Prop
Emery	Samuel		1836	StC	Prop
Emmonds	Elias	I	1840	Call	Poll
Emmons	Gibson	U	1840	Call	Poll
Emmons	Benjamin		1821	StC	Ct
Emmons	Ira	A	1830	Coop	Ct
Emmons	Young		1838	Ripl	DTL
Emouron, Sr	Benjamin		1836	StC	Prop
Endicutt	Samuel		1829	Mari	DTL
Engleson	John		1859	Reyn	DTL
English	Benjamin	F	1839	Plat	Prop
English	W	M	1839	Plat	Prop
English	Samuel		1837	Cass	DTL
English	Robert		1837	Cass	DTL
English	Frosty		1839	Lew	DTL
Ennet	John		1840	Call	Poll
Ennett	Joseph		1840	Call	Poll
Eno	Louis		1840	Call	Poll
Ensaw	Syndey		1836	StC	Prop
Ensign	William	H	1867	Reyn	DTL
Ensley	Coonrod		1843	Audr	Prop
Enyard	Silas		1817	How	Prop
Epps	R		1843	Char	DTL
Ernes	Anthony		1836	StC	Prop
Ernos	Francis		1840	Call	Poll
Ershine	David		1836	Carr	Prop
Ershine	David		1836	Carr	PrpPt
Esham	Daniel		1840	Call	Poll
Esler	Jonathan	E	1867	Reyn	DTL
Esler	Jonathan		1867	Reyn	DTL
Ess	Henry		1843	Audr	Prop
Estes	Richard		1827	Boon	Lisc
Estes	John		1840	Call	Poll
Estes	Thomas		1840	Call	Poll
Estes	John		1821	StC	Ct

74

Last Name	First Name	Int	Year	County	Type
Estes	William		1830	Jeff	DTL
Estes	Peter		1821	Ray	Prop
Estes	Thomas		1820	StL	Prop
Estes	William		1817	How	Prop
Estes	Henry		1817	How	Prop
Estes	Robert		1835	Barr	DTL
Esther	(Free Mullatto)		1818	StL	Real
Esther	(Free Mulatoo)		1820	StL	Prop
Estill	Benjamin		1817	How	Prop
Eubanks	David		1843	Audr	Prop
Eubanks	Elijah		1843	Audr	Prop
Eubanks	John		1843	Audr	Prop
Eubanks	Bethiel		1843	Audr	Prop
Eubanks	Joseph		1843	Audr	Prop
Eubanks	Elijah		1838	Audr	DTL
Eubanks	William		1838	Audr	DTL
Eubanks	David		1838	Audr	DTL
Euin	Elisha		1836	Carr	Prop
Euin	Elisha		1836	Carr	PrpPt
Eulenstine	Gustavus		1836	StC	Prop
Evans	Wm	B	1843	Audr	Prop
Evans	W	B	1843	Audr	Prop
Evans	W		1843	Audr	Prop
Evans	Amis		1818	Lawr	DTL
Evans	Joshua		1838	Cass	DTL
Evans	William		1836	Carr	Prop
Evans	William		1836	Carr	PrpPt
Evans	Augustus		1828	Boon	Lisc
Evans	Erastus		1840	Call	Poll
Evans	George		1840	Call	Poll
Evans	William		1840	Call	Poll
Evans	B	P	1840	Call	Poll
Evans	John		1821	Ray	Prop
Evans	William	B	1838	Audr	DTL
Evans	Andrew		1817	How	Prop
Evans	William		1830	Ray	Prop
Evans	George		1844	Osag	Real
Evans	Elizabeth		1844	Osag	Real
Evans	James		1834	Call	DTL
Evans	George		1834	Call	DTL
Eveland	Moses		1836	Carr	PrtPt
Evens	John	C	1836	StC	Prop

Last Name	First Name	Int	Year	County	Type
Everett	William		1822	Clay	Poll
Everett	Zacahriah		1822	Clay	Poll
Everett	Mathew		1822	Clay	Poll
Everheart	Martin		1843	Audr	Prop
Everheart	George		1818	StL	Real
Everitt's Heirs	John		1836	Carr	Prop
Everitt's Heirs	John		1836	Carr	PrpPt
Eversall	Jacob		1836	StC	Prop
Eversall	E	R	1836	StC	Prop
Evins	Robert	T	1839	Plat	Prop
Evins	Thomas	H	1839	Plat	Prop
Eweing	James		1840	Call	Poll
Eweing	Patrick		1840	Call	Poll
Eweing	William	H	1840	Call	Poll
Ewell	Thpmas		1836	Perr	Poll
Ewing	Robert	A	1827	Sali	DTL
Ewing	Marlhous		1836	Carr	Prop
Ewing	Marlhous		1836	Carr	PrpPt
Ewing	Samuel		1823	Call	NRP
Ewing	Robert	A	1829	Char	DTL
Exercise	Louis		1818	StL	Real
Ezell	Baloom		1836	Carr	Prop
Ezell	Baloom		1836	Carr	PrpPt
Faber	David	S	1840	Call	Poll
Faber	Joseph		1840	Call	Poll
Fache	Joseph		1780	StL	Mil
Fache	Luis		1780	StL	Mil
Faderhouse	Henry		1836	StC	Prop
Fagenburner	Adolph		1836	StC	Prop
Faget	Andre		1815	Ark	Prop
Fahee	Michael		1863	Jeff	Ass
Faields	Beverly		1843	Audr	Prop
Fain	Felipe		1791	StL	Span
Fain	Jonathan		1815	Ark	Prop
Faink	Lucy	A	1867	Reyn	DTL
Fair	James		1840	Call	Poll
Fair	Eliza		1820	StL	Prop
Fairhett	James		1836	Perr	Poll
Faliar	Luis		1780	StL	Mil
Fallis	Thomas		1818	StL	Real
Fanekin	William		1815	Ark	Prop
Fannery	John		1838	Audr	DTL

Last Name	First Name	Int	Year	County	Type
Fannon	Michael		1840	Call	Poll
Fant	A	B	1840	Call	Poll
Fant	George	B	1836	StC	Prop
Fare	Joseph		1836	StC	Prop
Farley	Tirnes		1863	Jeff	Ass
Farley	Patrick		1863	Jeff	Ass
Farmer	Thomas		1839	Plat	Prop
Farmer	Anson		1839	Plat	Prop
Farmer	Jesse		1840	Call	Poll
Farmer	John		1840	Call	Poll
Farmer	Joseph		1840	Call	Poll
Farmer	John		1836	StC	Prop
Farmer	Mary		1836	StC	Prop
Farmer	Samuel	B	1836	StC	Prop
Farnax	Joseph		1836	StC	Prop
Farnesworth	Bial		1836	StC	Prop
Farnesworth	Alden		1836	StC	Prop
Farnesworth's Heir	William		1836	StC	Prop
Farrar	John		1836	Perr	Poll
Farrar	Dr		1820	StL	Prop
Farrar	Barnard	G	1820	StL	Prop
Farrel	Ansil		1836	Perr	Poll
Farris	Aaron		1820	StL	Prop
Farriss	William		1840	Call	Poll
Farter's Heirs	Joseph		1836	StC	Prop
Fatunet	Daniel		1815	Ark	Prop
Faucet	John		1838	Audr	DTL
Faucett	Edward		1838	Audr	DTL
Faulkner	Jacob		1836	Carr	PrpPt
Faulkner	Josiah		1840	Call	Poll
Favarall	John		1836	Carr	Prop
Favarall	James		1836	Carr	Prop
Favarall	John		1836	Carr	PrpPt
Favarall	James		1836	Carr	PrpPt
Fayler	M	D	1839	Plat	Prop
Feagan	Zachariah		1827	Mari	Prop
Fealy	Thomas		1867	Reyn	DTL
Fear	Madam		1818	StL	Real
Feazle	Joshua		1827	Mari	Prop
Feckly	Benjamin		1836	StC	Prop
Feeham	Patrick		1867	Reyn	DTL
Feller	I	W	1816	How	Lic

Last Name	First Name	Int	Year	County	Type
Feneti	Andrea		1780	StL	Mil
Fenn	Dr Zero		1820	StL	Prop
Fenton	James	E	1828	Boon	Lisc
Fenton	Jas	E	1838	Audr	DTL
Fenwick	Leo		1836	Perr	Poll
Fenwick	Walter		1830	Jeff	DTL
Ferguson	George		1839	Plat	Prop
Ferguson	Joseph		1836	Carr	Prop
Ferguson	Thomas	H	1836	Carr	Prop
Ferguson	Joseph		1836	Carr	PrpPt
Ferguson	Thomas		1836	Carr	PrpPt
Ferguson	John	R	1840	Call	Poll
Ferguson	G	W	1818	StL	Real
Ferguson	????		1818	StL	Real
Ferguson	George	W	1820	StL	Prop
Ferguson	Joseph		1820	StL	Prop
Ferguson	Nancy		1844	Osag	Real
Ferguson	A	W	1831	Craw	DTL
Ferrel	Thomas		1818	Lawr	DTL
Ferrel	Hiram		1839	Plat	Prop
Ferrel	Ansel		1837	Perr	Lisc
Ferrel	Ansel		1837	Perr	Adv
Ferrel	Hutchens	B	1836	StC	Prop
Ferrel	Benjamin	P	1836	StC	Prop
Ferrel	Mary		1836	StC	Prop
Ferrell	Robert		1836	Carr	Prop
Ferrell	Robert		1836	Carr	PrpPt
Ferrell	Frederich		1836	StC	Prop
Ferrens	John		1821	Ray	Prop
Ferrier	Thomas		1840	Call	Poll
Ferrier	Samuel		1840	Call	Poll
Ferrier	Thomas	H	1840	Call	Poll
Ferrill	G	W	1840	Call	Poll
Ferrill	John		1817	How	Prop
Ferrill	Jas		1843	Char	DTL
Ferrin	Thomas		1840	Call	Poll
Ferrin	John		1867	Reyn	DTL
Fetch	Michael		1836	StC	Prop
Fetter	John		1836	StC	Prop
Fetter	Bernhardt		1836	StC	Prop
Fewgett	Sasil		1839	Plat	Prop
Ficett	Joseph		1836	StC	Prop

Last Name	First Name	Int	Year	County	Type
Fickle	Absolom		1839	Plat	Prop
Fickle	Abner		1839	Plat	Prop
Fidecharme	Andres		1780	StL	Mil
Field	B	A	1843	Audr	Prop
Field	John		1825	Char	DTL
Fields	Thomas		1839	Plat	Prop
Fields	Levi		1839	Plat	Prop
Fields	Benjamin		1839	Plat	Prop
Fields	Levy		1821	Ray	Prop
Fields	Ebenezer		1821	Ray	Prop
Fields	Stephen		1821	Ray	Prop
Fields	Thomas		1821	Ray	Prop
Fields	Joseph		1821	Ray	Prop
Fields	Paskil		1839	John	DTL
Fields	Barton		1827	Mari	Prop
Fields, Sr	John		1821	Ray	Prop
Fielter	William		1863	Jeff	Ass
Figitt	Melida		1817	How	Prop
Figitt	Nancy		1817	How	Prop
Finasaon	David		1834	Craw	DTL
Finch	John	P	1836	Perr	Poll
Fine	Joshua		1836	StC	Prop
Fine	Joshua		1836	StC	Prop
Finewalt	George		1844	Osag	Real
Finks	John		1843	Audr	Prop
Finks	Simeon		1843	Audr	Prop
Finley	Samuel		1839	Plat	Prop
Finley	John		1840	Call	Poll
Finley	Travis		1821	Ray	Prop
Finley	Dabney		1828	Sali	DTL
Finley	John		1827	Mari	Prop
Finley	William		1815	Ark	Prop
Finley	John		1844	Osag	Real
Finly	Ebenezer		1840	Call	Poll
Finly	J	W	1840	Call	Poll
Finly	Dabner		1823	Call	NRP
Finly	John		1823	Call	NRP
Finn	Robert		1867	Reyn	DTL
Finn	Robert		1860	Reyn	DTL
Fish	John		1840	Call	Poll
Fisher	Richard		1836	Bent	DTL
Fisher	James	D	1840	Call	Poll

79

Last Name	First Name	Int	Year	County	Type
Fisher	James	D	1840	Call	Poll
Fisher	Joseph		1840	Call	Poll
Fisher	John		1834	Pett	Prop
Fisher	John		1834	Pett	PrpPt
Fisher	Anthony		1834	Pett	PrpPt
Fisher	Peter		1834	Pett	PrpPt
Fisher	Coleman		1830	Howa	DTL
Fisher	Henry		1867	Reyn	DTL
Fisher	Jared		1867	Reyn	DTL
Fisher	Nancy		1836	StC	Prop
Fisher	Daniel		1836	StC	Prop
Fisher	Nicholas		1836	StC	Prop
Fisher	Samuel	P	1839	John	DTL
Fisher	William		1827	Mari	Prop
Fisher	Richard		1837	Bent	DTL
Fistzpatrick	G	W	1867	Reyn	DTL
Fitter	William		1820	StL	Prop
Fitzgerald	Pat		1859	Reyn	DTL
Fitzgerald	James		1836	Carr	PrtPt
Fitzgerrard	James		1830	Ray	Prop
Fitzgibbons	Daniel		1815	Ark	Prop
Fitzhugh	Alexander		1840	Call	Poll
Fitzhugh	John		1830	Coop	Ct
Fitzhugh	James		1830	Coop	CtS
Fitzpatrick	John		1836	Carr	Prop
Fitzpatrick	John		1836	Carr	PrpPt
Fitzpatrick	M		1867	Reyn	DTL
Fitzpatrick	Robert		1867	Reyn	DTL
Fitzsimmons	Jno		1863	Jeff	Ass
Fitzwater	S	M	1867	Reyn	DTL
Fitzwater	Moses		1831	Craw	DTL
Flaharty	Peter		1836	Perr	Poll
Flair	Joseph		1836	StC	Prop
Flanagan	Hugh		1810	Ark	Prop
Flandrin	Antonie		1820	StL	Prop
Flanegan	William		1810	Ark	Prop
Flanery	John		1843	Audr	Prop
Flannery	Washington		1838	Ripl	DTL
Flannery	Thomas		1838	Ripl	DTL
Flannery, Sr	James		1839	Plat	Prop
Flannery, Sr	Jas		1839	Plat	Prop
Flare	Joseph		1836	StC	Prop

Last Name	First Name	Int	Year	County	Type
Flare	Jos		1836	StC	Prop
Flaugherty	Rolf		1836	StC	Prop
Flaugherty' heirs	Jos		1836	StC	Prop
Fleetwood	William		1825	Char	DTL
Fleming	John		1839	Plat	Prop
Fleming	Jesse		1839	Plat	Prop
Fleming	Patrick		1840	Call	Poll
Fleming	Leem		1834	Lew	DTL
Flemming	Jonathan		1827	Mari	Prop
Fleshman	Larkin		1840	Call	Poll
Fleshman	Perry		1840	Call	Poll
Fletcher	Oliver		1836	Carr	PrpPt
Fletcher	James		1840	Call	Poll
Fletcher	John		1840	Call	Poll
Fletcher	John	F	1840	Call	Poll
Fletcher	Joseph		1840	Call	Poll
Fletcher	Jesse		1821	Ray	Prop
Fletcher	David		1821	Ray	Prop
Fletcher	Moses		1821	Ray	Prop
Fletcher	David		1817	How	Prop
Fletcher	Jeffery		1822	Clay	Poll
Fling	Richard		1836	Carr	Prop
Fling	Richard		1836	Carr	PrpPt
Fling	Patrick		1829	Char	DTL
Fling	Richard		1830	Ray	Prop
Floid	Peter		1836	Carr	Prop
Floid	Peter		1836	Carr	PrpPt
Flood	Thomas		1840	Call	Poll
Flore	Florence		1820	StL	Prop
Florence	Florence		1818	StL	Real
Floss	Elijah		1828	Sali	DTL
Floyd	Peter		1843	Audr	Prop
Floyd	Charles		1836	Carr	Prop
Floyd	Charles		1836	Carr	PrpPt
Flynn	Isaac		1836	Perr	Poll
Flynn	William		1836	Perr	Poll
Flynn	Martin		1867	Reyn	DTL
Foany	John		1818	StL	Real
Foasum	George		1835	Barr	DTL
Focke	Ferdinand		1836	StC	Prop
Foley	William		1836	Carr	Prop
Foley	William		1836	Carr	PrpPt

Last Name	First Name	Int	Year	County	Type
Foley	Abraham		1827	Boon	Lisc
Fontain	Felix		1820	StL	Prop
Fontaine	Petit		1818	StL	Real
Fooy	Benjamin		1810	Ark	Prop
Forbias	Riley		1867	Reyn	DTL
Forbias	Albert		1867	Reyn	DTL
Ford	Isaac		1843	Audr	Prop
Ford	George	W	1839	Plat	Prop
Ford	Samuel		1839	Plat	Prop
Ford	Alexander		1840	Call	Poll
Ford	Robert		1840	Call	Poll
Ford	Alexander		1821	StC	Ct
Ford	Edward		1836	StC	Prop
Ford	Mary		1836	StC	Prop
Foreman	Jacob		1839	Plat	Prop
Foris	John	M	1839	Plat	Prop
Foris	John	W	1839	Plat	Prop
Forman	S	M	1821	StC	CtS
Forman	William		1836	StC	Prop
Forman	Isaac		1827	Mari	Prop
Forman	William		1827	Mari	Prop
Forman	Isaac		1827	Mari	Prop
Forman	Benjamin		1827	Mari	Prop
Forster	William		1840	Call	Poll
Forsythe	Thomas		1820	StL	Prop
Fort	David	J	1843	Audr	Prop
Fort	Peter		1840	Call	Poll
Fort	Peter		1867	Reyn	DTL
Fort	David	I	1838	Audr	DTL
Fortuna	Jn Baptiste		1805	Steg	Prop
Fory	Francis		1840	Call	Poll
Fosset	John		1843	Audr	Prop
Fosset	Edward		1843	Audr	Prop
Fossett	John		1843	Audr	Prop
Foster	Isaac		1818	Lawr	DTL
Foster	Andrew		1839	Plat	Prop
Foster	Ambrose		1839	Plat	Prop
Foster	Newford		1836	Carr	Prop
Foster	James		1836	Carr	PrpPt
Foster	Edward		1840	Call	Poll
Foster	John	J	1840	Call	Poll
Foster	James	T	1840	Call	Poll

Last Name	First Name	Int	Year	County	Type
Foster	William	H	1840	Call	Poll
Foster	Robert		1840	Call	Poll
Foster	William		1839	John	DTL
Foster	George		1817	How	Prop
Foster	James	L	1817	How	Prop
Foster	Freeman		1817	How	Prop
Foster	John		1817	How	Prop
Foster	James		1830	Ray	Prop
Fotes	Oliver		1836	Carr	Prop
Fotes	Oliver		1836	Carr	PrpPt
Fourd	Charles		1830	Coop	Ct
Foushee	Mary		1836	StC	Prop
Fovrell	George		1836	Carr	PrpPt
Fowler	William		1818	Lawr	DTL
Fowler	Levi		1839	Plat	Prop
Fowler	Joseph		1821	Ray	Prop
Fowler	Henry		1837	Lew	DTL
Fowler	James		1817	How	Prop
Fowler, dec	Robert		1817	How	Prop
Fox	William		1839	Plat	Prop
Fox	James		1839	Plat	Prop
Fox	William	A	1839	Plat	Prop
Fox	William	M	1839	Plat	Prop
Fox	Thomas		1859	Reyn	DTL
Fox	Francis		1836	Carr	Prop
Fox	Francis		1836	Carr	PrpPt
Fox	Thomas	G	1840	Call	Poll
Fox	Andrew		1836	StC	Prop
Fox	Francis		1830	Ray	Prop
Frame	Wesley		1839	Plat	Prop
Frame	John		1831	Cole	DTL
France	Henry		1834	Pett	PrpPt
France	William		1836	StC	Prop
Francis	Elisha		1839	Plat	Prop
Francis	Ephraim		1836	Carr	Prop
Francis	Ephraim		1836	Carr	PrpPt
Francis	Carr		1820	StL	Prop
Francis	George		1830	Ray	Prop
Francois	Epraim		1830	Ray	Prop
Francoise	(Negro)		1818	StL	Real
Franklin	John		1836	Carr	Prop
Franklin	John		1836	Carr	PrpPt

Last Name	First Name	Int	Year	County	Type
Fraser	William		1817	How	Prop
Frasier	John		1834	Call	DTL
Fraynoth	John		1836	StC	Prop
Frazier	Joseph		1830	Howa	DTL
Frazier	Jno	W	1863	Jeff	Ass
Frazier	Julian		1863	Jeff	Ass
Frazier	Daniel		1810	Ark	Prop
Frazier	John	S	1829	Mari	DTL
Frazier	Simon		1829	Mari	DTL
Frazier (1)	Samuel		1863	Jeff	Ass
Frazier (2)	Samuel		1863	Jeff	Ass
Frazure	Stephen		1836	StC	Prop
Frazure	David		1836	StC	Prop
Frazure	Thomas		1810	Ark	Prop
Frederick	Leonard		1840	Call	Poll
Freefaman	L	A	1867	Reyn	DTL
Freefman	L	C	1867	Reyn	DTL
Freeland	Joseph		1840	Call	Poll
Freeman	Joshua		1828	Boon	Lisc
Freeman	William		1840	Call	Poll
Freeman	Daniel		1820	StL	Prop
French	Joseph		1836	Perr	Poll
French	Silas		1836	Perr	Poll
French	James		1821	StC	Ct
Frenth	Pinkney		1838	Audr	DTL
Frickle	Mathias		1839	Plat	Prop
Frifield	E		1867	Reyn	DTL
Frink	????	A	1859	Reyn	DTL
Frink	Lucy	A	1867	Reyn	DTL
Frink	Lucy Ann		1867	Reyn	DTL
Frink	John		1867	Reyn	DTL
Frizell	Allison		1838	John	DTL
Frost	George	E	1863	Jeff	Ass
Frost	Thomas		1821	Ray	Prop
Frsure	Peter		1819	Steg	Lic
Fruit	J	C	1843	Audr	Prop
Fry	John	F	1839	Plat	Prop
Fry	John		1840	Call	Poll
Frye	Benjamin		1827	Mari	Prop
Frye	Abraham	K	1827	Mari	Prop
Fryer	John		1836	Carr	Prop
Fryer	John		1836	Carr	PrpPt

Last Name	First Name	Int	Year	County	Type
Fryer	John		1830	Ray	Prop
Fugate	Josiah		1838	Audr	DTL
Fuge	George		1843	Char	DTL
Fuget	Josiah		1843	Audr	Prop
Fugett	Ezekial		1839	Plat	Prop
Fulcher	Jefferson		1817	How	Prop
Fulkerson	James		1839	Plat	Prop
Fulkerson	James	P	1825	CGir	Lisc
Fulkerson	Richard		1827	Boon	Lisc
Fulkerson	William	N	1836	StC	Prop
Fulkerson	J	P	1829	Char	DTL
Fulkerson	R	H C	1838	Audr	DTL
Fulkerson	Richard		1817	How	Prop
Fulkerson's Heirs	Isaac		1836	StC	Prop
Fuller	John		1836	Carr	Prop
Fuller	John		1836	Carr	PrpPt
Fuller	James		1834	Pett	Prop
Fuller	George	W	1867	Reyn	DTL
Fullington	L	C	1836	StC	Prop
Fulsom	Elizzear		1810	Ark	Prop
Fulton	William		1839	Plat	Prop
Fulton's Heirs	Tabitha		1836	StC	Prop
Funderbark	Washington		1839	Plat	Prop
Funderbark	George		1839	Plat	Prop
Funk	Fred		1867	Reyn	DTL
Funk	Thompson		1837	Lew	DTL
Funnels	Joseph		1836	Carr	PrpPt
Furgerson	Allen		1839	Plat	Prop
Furgerson	Archibald	B	1840	Call	Poll
Furgerson	W	P	1840	Call	Poll
Furgerson	Swan		1840	Call	Poll
Furgesson	Critidon		1837	Lew	DTL
Furgison	James		1840	Call	Poll
Furgison	T	J	1840	Call	Poll
Furguson	Thomas		1831	Cole	DTL
Furline	Noble		1836	StC	Prop
Furrell	George	L	1836	Carr	PrpPt
Futral	Daniel		1810	Ark	Prop
Gafferson	Gregg		1839	Plat	Prop
Gage's Heirs	William		1836	Carr	Prop
Gage's Heirs	William		1836	Carr	PrpPt
Gagnier	Amable		1791	StL	Span

Last Name	First Name	Int	Year	County	Type
Gagnon	Pedro		1791	StL	Span
Gagnon	Baptiste		1818	StL	Real
Gaines	Edward	P	1840	Call	Poll
Gaines	Gideon		1840	Call	Poll
Gains	J	J	1843	Audr	Prop
Gains	Franklin		1828	Boon	Lisc
Gains	James		1838	Ripl	DTL
Gainsay	David		1821	StC	Ct
Galbreath	Alfred		1843	Audr	Prop
Galbreath	Angus		1840	Call	Poll
Galbreth	Alfred		1838	Audr	DTL
Galbreth	Daniel		1838	Audr	DTL
Gales	William		1836	Carr	Prop
Gales	William		1836	Carr	PrpPt
Gallaher	Charles		1818	Lawr	DTL
Gallaspie	John	R	1838	John	DTL
Gallatin	Abraham		1820	StL	Prop
Gallation	Abraham		1818	StL	Real
Galph	Thos		1843	Audr	Prop
Galve, Jr	Antonia		1780	StL	Mil
Galve. Sr	Antonia		1780	StL	Mil
Gamble	Archibald		1820	StL	Prop
Gamel	Jno	H	1863	Jeff	Ass
Gamerdinger	Jacob		1867	Reyn	DTL
Ganaty	Joseph	W	1821	StC	Ct
Ganett	????		1818	StL	Real
Ganett	E	L	1818	StL	Real
Gann	Jackson		1839	Plat	Prop
Gann	Thornton		1839	Plat	Prop
Ganon	Felizberto		1780	StL	Mil
Ganon	Pedro		1780	StL	Mil
Gant	Josiah		1843	Audr	Prop
Gant	Thos	R	1843	Audr	Prop
Gapper	Edmund		1838	Cass	DTL
Gardheafair	Modest		1836	StC	Prop
Gardick	Rueben		1830	Ray	Prop
Gardner	Isadore		1836	StC	Prop
Gardner	William		1830	Call	DTL
Gardner	Foushe		1821	Ray	Prop
Gardner	William	G	1829	Mari	DTL
Gardner	James		1827	Mari	Prop
Garlich	Hemon		1836	StC	Prop

Last Name	First Name	Int	Year	County	Type
Garlick	Reuben		1836	Carr	Prop
Garlick	Reuben		1836	Carr	PrpPt
Garlick	Rueben		1836	Carr	PrpPt
Garman	Louis		1836	StC	Prop
Garner	Cornelius		1843	Audr	Prop
Garner	J	V	1818	StL	Real
Garner	William		1827	Mari	Prop
Garner	John		1827	Mari	Prop
Garnier	Joseph	V	1820	StL	Prop
Garret	William		1818	Lawr	DTL
Garrett	William	B	1840	Call	Poll
Garrett	Maryland	H	1840	Call	Poll
Garrison	William		1836	Carr	Prop
Garrison	William		1836	Carr	PrpPt
Garrison	William		1830	Ray	Prop
Garrison	John		1834	Craw	DTL
Garrot	Isam	A R	1843	Audr	Prop
Garvin	Alexander		1821	StC	Ct
Garvin	John		1821	StC	CtS
Garvin	John	B	1836	StC	Prop
Garvin's Heirs	Alexander		1836	StC	Prop
Garvis	James		1867	Reyn	DTL
Gary	John	B	1828	Sali	DTL
Gascou	Battest		1836	StC	Prop
Gash	John		1827	Mari	Prop
Gash	William		1827	Mari	Prop
Gash, Jr	Martin		1827	Mari	Prop
Gash, Jr	Joseph	D	1827	Mari	Prop
Gash, Sr	Martin		1827	Mari	Prop
Gash, Sr	Joseph	D	1827	Mari	Prop
Gask	George	W	1867	Reyn	DTL
Gason	George	W	1839	Plat	Prop
Gass	Jas	R C	1843	Audr	Prop
Gass	Saml	B	1843	Audr	Prop
Gasway	Upton	T	1837	Lew	DTL
Gata	George	N	1836	StC	Prop
Gata, Sr	John		1836	StC	Prop
Gates	Joseph		1836	Carr	Prop
Gates	Joseph		1836	Carr	PrpPt
Gatewood	Ignatius		1836	Carr	Prop
Gatewood	Ignatius		1836	Carr	PrpPt
Gather	Washington		1836	Perr	Poll

87

Last Name	First Name	Int	Year	County	Type
Gathing	Joseph		1836	Carr	Prop
Gathing	Joseph		1836	Carr	PrpPt
Gathright	M	W	1840	Call	Poll
Gauge	Joseph		1821	Ray	Prop
Gay	Wid		1820	StL	Prop
Gay	Green		1831	Craw	DTL
Geary	Edward		1867	Reyn	DTL
Gee	John		1843	Audr	Prop
Gee	Aaron		1840	Call	Poll
Gee	Standford		1840	Call	Poll
Gee	John		1840	Call	Poll
Gee	Silas	W	1840	Call	Poll
Gelting	Joseph		1836	Carr	PrpPt
Gennings	Josiah		1817	How	Prop
Gentry	Woodson	H	1843	Audr	Prop
Gentry	George	W	1838	Cass	DTL
Gentry	Ruben	E	1834	Pett	Prop
Gentry	D		1834	Pett	PrpPt
Gentry	Rueben	E	1834	Pett	PrpPt
Gentry	Reuben		1817	How	Prop
Gentry	Moses		1827	Mari	Prop
Gentry	Joshua		1827	Mari	Prop
Gentry	Jesse		1827	Mari	Prop
Gentry	Moses		1827	Mari	Prop
Gentry	Mrs Jane		1836	Char	DTL
Geobburd	Eugene		1839	Wash	Lisc
Geoffrey	Celeste		1820	StL	Prop
Geofry	Celeste		1818	StL	Real
Geogg	Archibald		1843	Audr	Prop
George	Alfred		1840	Call	Poll
George	William	M	1840	Call	Poll
George	Baley		1821	Ray	Prop
George	Bailey		1822	Clay	Poll
George	Leawood	F	1835	Barr	DTL
Gerard	Baptiste		1818	StL	Real
Gettis	David		1836	Carr	Prop
Gettis	David		1836	Carr	PrpPt
Gevero	Michel		1805	Steg	Prop
Geyer	John	S	1827	Boon	Lisc
Geyer	H	S	1818	StL	Real
Geyer	Henry		1817	How	Prop
Geynon	????		1818	StL	Real

Last Name	First Name	Int	Year	County	Type
Gibbony	John		1840	Call	Poll
Gibbs	Stephen		1839	Plat	Prop
Gibbs	C	I	1840	Call	Poll
Gibbs	Robert	F	1840	Call	Poll
Gibbs	Samuel		1840	Call	Poll
Gibbs	Thomas	J	1840	Call	Poll
Gibbs	Samuel		1834	Pett	Prop
Gibbs	Saml		1834	Pett	PrpPt
Gibbs	Parthenia		1817	How	Prop
Gibbs	Samuel		1817	How	Prop
Gibbs	Samuel		1817	How	Prop
Gibor	August		1818	StL	Real
Gibson	Jesse		1839	Plat	Prop
Gibson	William		1839	Plat	Prop
Gibson	James		1839	Plat	Prop
Gibson	Isaac	W	1839	Plat	Prop
Gibson	James		1831	Jack	DTL
Gibson	Humphrey		1817	How	Prop
Gibson	William	M	1844	Osag	Real
Giddings	Salmon		1818	StL	Real
Giddings	Solman		1820	StL	Prop
Gigaire	Jean	B	1818	StL	Real
Giguiere	Baptiste		1818	StL	Real
Gilbert	James		1840	Call	Poll
Gilbert	Kemuel	C	1840	Call	Poll
Gilbert	Michael		1840	Call	Poll
Gilbert	William	H H	1840	Call	Poll
Gilbert	P	D	1840	Call	Poll
Gilian	Robert	P	1839	Plat	Prop
Gill	Philip	E	1839	Plat	Prop
Gill	Presley		1840	Call	Poll
Gill	A	F	1867	Reyn	DTL
Gill	A		1867	Reyn	DTL
Gill	John		1836	StC	Prop
Gill	Joseph		1829	Char	DTL
Gill	Joseph		1821	Ray	Prop
Gillasby	Angel		1838	Audr	DTL
Gillchrist	Thomas		1867	Reyn	DTL
Gillespi	John		1839	John	DTL
Gillespi	John		1839	John	DTL
Gillett	Benona	R	1821	StC	CtS
Gillett	Phileo		1836	StC	Prop

Last Name	First Name	Int	Year	County	Type
Gillett	Leonard		1836	StC	Prop
Gilliam	Cornelius		1821	Ray	Prop
Gilliam	John		1821	Ray	Prop
Gilliam	Jesse		1821	Ray	Prop
Gilliam	Robert		1822	Clay	Poll
Gillian	John		1839	Plat	Prop
Gilligan	Anthiny		1830	Ray	Prop
Gillmore	James		1821	Ray	Prop
Gillum	Jesse		1839	Plat	Prop
Gilman	William	J	1840	Call	Poll
Gilman	John	P	1844	Osag	Real
Gilman	Robert	J	1829	NMad	DTL
Gilmore	James		1840	Call	Poll
Gilmore	Robert		1840	Call	Poll
Gilmore	W	H	1840	Call	Poll
Gilmore	Thomas		1836	StC	Prop
Gilmore	John		1836	StC	Prop
Gilpin	Nancy		1843	Audr	Prop
Gilvar	Juan		1780	StL	Mil
Ginder	John		1859	Reyn	DTL
Ginnard	Alex		1836	StC	Prop
Ginnard	Louis		1836	StC	Prop
Gipson	John		1840	Call	Poll
Giquiere	Baptiste		1820	StL	Prop
Giratal	William		1859	Reyn	DTL
Givens	John		1818	Lawr	DTL
Givens	W	R	1840	Call	Poll
Givens	Samuel		1836	StC	Prop
Gizas	Aaron		1815	Ark	Prop
Gladden	David		1839	Plat	Prop
Gladen	William		1838	Ripl	DTL
Gladwill	John		1840	Call	Poll
Glascock	Robert	L	1836	Perr	Poll
Glass	Smith		1867	Reyn	DTL
Glass	Samuel		1836	StC	Prop
Glass	William	H	1810	Ark	Prop
Glasscock	Harmon		1839	Plat	Prop
Glasscock	Robert	L	1836	Perr	Lisc
Glassgow	Nathan		1840	Call	Poll
Glaun	John		1836	Carr	PrpPt
Glaze	Jas	G	1863	Jeff	Ass
Glem	Silas		1839	Plat	Prop

90

Last Name	First Name	Int	Year	County	Type
Glenday	Thomas		1836	StC	Prop
Glenday	Thomas		1829	Mari	DTL
Glenday	James		1829	Mari	DTL
Glover	William		1840	Call	Poll
Glover	James	M	1840	Call	Poll
Glover	Chesley		1840	Call	Poll
Glover	Jesse		1840	Call	Poll
Glover	Robert		1840	Call	Poll
Glover	H	B	1863	Jeff	Ass
Goally	John		1838	Audr	DTL
Goatly	J		1843	Audr	Prop
Goatty	John		1843	Audr	Prop
Goble's Heirs	Stephen		1836	Carr	Prop
Goble's Heirs	Stephen		1836	Carr	PrpPt
Godair	Andrew		1836	Carr	Prop
Godair	Baptist		1818	StL	Real
Godair	Augustine		1818	StL	Real
Godair	Antoine		1820	StL	Prop
Godair	Baptist		1820	StL	Prop
Godair	Andrew		1830	Ray	Prop
Godak	Andrew		1827	Jack	DTL
Godding	Henry		1836	Carr	PrpPt
Godfrey	Louis		1836	StC	Prop
Godsey	Burley		1836	Carr	Prop
Godsey	Burley		1836	Carr	PrpPt
Godsey	Burton		1836	Carr	Prop
Godsey	Burton		1836	Carr	PrpPt
Godsey	Burton		1830	Ray	Prop
Godson	G	P	1818	StL	Real
Goe	Noble		1836	Carr	Prop
Goff	Thomas		1840	Call	Poll
Goforth	Benjamin		1838	Ripl	DTL
Golair	James		1822	NMad	Lisc
Golternart	Earnest		1836	StC	Prop
Gonon	Pedro		1780	StL	Mil
Gooch	Martin		1839	John	DTL
Good	Edward		1830	Howa	DTL
Good	Edward		1817	How	Prop
Goodale	Leonads		1859	Reyn	DTL
Goodall	John		1829	Char	DTL
Gooden	John		1840	Call	Poll
Gooden	Walter		1840	Call	Poll

Last Name	First Name	Int	Year	County	Type
Goodlett	Chas		1867	Reyn	DTL
Goodlove	Orth		1867	Reyn	DTL
Goodly	John		1867	Reyn	DTL
Goodman	Peter		1839	John	DTL
Goodman	Robert		1844	Osag	Real
Goodman	David		1844	Osag	Real
Goodnight	Edward		1843	Audr	Prop
Goodnight	Harison		1843	Audr	Prop
Goodnight	John	B	1843	Audr	Prop
Goodrich	D	W	1859	Reyn	DTL
Goodrich	????		1836	StC	Prop
Goodrich	Elijah	R	1836	StC	Prop
Goodrich	James		1836	StC	Prop
Goodwin	Abram		1823	How	DTL
Gooman	Thomas		1836	Carr	Prop
Gooman	Thomas		1836	Carr	PrpPt
Gordan	Thomas		1834	Call	DTL
Gordon	George		1818	Lawr	DTL
Gordon	A		1839	Plat	Prop
Gordon	John	B	1828	Boon	Lisc
Gordon	Robert		1867	Reyn	DTL
Gordon	William		1836	StC	Prop
Gordon	David		1820	StL	Prop
Gordon	William		1820	StL	Prop
Gordon	Avely		1838	Ripl	DTL
Gossett	John		1810	Ark	Prop
Gotio	Antonio		1780	StL	Mil
Govero	Louis		1805	Steg	Prop
Govero	Etienne		1805	Steg	Prop
Govers	Henry		1805	Steg	Prop
Govers	Jo		1805	Steg	Prop
Gowan	Thomas		1867	Reyn	DTL
Gowen	Christian		1830	Ray	Prop
Gower	Christian		1836	Carr	Prop
Gower	Christian		1836	Carr	PrpPt
Goza	Aaron		1810	Ark	Prop
Grabier	Baptiste		1815	Ark	Prop
Grace	Peter		1836	StC	Prop
Grady	George		1836	StC	Prop
Gragg	John		1818	Lawr	DTL
Gragg	Benjamin		1821	Ray	Prop
Gragg	Henry		1821	Ray	Prop

Last Name	First Name	Int	Year	County	Type
Graham	Jno		1837	Sali	DTL
Graham	John		1859	Reyn	DTL
Graham	Thos		1837	Cass	DTL
Graham	William		1827	Boon	Lisc
Graham	Michl		1863	Jeff	Ass
Graham	David		1867	Reyn	DTL
Graham	Beriah		1836	StC	Prop
Graham	Major		1818	StL	Real
Graham	R		1828	Sali	DTL
Graham	Richard	N	1836	Perr	Poll
Graham	Francis		1829	Mari	DTL
Graham	Mary		1815	Ark	Prop
Gramer	George		1859	Reyn	DTL
Gramsica	Frances		1844	Osag	Real
Grander	Augustin		1810	Ark	Prop
Grant	Israel	B	1840	Call	Poll
Grant	James		1840	Call	Poll
Grant	Squire		1823	Call	NRP
Grant	J	P	1829	Char	DTL
Grant	William		1829	Char	DTL
Grant	Josiah		1838	Audr	DTL
Grantham	T	P	1836	StC	Prop
Gratiot	Carlos		1791	StL	Span
Gratiot	Charles		1820	StL	Prop
Graves	Alvey		1839	Plat	Prop
Graves	Geo	W	1837	Lew	DTL
Graves	Elias		1839	Lew	DTL
Graviene's Heirs	Joseph		1836	StC	Prop
Gravier	Joseph		1810	Ark	Prop
Gravier	Joseph		1815	Ark	Prop
Gray	Elijah		1843	Audr	Prop
Gray	Thomas		1816	How	Lic
Gray	Caswell	R	1839	Plat	Prop
Gray	Charles		1839	Plat	Prop
Gray	James		1839	Plat	Prop
Gray	James	S	1840	Call	Poll
Gray	John	B	1840	Call	Poll
Gray	George		1840	Call	Poll
Gray	????		1840	Call	Poll
Gray	H	A	1867	Reyn	DTL
Gray	Henry		1823	Call	NRP
Gray	John		1823	Call	NRP

Last Name	First Name	Int	Year	County	Type
Gray	Presely		1823	Call	NRP
Gray	Thomas		1810	Ark	Prop
Gray	Thomas		1817	How	Prop
Gray	Nathaniel		1834	Call	DTL
Grayham	Nathaniel		1836	Carr	Prop
Grayham	William		1836	Carr	Prop
Grayham	Richard		1836	Carr	Prop
Grayham	Richard		1836	Carr	PrpPt
Grayham	John		1828	Boon	Lisc
Grayson	G	W	1843	Audr	Prop
Grayson	W	S	1824	Boon	Deed
Grayson	Hyacinthe		1828	Sali	DTL
Grayson	William		1815	Ark	Prop
Grayum	John		1817	How	Prop
Grear	Thomas	F	1840	Call	Poll
Greason	John	I	1838	Audr	DTL
Gredley	Judah		1859	Reyn	DTL
Green	Elisha		1839	Plat	Prop
Green	Benjamin		1839	Plat	Prop
Green	Duff		1827	Sali	DTL
Green	Vincent		1836	Perr	Poll
Green	William		1836	Carr	PrpPt
Green	William		1840	Call	Poll
Green	John		1821	StC	CtS
Green	Willis		1830	How	DTL
Green	John		1830	How	DTL
Green	Squire		1836	StC	Prop
Green	John		1836	StC	Prop
Green	John		1830	Linc	DTL
Green	Robert		1830	Linc	DTL
Green	Thomas		1810	Ark	Prop
Green	Duff		1829	Sali	DTL
Green	Duff		1828	Sali	DTL
Green	Duff		1817	How	Prop
Green	James	I	1839	Lew	DTL
Green	William		1839	Lew	DTL
Green	Luin		1822	Clay	Poll
Green	Liburn	B	1833	Lew	DTL
Green	Zenge		1833	Lew	DTL
Green, Jr	James		1836	StC	Prop
Greene	John		1839	Plat	Prop
Greene	Charles		1859	Reyn	DTL

Last Name	First Name	Int	Year	County	Type
Greenlee	Asa		1834	Craw	DTL
Greenup	Jackman		1843	Audr	Prop
Greenwalt	Anna		1810	Ark	Prop
Greffey	William		1844	Osag	Real
Gregg	Riley		1839	Plat	Prop
Gregg	David		1839	Plat	Prop
Gregg	James		1839	Plat	Prop
Gregg	Hugh		1838	Audr	DTL
Gregg	Harmon		1817	How	Prop
Gregg	Rebecca		1817	How	Prop
Gregg, dec	William		1827	Sali	DTL
Gregor	Bannister		1827	Mari	Prop
Gregory	Ambrose		1840	Call	Poll
Gregory, Jr	John		1840	Call	Poll
Greman	Alexandre		1818	StL	Real
Grene	Francisco		1780	StL	Mil
Greor	W	H	1840	Call	Poll
Grey	Wm		1840	Call	Poll
Grey	William		1840	Call	Poll
Grey	James		1840	Call	Poll
Gribble	James	H	1839	Plat	Prop
Griffay	Clerma		1836	StC	Prop
Griffeith	Pugh		1867	Reyn	DTL
Griffeth	James		1839	Plat	Prop
Griffin	Jas		1843	Audr	Prop
Griffin	Lewis		1840	Call	Poll
Griffin	James	A	1840	Call	Poll
Griffin	John		1840	Call	Poll
Griffin	Carter		1836	StC	Prop
Griffin	Sinclear		1836	StC	Prop
Griffin	Asa		1836	StC	Prop
Griffin	Daniel		1836	StC	Prop
Griffin	John		1836	StC	Prop
Griffin	Joel		1836	StC	Prop
Griffin	Conrad		1836	StC	Prop
Griffin	Patrick		1829	Char	DTL
Griffith	John	A	1840	Call	Poll
Griffith	Martin		1840	Call	Poll
Griffith	David		1840	Call	Poll
Grigg	Archibald		1838	Audr	DTL
Griggs	Ambrose		1836	StC	Prop
Griman	Alexander		1820	StL	Prop

Last Name	First Name	Int	Year	County	Type
Grimes	Randolph		1836	Carr	Prop
Grimes	Randolph		1836	Carr	PrpPt
Grimes	Joshua		1836	StC	Prop
Grimes	????		1836	StC	Prop
Grimes	Daniel		1836	StC	Prop
Grimon	Alexander		1818	StL	Real
Gringo	Emaniel		1867	Reyn	DTL
Griseau	Adolph		1836	StC	Prop
Grisham	William		1840	Call	Poll
Grisley	H	H	1867	Reyn	DTL
Grober	Daniel		1839	Plat	Prop
Groce	Samuel		1836	Carr	Prop
Groce	John		1836	Carr	Prop
Groce	Samuel		1836	Carr	PrpPt
Groce	John		1836	Carr	PrpPt
Groce	Elizabeth		1836	StC	Prop
Groce	David		1836	StC	Prop
Groce	Isaac		1836	StC	Prop
Groce	Lewis		1836	StC	Prop
Groffoth	Isaac	H	1818	StL	Real
Grooms	John		1839	Plat	Prop
Grooms	William		1821	Ray	Prop
Grooms	Francis		1821	Ray	Prop
Grooms	Abraham		1821	Ray	Prop
Grooms	Isam		1822	Clay	Poll
Gross	John		1867	Reyn	DTL
Grounds	Henry		1836	Perr	Poll
Grounds	Peter		1836	Perr	Poll
Grover	Herrod		1836	StC	Prop
Grover	William		1839	Lew	DTL
Grover	Daniel		1844	Osag	Real
Groves	George		1839	Lew	DTL
Grugin	Thos		1843	Audr	Prop
Guard	P	C	1867	Reyn	DTL
Guarren	Thomas		1867	Reyn	DTL
Gudard	Bicnent		1818	StL	Real
Guenelle	Frances		1818	StL	Real
Gueret	Peter		1818	StL	Real
Guerette	Pierre		1818	StL	Real
Guerrett	Pierre		1820	StL	Prop
Guerrier	Charles		1818	StL	Real
Guettramt	Stephen		1840	Call	Poll

Last Name	First Name	Int	Year	County	Type
Gugitt	Hiram		1817	How	Prop
Guibord	Augustin		1820	StL	Prop
Guiersero	Gregorio		1780	StL	Mil
Guinell	Francois		1820	StL	Prop
Guinelle	Francis		1818	StL	Real
Guion	Nicolas		1780	StL	Mil
Guion	Amable		1780	StL	Mil
Guion	Amable		1791	StL	Span
Guion	Hubert		1820	StL	Prop
Guion	Davins		1820	StL	Prop
Guish	Michael		1859	Reyn	DTL
Guitar	Pablo		1780	StL	Mil
Guitar	Louis		1818	StL	Real
Guitard	Pablo		1791	StL	Span
Guitard	Louis		1818	StL	Real
Guitard	Paul	L	1818	StL	Real
Guitard	Louis		1820	StL	Prop
Guitard	Vincent		1820	StL	Prop
Guitard	Paul Lagrandeur		1820	StL	Prop
Guitard	Paul		1820	StL	Prop
Gullet	Rice		1818	Lawr	DTL
Guman	James	R	1859	Reyn	DTL
Gunn	Henry		1839	Plat	Prop
Gunn	David		1839	Plat	Prop
Gunn	Rebecca		1839	Plat	Prop
Gunn	Berryman		1822	Clay	Poll
Gush	Michael		1867	Reyn	DTL
Gutheridge	Elija	W	1836	StC	Prop
Gutherie	Samuel	T	1840	Call	Poll
Gutherie	Robert		1836	StC	Prop
Guy	John		1840	Call	Poll
Guy	John	R	1818	StL	Real
Guy	John	R	1820	StL	Prop
Guyer	Jacob		1839	Plat	Prop
Guyol	Francois	M	1820	StL	Prop
Guyon	Amable		1830	Howa	DTL
Guyori	Phillip		1820	StL	Prop
Guyory	Alexander		1818	StL	Real
Gyle	John	K	1839	Plat	Prop
Habb	Victor		1818	StL	Real
Hacker	Absalom		1830	Ray	Prop
Hacket	Madam		1810	Ark	Prop

Last Name	First Name	Int	Year	County	Type
Haclum	(Negro)		1818	StL	Real
Haden	Anthony		1810	Ark	Prop
Haden	Elijah		1827	Mari	Prop
Haden	Henderson		1815	Ark	Prop
Haden	Anthony		1815	Ark	Prop
Hagan	Isadore		1836	Perr	Poll
Hagan	Edward		1836	Perr	Poll
Hagan	Mitchael		1836	Perr	Poll
Hagan	James		1863	Jeff	Ass
Hagen	Edmund		1810	Ark	Prop
Haines	Benjamin		1836	Carr	Prop
Haines	Benjamin		1836	Carr	PrpPt
Halbert	Philip		1836	Carr	Prop
Halbert	Philip		1836	Carr	PrpPt
Halbert	John		1829	Char	DTL
Halderman	Peter		1818	StL	Real
Hale	John		1840	Call	Poll
Hale	Abijah		1818	StL	Real
Hale	Philip		1831	Cole	DTL
Haley	John		1843	Audr	Prop
Haley	William		1859	Reyn	DTL
Halford	James		1839	Plat	Prop
Hall	William		1843	Audr	Prop
Hall	Levi		1843	Audr	Prop
Hall	Elihu		1843	Audr	Prop
Hall	Banks	B	1843	Audr	Prop
Hall	Elisha		1843	Audr	Prop
Hall	Edward	B	1825	Clay	DTL
Hall	Seth		1836	Perr	Poll
Hall	Thomas		1836	Carr	Prop
Hall	Thomas		1836	Carr	PrpPt
Hall	Nathaniel		1836	Carr	PrpPt
Hall	Henry		1840	Call	Poll
Hall	Matthew		1840	Call	Poll
Hall	Samuel		1840	Call	Poll
Hall	Ann		1834	Pett	Prop
Hall	B		1834	Pett	PrpPt
Hall	S		1834	Pett	PrpPt
Hall	Joseph		1836	StC	Prop
Hall	William		1821	Ray	Prop
Hall	Elisha		1821	Ray	Prop
Hall	Elihu		1838	Audr	DTL

98

Last Name	First Name	Int	Year	County	Type
Hall	William		1838	Audr	DTL
Hall	John		1818	StL	Real
Hall	David		1818	StL	Real
Hall	J	B	1837	Lew	DTL
Hall	John		1820	StL	Prop
Hall	William		1829	Mari	DTL
Hall	Charles	R	1830	Ray	Prop
Hall	Joseph		1830	Ray	Prop
Hall	Peter	A	1839	Lew	DTL
Hall	James	E	1822	Clay	Poll
Hall	Edward	V	1822	Clay	Poll
Hallet	Moses		1817	How	Prop
Ham	Abram		1836	Perr	Poll
Ham	James		1838	Steg	DTL
Ham	John	D	1836	Carr	PrpPt
Ham	Joseph		1840	Call	Poll
Ham	S	B	1840	Call	Poll
Ham	Tice		1823	How	DTL
Hamblin	George		1840	Call	Poll
Hambry	William		1836	Carr	Prop
Hambry	William		1836	Carr	PrpPt
Hamelin	Alexis		1820	StL	Prop
Hamer	Green		1859	Reyn	DTL
Hamilin	James		1839	Plat	Prop
Hamilin	Henry		1839	Plat	Prop
Hamilton	David		1839	Plat	Prop
Hamilton	James	C	1840	Call	Poll
Hamilton	Robert		1840	Call	Poll
Hamilton	William	B	1840	Call	Poll
Hamilton	Joseph		1817	How	Prop
Hamilton	Harrison		1839	Lew	DTL
Hamilton	Andrew		1844	Osag	Real
Hamilton	Robert	M	1834	Call	DTL
Hamilton, Jr	John		1840	Call	Poll
Hamilton, Sr	James		1840	Call	Poll
Hamington	Bartley		1810	Ark	Prop
Hammond	James		1836	Carr	Prop
Hammond	James		1836	Carr	PrpPt
Hammond	Allen		1840	Call	Poll
Hammond	Samuel		1823	Call	NRP
Hammond	Samuel		1820	StL	Prop
Hampton	Thomas		1840	Call	Poll

Last Name	First Name	Int	Year	County	Type
Hampton	John		1810	Ark	Prop
Hanah	John		1840	Call	Poll
Hanah	Samuel		1840	Call	Poll
Hanaley	Samuel		1835	Barr	DTL
Hancock	Robert		1830	Howa	DTL
Hancock	John	C	1836	StC	Prop
Hancock	Benjamin		1836	StC	Prop
Hancock	John		1817	How	Prop
Hancock	Robert		1817	How	Prop
Hancock	Rawley	A	1844	Osag	Real
Handson	John		1836	Carr	PrtPt
Hanes	Joel		1843	Audr	Prop
Haney	Charles		1830	Ray	Prop
Hangers	Washington		1838	Ripl	DTL
Hank's Heirs	George		1836	Carr	Prop
Hank's Heirs	George		1836	Carr	PrpPt
Hanks	James	M	1836	Carr	Prop
Hanks	James		1836	Carr	PrpPt
Hanks	James		1810	Ark	Prop
Hanley	Archibald		1840	Call	Poll
Hanley	Thomas		1820	StL	Prop
Hanna	Samuel		1827	Boon	Lisc
Hannah	John	A	1840	Call	Poll
Hannon	Thomas		1827	Mari	Prop
Hanse	Robert		1840	Call	Poll
Hansen	L		1840	Call	Poll
Hapson	Joseph		1833	Lew	DTL
Hard	Richard	L	1840	Call	Poll
Hardeman	Thomas		1817	How	Prop
Harden	Elihu		1840	Call	Poll
Harden	George		1840	Call	Poll
Harden	Moris		1840	Call	Poll
Harden	William		1840	Call	Poll
Hardey	William		1839	Plat	Prop
Hardin	William		1843	Audr	Prop
Hardin	George	W	1823	How	DTL
Hardwick	John		1822	Clay	Poll
Hardwick	Alex		1822	Clay	Poll
Hardwick	Lewis		1822	Clay	Poll
Hardy	Benjamin		1836	Carr	Prop
Hardy	Joel		1836	Carr	Prop
Hardy	Benjamin		1836	Carr	PrpPt

Last Name	First Name	Int	Year	County	Type
Hardy	Joel		1836	Carr	PrpPt
Hardy	Benjamin		1836	Carr	PrpPt
Harison	William	D	1843	Audr	Prop
Harison	William	P	1843	Audr	Prop
Harison	Jas		1843	Audr	Prop
Harison	Thos		1843	Audr	Prop
Harison	W	D	1843	Audr	Prop
Harison, dec	T		1843	Audr	Prop
Hark	George	C	1827	Sali	DTL
Harkins, Sr	Hiram	C	1840	Call	Poll
Harland	Aaron		1837	Lew	DTL
Harler	Nathaniel		1840	Call	Poll
Harless	Henry		1836	StC	Prop
Harless	Edward		1836	StC	Prop
Harman	Jas	H	1843	Audr	Prop
Harman	C	P	1867	Reyn	DTL
Harman	David		1831	Cole	DTL
Harmon	A	D	1836	StC	Prop
Harness	Chrisley		1818	Lawr	DTL
Harness	Addam		1836	StC	Prop
Harney	Henry	L	1836	StC	Prop
Harold	Leonard		1836	StC	Prop
Harper	William		1843	Audr	Prop
Harper	Thomas		1836	Carr	PrpPt
Harper	Robert		1840	Call	Poll
Harper	Edward		1840	Call	Poll
Harper	N	D	1840	Call	Poll
Harper	William		1818	StL	Real
Harper	William		1820	StL	Prop
Harper	Wm		1820	StL	Prop
Harper	Edward		1844	Osag	Real
Harper	John		1836	Char	DTL
Harriet	Ameline		1830	Wash	DTL
Harriman	John		1821	StC	Ct
Harrington	Thomas		1839	Plat	Prop
Harrington	Miles		1839	Plat	Prop
Harris	Joseph	B	1843	Audr	Prop
Harris	Jefferson		1839	Plat	Prop
Harris	John		1839	Plat	Prop
Harris	Charles	A	1836	Perr	Poll
Harris	Winens		1836	Carr	PrpPt
Harris	Alexander		1836	Carr	Prop

Last Name	First Name	Int	Year	County	Type
Harris	Zacariah		1836	Carr	Prop
Harris	Alexander		1836	Carr	PrpPt
Harris	Zacariah		1836	Carr	PrpPt
Harris	James		1827	Boon	Lisc
Harris	P		1828	Boon	Lisc
Harris	William	P	1828	Boon	Lisc
Harris	George		1828	Boon	Lisc
Harris	George		1840	Call	Poll
Harris	John		1840	Call	Poll
Harris	Peter		1840	Call	Poll
Harris	Mastus		1840	Call	Poll
Harris	Reubin	B	1830	Coop	Ct
Harris	Reubin	B	1830	Coop	CtS
Harris	Moses		1829	Char	DTL
Harris	John		1821	Ray	Prop
Harris	Hezekiah		1828	Sali	DTL
Harris	James		1817	How	Prop
Harris' Heirs	Barnabas		1823	Call	NRP
Harrison	John		1840	Call	Poll
Harrison	M	V	1840	Call	Poll
Harrison	Mathew	G	1840	Call	Poll
Harrison	Cuthbert		1829	Mari	DTL
Harrison	Joseph	V	1839	Lew	DTL
Harrison	Aristedes		1834	Craw	DTL
Harriss	George	W	1840	Call	Poll
Harriss	Hamilton	H	1840	Call	Poll
Harriss	Thomas	B	1840	Call	Poll
Harriss	Thomas	D	1840	Call	Poll
Harry	Hiram		1838	Audr	DTL
Harson	Gideon		1839	Plat	Prop
Harst	Joshua		1837	Cass	DTL
Hart	Alford	E	1840	Call	Poll
Hart	Richard		1867	Reyn	DTL
Hart	Richard		1867	Reyn	DTL
Hartkoff	Daniel		1867	Reyn	DTL
Hartkoff	Daniel		1867	Reyn	DTL
Hartley	James		1839	Lew	DTL
Hartman	Henry		1836	StC	Prop
Hartt	George	C	1830	Coop	Ct
Harvey	Saml	L	1843	Audr	Prop
Harvey	Saml		1843	Audr	Prop
Harvey	J		1836	Carr	Prop

Last Name	First Name	Int	Year	County	Type
Harvy	William		1843	Audr	Prop
Hase	Frederick	C	1836	Perr	Poll
Hassel	Hahn		1817	How	Prop
Hastings	????		1820	StL	Prop
Haston	Robert		1839	Plat	Prop
Hatch	William	T	1827	Boon	Lisc
Hater	Solomon		1839	Plat	Prop
Hatfield	George	H	1859	Reyn	DTL
Hatfield	Thomas		1859	Reyn	DTL
Hatfield	S		1859	Reyn	DTL
Hatfield	John	O	1859	Reyn	DTL
Hatfield	Allen	P	1867	Reyn	DTL
Hathway	William		1867	Reyn	DTL
Hatley	Elisha		1839	Plat	Prop
Hatt	Thomas		1859	Reyn	DTL
Hatten	Milton		1843	Audr	Prop
Hatten	Jonah	B	1843	Audr	Prop
Hatten	David		1843	Audr	Prop
Hatten	D		1843	Audr	Prop
Hatten	David		1838	Audr	DTL
Hatten	Jonah	B	1838	Audr	DTL
Hatten	Milton		1838	Audr	DTL
Hatton	Samuel	P	1834	Call	DTL
Haupt	Charles		1836	StC	Prop
Haupt	Jacob		1838	Audr	DTL
Hause	Charles	W	1836	Carr	Prop
Hause	Charles		1836	Carr	PrpPt
Havans	William		1867	Reyn	DTL
Havnans	William		1867	Reyn	DTL
Hawford	F	C	1867	Reyn	DTL
Hawken	Jacob		1820	StL	Prop
Hawkins	H	H	1839	Wash	Lisc
Hawkins	Willis		1828	Boon	Lisc
Hawkins	James		1823	How	DTL
Hawkins	James	H	1844	Osag	Real
Hawks	Mary	M	1867	Reyn	DTL
Hawver's Heirs	Isaac		1836	Carr	Prop
Hawver's Heirs	Isaac		1836	Carr	PrpPt
Hayden	S	T	1843	Audr	Prop
Hayden	Charles		1836	Perr	Poll
Hayden	Clement		1836	Perr	Poll
Hayden	George		1836	Perr	Poll

Last Name	First Name	Int	Year	County	Type
Hayden	William		1840	Call	Poll
Hayden	Rawlenger		1840	Call	Poll
Hayden	William		1840	Call	Poll
Hayden	Samuel		1840	Call	Poll
Hayden	Newel		1831	Craw	DTL
Hayes	William	H	1839	Plat	Prop
Hayes	Jacob		1839	Plat	Prop
Hayes	S	C	1839	Plat	Prop
Hayes	D	R	1839	Plat	Prop
Hayes	G		1829	Char	DTL
Hayes	Andrew	B B	1838	Audr	DTL
Haynes	Joel		1843	Audr	Prop
Haynes	Wm		1830	Wash	DTL
Haynes	Osburn		1836	Carr	PrtPt
Haynes	Luther		1867	Reyn	DTL
Haynes	Joel		1838	Audr	DTL
Hays	A	B R	1843	Audr	Prop
Hays	John		1840	Call	Poll
Hays	William		1867	Reyn	DTL
Hays	Robert		1829	Char	DTL
Hays	Charles		1823	How	DTL
Hays	Chas		1823	How	DTL
Hays	William		1817	How	Prop
Hazelrig	Green		1840	Call	Poll
Head	William	H	1834	Pett	Prop
Head	Mark		1834	Pett	PrpPt
Head	Natahn		1830	Linc	DTL
Head	Anthony		1817	How	Prop
Head	Gaven		1817	How	Prop
Head	James		1830	Ray	Prop
Headerick	George		1836	StC	Prop
Headerick	Joseph		1836	StC	Prop
Heady	Thomas	B	1834	Call	DTL
Heald	Johnas		1836	StC	Prop
Heald	Rebecca		1836	StC	Prop
Heald's Heirs	Nathaniel		1836	StC	Prop
Heart	Samuel		1836	StC	Prop
Heartment	Heirock		1836	StC	Prop
Heath	Robert	A	1830	How	DTL
Heath	John		1817	How	Prop
Heath	Robert		1817	How	Prop
Heath	B	S	1839	Lew	DTL

Last Name	First Name	Int	Year	County	Type
Heath's Heirs	John		1836	Carr	Prop
Heath's Heirs	John		1836	Carr	PrpPt
Heather	Michael	B	1827	Mari	Prop
Hebbert	Charles		1831	Cole	DTL
Hebert	Hyacinthe		1818	StL	Real
Hebert	Yaeinthe		1820	StL	Prop
Heckel	Wm		1843	Audr	Prop
Hedges	G	C B	1840	Call	Poll
Hedges	J		1831	Craw	DTL
Heeling	Walker	D	1840	Call	Poll
Heilfrech	Charles		1836	StC	Prop
Heilfrech	John	M	1836	StC	Prop
Heiskell	William		1823	Call	NRP
Heity	Lewis		1867	Reyn	DTL
Hellerbrand	P		1863	Jeff	Ass
Helman	Henry		1836	StC	Prop
Helms	Hiram		1837	Cass	DTL
Hemmerly	Joseph		1830	Ray	Prop
Hemphill	Hugh		1867	Reyn	DTL
Hemphill	John		1810	Ark	Prop
Hemphill	John		1815	Ark	Prop
Hempstead	Thomas		1820	StL	Prop
Hempstead	Charles	S	1820	StL	Prop
Hempstead	Thomas		1820	StL	Prop
Henderson	Dorman		1839	Plat	Prop
Henderson	John		1839	Plat	Prop
Henderson	Joseph		1839	Plat	Prop
Henderson	Giles		1839	Plat	Prop
Henderson	Thomas		1839	Plat	Prop
Henderson	Cyrus		1825	CGir	Lisc
Henderson	John		1836	Carr	Prop
Henderson	John		1836	Carr	PrpPt
Henderson	I		1828	Boon	Lisc
Henderson	A	H	1840	Call	Poll
Henderson	James	A	1840	Call	Poll
Henderson	David		1840	Call	Poll
Henderson	Jas	S	1840	Call	Poll
Henderson	William		1840	Call	Poll
Henderson	John		1830	Jeff	DTL
Henderson	Joseph		1818	StL	Real
Henderson	William		1844	Osag	Real
Henderson	Nathaniel		1838	Ripl	DTL

Last Name	First Name	Int	Year	County	Type
Henderson, Jr	William		1821	Ray	Prop
Hendon	John		1836	Char	DTL
Hendreson	Joseph		1818	StL	Real
Hendricks	Peter		1839	Plat	Prop
Hendricks	John		1836	Carr	Prop
Hendricks	John		1836	Carr	PrpPt
Hendricks	John		1830	Ray	Prop
Hendricks	Jesse		1834	Craw	DTL
Hendricks	Edwin		1829	NMad	DTL
Hendrickson	John		1838	Steg	DTL
Hendrix	John		1837	Lew	DTL
Hendrix	James		1839	Lew	DTL
Hene	Henry		1840	Call	Poll
Henete	Baptista		1780	StL	Mil
Henley	Thomas		1836	Char	DTL
Henlsey	J	M	1863	Jeff	Ass
Henny	James		1810	Ark	Prop
Henricks	John		1839	Plat	Prop
Henry	Andrew		1830	Wash	DTL
Henry	Henry	J	1831	Jack	DTL
Henry	Conrad		1836	Carr	PrpPt
Henry	James		1836	Carr	Prop
Henry	James		1836	Carr	PrpPt
Henry	Ezekiel		1810	Ark	Prop
Henry	Isaac	N	1820	StL	Prop
Henry	Hugh		1827	Mari	Prop
Henry	William		1827	Mari	Prop
Henry	Ezkiel		1815	Ark	Prop
Henry	Patrick		1839	Lew	DTL
Henry	James		1822	Clay	Poll
Henshaw	James		1839	Plat	Prop
Hensley	John		1825	Clay	DTL
Hensley	Samuel		1840	Call	Poll
Hensley	A	W	1863	Jeff	Ass
Hensley	Jas	O	1863	Jeff	Ass
Hensley	John		1817	How	Prop
Hensley	William		1817	How	Prop
Hensley	Samuel		1822	Clay	Poll
Henson	Andrew		1839	Plat	Prop
Henson	William	E	1839	Plat	Prop
Hepler	Joseph		1843	Audr	Prop
Her	Henry		1839	Plat	Prop

Last Name	First Name	Int	Year	County	Type
Her	Richard		1839	Plat	Prop
Her	Jacob		1839	Plat	Prop
Herman	Bernard		1867	Reyn	DTL
Heron	Saml	J	1845	Sali	Lisc
Herrick	Isaac		1843	Audr	Prop
Herring	George		1840	Call	Poll
Herring	John		1840	Call	Poll
Herring	James	C	1840	Call	Poll
Herring	John	B	1840	Call	Poll
Herrington	Levi	B	1859	Reyn	DTL
Herrington	Albert		1867	Reyn	DTL
Herron	John		1839	Plat	Prop
Herron	Silas		1836	Carr	Prop
Herron	Silas		1836	Carr	PrpPt
Herron	James		1829	NMad	DTL
Herron	Wilson		1829	NMad	DTL
Hertzog	Joseph		1820	StL	Prop
Heslnell	John		1818	StL	Real
Hever	Augustin		1780	StL	Mil
Hewes	John		1867	Reyn	DTL
Hewes	John		1867	Reyn	DTL
Hewit	Jos		1845	Sali	Lisc
Hewlit	Benj		1837	Lew	DTL
Hewlit	Jeptha		1837	Lew	DTL
Hiatt	James		1821	Ray	Prop
Hiatt	Joseph		1817	How	Prop
Hiatt	Moses		1817	How	Prop
Hibler	Henry	R	1844	Osag	Real
Hibler	Sharlotte		1844	Osag	Real
Hibler	Henry	R	1844	Osag	Real
Hickman	J		1826	Coop	DTL
Hickman	James		1830	Howa	DTL
Hickman	Henry		1836	StC	Prop
Hickman	J		1826	Coop	DTL
Hickox	Benjamin	T	1830	Coop	CtS
Hicks	D	C	1867	Reyn	DTL
Hicks	Absalom		1817	How	Prop
Higgins	John		1839	Plat	Prop
Higgins	Philomon		1839	Plat	Prop
Higgins	Josiah		1839	Plat	Prop
Higgins	Jacob		1839	Plat	Prop
Higgins	Philemon		1836	Perr	Poll

Last Name	First Name	Int	Year	County	Type
Higgins	John	W	1836	Carr	PrpPt
Higgins	Josiah		1817	How	Prop
Highland	John		1867	Reyn	DTL
Highland	Stephen		1829	NMad	DTL
Hignight	Abner		1810	Ark	Prop
Hilbert	Charles	A	1836	Carr	Prop
Hilbert	Charles		1836	Carr	PrpPt
Hilbert	A	C	1836	StC	Prop
Hill	Alison		1839	Plat	Prop
Hill	Archibald		1839	Plat	Prop
Hill	Thomas		1827	Sali	DTL
Hill	Irwin	W	1838	Cass	DTL
Hill	A		1827	Boon	Lisc
Hill	Benjamin		1840	Call	Poll
Hill	Robert	C	1840	Call	Poll
Hill	Charles		1840	Call	Poll
Hill	Richard		1840	Call	Poll
Hill	Willis		1840	Call	Poll
Hill	Wright		1830	Howa	DTL
Hill	James		1821	Ray	Prop
Hill	????		1820	StL	Prop
Hill	Charles	D	1823	How	DTL
Hillen	John		1844	Osag	Real
Hillencamp	Francis		1836	StC	Prop
Hiller	Daniel		1840	Call	Poll
Hilsey	Jacob		1836	Carr	Prop
Hilsey	Jacob		1836	Carr	PrpPt
Hilton	Isaac		1844	Osag	Real
Hilton, Sr	James		1844	Osag	Real
Hinch	Michael		1823	How	DTL
Hinch	Michael		1817	How	Prop
Hinch, dec	Samuel		1817	How	Prop
Hincher	Jonathan		1839	Plat	Prop
Hinds	Jessie	P	1867	Reyn	DTL
Hines	William		1836	Carr	Prop
Hines	William		1836	Carr	PrpPt
Hines	John		1867	Reyn	DTL
Hines	John		1817	How	Prop
Hinkley	Thos	G	1859	Reyn	DTL
Hinkson	Robt		1805	Steg	Prop
Hinston	Harlow		1821	Ray	Prop
Hinton	John		1840	Call	Poll

Last Name	First Name	Int	Year	County	Type
Hirtlin	James		1840	Call	Poll
Hisey	Jacob	G	1840	Call	Poll
Hitchock	Isaac		1827	Jack	DTL
Hix	F		1829	Char	DTL
Hixson	Thomas		1821	Ray	Prop
Hixton	Andrew		1821	Ray	Prop
Hoard	Alexander		1840	Call	Poll
Hobaugh	Hiram		1838	Ripl	DTL
Hobbs	Jas	H	1843	Audr	Prop
Hobby	W		1829	Char	DTL
Hobs	John		1818	Lawr	DTL
Hobson	Jonathan		1834	Craw	DTL
Hockaday	J	O	1840	Call	Poll
Hockaday	James		1840	Call	Poll
Hockaday, Sr	Isaac	N	1840	Call	Poll
Hodge	John		1821	Ray	Prop
Hodge	J	B	1844	Osag	Real
Hodges	Samuel		1817	How	Prop
Hodges	Daniel		1817	How	Prop
Hoduston	David		1840	Call	Poll
Hoel	Barnabas		1867	Reyn	DTL
Hoelsclaw	Obed		1836	StC	Prop
Hofflinger	James		1837	Bent	DTL
Hofflingler	James		1836	Bent	DTL
Hoffman	George	W	1836	StC	Prop
Hogan	John		1859	Reyn	DTL
Hogan	Jno		1859	Reyn	DTL
Hogan	James	H	1859	Reyn	DTL
Hogan	John		1867	Reyn	DTL
Hogan	James		1867	Reyn	DTL
Hogard	Austin		1836	Perr	Poll
Hogard	William		1836	Perr	Poll
Hogard	Alexander		1836	Perr	Poll
Hoglesbach	Francis		1844	Osag	Real
Hognight	John		1839	Plat	Prop
Hoit	William		1820	StL	Prop
Holbrock	John		1820	StL	Prop
Holcomb	Kinsey		1837	Lew	DTL
Hold	Jacob		1825	Char	DTL
Holden	Henry		1836	Carr	Prop
Holden	Henry		1836	Carr	PrpPt
Holden	E	M	1831	Cole	DTL

Last Name	First Name	Int	Year	County	Type
Holderfield	John		1836	Carr	PrpPt
Holderman	Ferdinand		1844	Osag	Real
Holdra	Harmon		1836	StC	Prop
Holdraugh	Harmon		1836	StC	Prop
Hole	William		1867	Reyn	DTL
Holeman	James		1839	Plat	Prop
Holeman	Ruben		1831	Jack	DTL
Holeman	Henry		1840	Call	Poll
Holeman	Oliver	W	1844	Osag	Real
Holeman, dec	Christian		1844	Osag	Real
Holland	Benjamin		1839	Plat	Prop
Holland	Thomas	L	1839	Plat	Prop
Holland	Robert	W	1839	Plat	Prop
Holland	Nathaniel		1839	Plat	Prop
Hollend	Peter	H	1840	Call	Poll
Holliday	Thomas		1817	How	Prop
Holliman	David		1834	Craw	DTL
Holloman	Daniel		1859	Reyn	DTL
Holloway	Nathan		1817	How	Prop
Holly	John		1836	Carr	Prop
Holly	John		1836	Carr	PrpPt
Holmes	John		1827	Sali	DTL
Holmes	James		1836	Carr	PrpPt
Holmes	Lorenzo	B	1836	StC	Prop
Holmes	Ellen		1836	StC	Prop
Holmes	Samuel		1836	StC	Prop
Holms	Oliver		1820	StL	Prop
Holoway	Absalom		1844	Osag	Real
Holsa	John		1836	Char	DTL
Holt	David	R	1839	Plat	Prop
Holt	James		1836	Carr	PrpPt
Holt	Abner		1840	Call	Poll
Holt	Hiram		1840	Call	Poll
Holt	Abner	C	1840	Call	Poll
Holt	John		1840	Call	Poll
Holt	John	D	1840	Call	Poll
Holt	Robert		1840	Call	Poll
Holt	Hiram		1829	Char	DTL
Holt	nathaniel		1830	Ray	Prop
Holt	James		1830	Ray	Prop
Holt, Jr	William	P	1840	Call	Poll
Holt, Sr	William	P	1840	Call	Poll

110

Last Name	First Name	Int	Year	County	Type
Holterfield	Richard		1836	Carr	Prop
Holterfield	Richard		1836	Carr	PrpPt
Homes	David		1821	Ray	Prop
Honore	Luis		1780	StL	Mil
Honore	Francisco		1780	StL	Mil
Honore	Luis		1791	StL	Span
Honory	Silvest		1836	StC	Prop
Honory	Madden Francis		1836	StC	Prop
Honory	Tesent		1836	StC	Prop
Honory	Louis		1836	StC	Prop
Honslow	John		1836	Carr	PrtPt
Hoober	William		1844	Osag	Real
Hood	W	G	1829	Char	DTL
Hook	Thos		1843	Audr	Prop
Hook	Thomas		1840	Call	Poll
Hook	William		1840	Call	Poll
Hook	Zadick		1840	Call	Poll
Hook	Thomas		1838	Audr	DTL
Hooke	William		1845	Sali	Lisc
Hooker	Samuel		1840	Call	Poll
Hoon	Joseph		1836	Carr	PrtPt
Hooper	David		1844	Osag	Real
Hooper	John		1844	Osag	Real
Hoops	David		1844	Osag	Real
Hoover	Arealas		1840	Call	Poll
Hoover	Perry		1840	Call	Poll
Hopkins	George	B	1840	Call	Poll
Hopkins	James		1815	Ark	Prop
Hopper	Charles		1837	Cass	DTL
Hormsby	William		1838	Cass	DTL
Horn	Adam		1830	Coop	Ct
Horn	William		1830	Coop	Ct
Horn	Amos		1830	Coop	CtS
Horn	William		1830	Coop	CtS
Hornback	Adam		1839	Plat	Prop
Hornbuckle	R	S	1840	Call	Poll
Hornbuckle	Alfred		1840	Call	Poll
Hornbuckle (1)	Harden	F	1840	Call	Poll
Hornbuckle (2)	Harden	F	1840	Call	Poll
Horns	Christen		1836	Perr	Poll
Horocks	Edward		1820	StL	Prop
Horrell	Bernard		1836	Perr	Poll

111

Last Name	First Name	Int	Year	County	Type
Horrow	Even		1818	Lawr	DTL
Hortez	Juan Bapt		1780	StL	Mil
Hortez	Juan Bapt		1791	StL	Span
Hortez	Josef		1791	StL	Span
Hortiz	Wid		1818	StL	Real
Hortiz	J	B	1818	StL	Real
Hortiz	Wid Margaret		1820	StL	Prop
Hortiz	Jean Baptiste		1820	StL	Prop
Horton	A	J	1843	Char	DTL
Hosely	Catherine		1829	NMad	DTL
Hosley	David		1829	NMad	DTL
Hosper	Conrad		1836	StC	Prop
Hosteter	Francis		1836	StC	Prop
Hostetor's Heirs	Christian		1836	StC	Prop
Hostey	John		1831	Cole	DTL
Hot	Carlos		1780	StL	Mil
Houchen	John		1843	Audr	Prop
Houf	Henry		1840	Call	Poll
Hough	Jacob		1843	Audr	Prop
Houp	A		1843	Audr	Prop
House	William		1843	Audr	Prop
House	Charles	W	1830	Ray	Prop
Housen	Candy		1843	Audr	Prop
Housen	John	H	1836	StC	Prop
Houshaw	Jesse		1838	Cass	DTL
How	Alfred		1843	Audr	Prop
Howans	William		1867	Reyn	DTL
Howard	Enoch		1839	Plat	Prop
Howard	John		1839	Plat	Prop
Howard	A	H	1859	Reyn	DTL
Howard	Joseph	B	1828	Boon	Lisc
Howard	Joseph		1828	Boon	Lisc
Howard	A	H	1867	Reyn	DTL
Howard	James	P	1810	Ark	Prop
Howard	William		1838	Audr	DTL
Howard	William		1817	How	Prop
Howdeshell	John		1823	Call	NRP
Howe	Isaac	P	1840	Call	Poll
Howe	Thomas		1840	Call	Poll
Howel	Benjamin		1836	StC	Prop
Howel	Larkin		1836	StC	Prop
Howel	Alzono	A	1836	StC	Prop

Last Name	First Name	Int	Year	County	Type
Howel	James		1836	StC	Prop
Howel	Thomas		1836	StC	Prop
Howel	Frances		1836	StC	Prop
Howel	Lewis		1836	StC	Prop
Howel	John		1836	StC	Prop
Howel, Sr	Pizaro		1836	StC	Prop
Howell	Jas		1810	Ark	Prop
Howell	James		1817	How	Prop
Howell	John		1827	Mari	Prop
Howland	????		1829	Char	DTL
Howlin	Samuel		1836	StC	Prop
Hoy	Samuel		1839	Plat	Prop
Hubbard	Asaph	E	1843	Audr	Prop
Hubbard	Henry	C	1843	Audr	Prop
Hubbard	Flemming	B	1843	Audr	Prop
Hubbard	Thomas		1836	Carr	Prop
Hubbard	David		1836	Carr	Prop
Hubbard	Thomas		1836	Carr	PrpPt
Hubbard	David		1836	Carr	PrpPt
Hubbard	Durett		1827	Boon	Lisc
Hubbard	E		1828	Boon	Lisc
Hubbard	Jabez		1830	Coop	Ct
Hubbard	Jabez		1830	Coop	Ct
Hubbard	H	R	1867	Reyn	DTL
Hubbard	Flemming	B	1838	Audr	DTL
Hubbard	????		1820	StL	Prop
Hubbard	Aspah		1817	How	Prop
Hubbard	Thomas		1817	How	Prop
Hubble	Jonathan		1818	Lawr	DTL
Huber	Charles		1844	Osag	Real
Hublec	Ichabuf		1818	Lawr	DTL
Huckner	Wid Frederick		1844	Osag	Real
Huddleston	Findley		1836	Carr	PrpPt
Huder	Antonio		1780	StL	Mil
Hudgens	John		1818	Lawr	DTL
Hudsell	Joseph		1810	Ark	Prop
Hudson	Hezekiah		1836	Carr	Prop
Hudson	Hezekiah		1836	Carr	PrpPt
Hudson	William		1840	Call	Poll
Hudson	John		1840	Call	Poll
Hudson	James		1840	Call	Poll
Hudson	Thomas		1840	Call	Poll

113

Last Name	First Name	Int	Year	County	Type
Hudson	James		1818	StL	Real
Hudspeth	A	W	1830	Wash	DTL
Huff	John		1836	Carr	PrpPt
Huff	David		1840	Call	Poll
Huff	Peter		1840	Call	Poll
Huff	Nathan		1830	Coop	Ct
Huff	John		1821	Ray	Prop
Huff	William		1838	Ripl	DTL
Huffington	J	B	1840	Call	Poll
Huffman	William		1839	Plat	Prop
Huffman	John		1836	Perr	Poll
Huffman	Adam		1836	Carr	Prop
Huffman	Adam		1836	Carr	PrpPt
Huffman	George		1836	StC	Prop
Huffman	J		1836	StC	Prop
Huffman	Peter		1836	StC	Prop
Huffman	John		1836	StC	Prop
Huffman	Uriah		1821	Ray	Prop
Huffman	Ezekiel		1821	Ray	Prop
Huffman	Joseph		1827	Mari	Prop
Huffman	Adam		1830	Ray	Prop
Hufftaker	George		1822	Clay	Poll
Huge	Dominique		1820	StL	Prop
Hugginnin	Susanah		1867	Reyn	DTL
Hugh	James		1838	Ripl	DTL
Hughe	Dominique		1818	StL	Real
Hughes	Aaron		1818	Lawr	DTL
Hughes	Samuel		1830	Wash	DTL
Hughes	B	M	1839	Plat	Prop
Hughes	Alfred	W	1839	Plat	Prop
Hughes	Mathias	M	1839	Plat	Prop
Hughes	Allen		1824	Boon	Deed
Hughes	Miles		1836	Perr	Poll
Hughes	James		1836	Carr	Prop
Hughes	Sandford		1836	Carr	Prop
Hughes	James		1836	Carr	PrpPt
Hughes	Sandford		1836	Carr	PrpPt
Hughes	Allen		1828	Boon	Lisc
Hughes	Thomas		1828	Boon	Lisc
Hughes	J	F	1840	Call	Poll
Hughes	David		1818	StL	Real
Hughes	William		1817	How	Prop

114

Last Name	First Name	Int	Year	County	Type
Hughes	Flemming		1843	Char	DTL
Hughes	Elijah		1838	Ripl	DTL
Hughett	Elias		1836	Carr	PrpPt
Hughs	John	N	1828	Boon	Lisc
Hughs	William		1810	Ark	Prop
Hughs	David		1818	StL	Real
Hughs	Jas	A	1834	Craw	DTL
Hughs	Lewis		1837	Mill	DTL
Huiller	Stephen	L	1828	Sali	DTL
Huinn	G		1837	Boon	PM
Huinn	T		1837	Boon	PM
Hukel	William		1843	Audr	Prop
Hulbert	Henry		1867	Reyn	DTL
Hulbert	Henry		1867	Reyn	DTL
Hulbert's Heirs	Ethan		1836	Carr	Prop
Hulbert's Heirs	Ethan		1836	Carr	PrpPt
Hulbert's Heirs	Ethan		1830	Ray	Prop
Hulen	Walter		1836	Carr	Prop
Hulen	Walter		1836	Carr	PrpPt
Hulet	Orum		1839	Plat	Prop
Hulkey	Stephen		1836	StC	Prop
Hull	James		1839	Plat	Prop
Hull	John	H	1840	Call	Poll
Hull	Welton		1840	Call	Poll
Hull	Abijah		1818	StL	Real
Hull	Abijah		1820	StL	Prop
Hull	John	H	1844	Osag	Real
Hull	M		1844	Osag	Real
Hulp	William		1859	Reyn	DTL
Humet	Bapt		1780	StL	Mil
Humphrey	Nathan		1837	Mill	DTL
Humphreys	Thomas		1840	Call	Poll
Humphreys	Samuel		1840	Call	Poll
Humphreys	James		1840	Call	Poll
Humphries	John		1840	Call	Poll
Hundle	Thomas		1838	Audr	DTL
Hungate	John		1843	Audr	Prop
Hungate	P		1843	Audr	Prop
Hungate	John		1838	Audr	DTL
Hungerford	Charles		1839	Plat	Prop
Hungerford	Anna		1839	Plat	Prop
Hungerford	W	B	1839	Plat	Prop

Last Name	First Name	Int	Year	County	Type
Hunker	Casper		1836	Perr	Poll
Hunn	George		1836	StC	Prop
Hunn	Martin		1836	StC	Prop
Hunn	Francis		1836	StC	Prop
Hunneby	James		1836	Carr	PrpPt
Hunnwell	John		1836	StC	Prop
Huno	Luis		1780	StL	Mil
Hunquel	William		1838	Audr	DTL
Hunsaker	Daniel		1839	Plat	Prop
Hunsaker	Isaac		1839	Plat	Prop
Hunsaker	Joseph		1839	Plat	Prop
Hunt	Daniel		1843	Audr	Prop
Hunt	Sylvester		1839	Plat	Prop
Hunt	Valentine		1859	Reyn	DTL
Hunt	Nathaniel		1836	Carr	Prop
Hunt	Phelemon		1836	Carr	Prop
Hunt	Eliphalt	B	1836	Carr	Prop
Hunt	Theoderick		1836	Carr	Prop
Hunt	Phelemon		1836	Carr	PrpPt
Hunt	Eliphalt		1836	Carr	PrpPt
Hunt	Theoderick		1836	Carr	PrpPt
Hunt	Daniel		1836	StC	Prop
Hunt	Monty		1836	StC	Prop
Hunt	Theodore		1820	StL	Prop
Hunt	William		1817	How	Prop
Hunt	Theodore		1817	How	Prop
Hunt	William		1817	How	Prop
Hunter	George		1839	Plat	Prop
Hunter	David		1822	NMad	Lisc
Hunter	Perry		1840	Call	Poll
Hunter	Samuel	A	1840	Call	Poll
Hunter	William	M	1840	Call	Poll
Hunter	C	W	1818	StL	Real
Huntsberry	Abraham		1827	Mari	Prop
Hurcheson's Heirs	G	W	1836	StC	Prop
Hurcules	Jonas		1836	StC	Prop
Hurd	Calvin		1836	Carr	Prop
Hurd	Calvin		1836	Carr	PrpPt
Hurd	James		1844	Osag	Real
Hurd	John		1844	Osag	Real
Hurd, Sr	John		1844	Osag	Real
Hurdle	Thos		1843	Audr	Prop

116

Last Name	First Name	Int	Year	County	Type
Hurt	William		1838	Ripl	DTL
Husah	John		1836	Carr	PrpPt
Huskey	Jefferson		1863	Jeff	Ass
Husky	Andrew		1863	Jeff	Ass
Huston	John		1840	Call	Poll
Huston	Jos		1845	Sali	Lisc
Huston	Stephen		1867	Reyn	DTL
Hutchance	Samuel		1822	Clay	Poll
Hutchance	Joseph		1822	Clay	Poll
Hutchens	Adam		1836	StC	Prop
Hutchens	Greenbury		1836	StC	Prop
Hutchens	Christopher		1836	StC	Prop
Hutchens	A	G	1836	StC	Prop
Hutcherson	John		1840	Call	Poll
Hutcherson	Zorado		1836	StC	Prop
Hutcheson	Nathaniel		1830	Howa	DTL
Hutcheson	Charles		1836	StC	Prop
Hutchings	John		1821	Ray	Prop
Hutchings	Smith		1821	Ray	Prop
Hutchings	Moses		1821	Ray	Prop
Hutchins	Moses		1822	Clay	Poll
Hutchinson	John		1817	How	Prop
Hutz	Lorenzo		1840	Call	Poll
Hyatt	Samuel		1822	Clay	Poll
Hyland	John		1867	Reyn	DTL
Hyton	Simpson		1840	Call	Poll
Iavoetas	John		1815	Ark	Prop
Iavoetas	Alexander		1815	Ark	Prop
Icenhour	Ann		1836	StC	Prop
Ilor	Daniel		1836	StC	Prop
Ilor	Stephen		1836	StC	Prop
Iman	Almenda		1836	StC	Prop
Imbau	Joseph		1810	Ark	Prop
Immone	Hyram		1837	Lew	DTL
Indicott	William		1839	Plat	Prop
Indicott	Richard	B	1839	Plat	Prop
Indrou	Alexander		1815	Ark	Prop
Inglish	Thomas		1821	Ray	Prop
Ingraham	Amiaziah		1836	Carr	Prop
Ingraham	Amiaziah		1836	Carr	PrpPt
Ingraham	Charles		1810	Ark	Prop
Ingram	William		1829	Mari	DTL

117

Last Name	First Name	Int	Year	County	Type
Inman	Levi		1836	Carr	Prop
Inman	Levi		1836	Carr	PrpPt
Inman	Daniel		1836	StC	Prop
Irons	Peyer		1821	Ray	Prop
Irvin	Benjamin		1823	How	DTL
Irvine	R		1843	Audr	Prop
Irvine	Robert		1827	Mari	Prop
Irwin	Jas		1818	StL	Real
Irwin	James		1818	StL	Real
Irwin	James		1820	StL	Prop
Isadore	Boyer		1836	StC	Prop
Isbell	Zacariah		1844	Osag	Real
Ish	John		1816	How	Lic
Ish	William		1839	Plat	Prop
Ish	Jacob		1817	How	Prop
Isonhour	Peter		1840	Call	Poll
Jacabo	Lewis		1838	Steg	DTL
Jack	Alfred		1839	Plat	Prop
Jack	William		1817	How	Prop
Jack, Jr	William		1839	Plat	Prop
Jack, Sr	William		1839	Plat	Prop
Jackman	Greenes		1838	Audr	DTL
Jackman	William		1837	Lew	DTL
Jacks	Thomas		1821	Ray	Prop
Jackson	John	J	1843	Audr	Prop
Jackson	Zacariah		1843	Audr	Prop
Jackson	Thomas		1843	Audr	Prop
Jackson	James		1843	Audr	Prop
Jackson	Daniel		1839	Plat	Prop
Jackson	Wallis		1839	Plat	Prop
Jackson	Nathan		1836	Perr	Poll
Jackson	Sheldon		1836	Carr	Prop
Jackson	Sheldon		1836	Carr	PrpPt
Jackson	William	J	1840	Call	Poll
Jackson	Richard	B	1840	Call	Poll
Jackson	Calvin		1840	Call	Poll
Jackson	Elisha		1830	Howa	DTL
Jackson	William		1867	Reyn	DTL
Jackson	William		1836	StC	Prop
Jackson	Slocum		1838	Audr	DTL
Jackson	Jas		1838	Audr	DTL
Jackson	Bacanah		1838	Audr	DTL

Last Name	First Name	Int	Year	County	Type
Jackson	Moses		1830	Ray	Prop
Jackson	Sheldon		1830	Ray	Prop
Jackson	James		1835	Barr	DTL
Jackson, dec	John		1844	Osag	Real
Jackson, Jr	James		1839	Plat	Prop
Jacob	T	F	1867	Reyn	DTL
Jacobs	William		1836	Carr	PrpPt
Jacobs	David		1829	Mari	DTL
Jacobs	David		1839	Lew	DTL
Jacoby	John		1821	StC	Ct
Jacoby	John		1820	StL	Prop
James	William		1843	Audr	Prop
James	Levi	A	1843	Audr	Prop
James	Ross		1805	Steg	Prop
James	David		1839	Plat	Prop
James	Henry		1839	Plat	Prop
James	Joseph		1836	Perr	Poll
James	William		1836	Carr	Prop
James	William		1836	Carr	PrpPt
James	Levy		1840	Call	Poll
James	J	J	1867	Reyn	DTL
James	James		1821	Ray	Prop
James	James		1815	Ark	Prop
James	James		1822	Clay	Poll
Jameson	James		1840	Call	Poll
Jameson	Samuel		1840	Call	Poll
Jameson	Sandford		1840	Call	Poll
Jaminson	George	W	1840	Call	Poll
Jamison	Sanford		1843	Audr	Prop
Jamison	Harrison		1828	Boon	Lisc
Jamison	Thomas		1840	Call	Poll
Janels	Alexis		1810	Ark	Prop
Janes	????		1818	StL	Real
Janes	Joseph		1820	StL	Prop
Janie	Antwine		1836	StC	Prop
Janis	Nicholas		1836	StC	Prop
Janks	James		1830	Ray	Prop
Jans' Heirs	Ant		1836	StC	Prop
January	Ephraim		1836	Carr	Prop
January	Ephraim		1836	Carr	PrpPt
Jardeus	John		1810	Ark	Prop
Jarmon	Edward		1843	Audr	Prop

119

Last Name	First Name	Int	Year	County	Type
Jarvey	Hill	H	1836	StC	Prop
Jaynes	H	F	1867	Reyn	DTL
Jeanette	Susan		1820	StL	Prop
Jeans	Alex	D	1840	Call	Poll
Jeans	Alexander	D	1834	Call	DTL
Jeffers	Brooking		1839	Plat	Prop
Jeffers	Raessard		1836	Carr	PrpPt
Jeffers	George		1821	Ray	Prop
Jefferson	B	L	1867	Reyn	DTL
Jen	James		1844	Osag	Real
Jenkins	Uptiam		1839	Plat	Prop
Jenkins	Simon		1836	Carr	Prop
Jenkins	Thomas		1836	Carr	Prop
Jenkins	Simon		1836	Carr	PrpPt
Jenkins	Thomas		1836	Carr	PrpPt
Jenkins	Hiram		1834	Pett	Prop
Jenkins	Hiram		1834	Pett	PrpPt
Jenkins	James		1818	StL	Real
Jenkins	James		1839	Lew	DTL
Jennings	Moses		1839	Plat	Prop
Jennings	Benjamin		1831	Jack	DTL
Jerrold	Gideon		1836	Carr	Prop
Jerrold	Gideon		1836	Carr	PrpPt
Jerrt	Thomas		1836	Carr	Prop
Jerrt	Thomas		1836	Carr	PrpPt
Jesse	John		1843	Audr	Prop
Jesse	William		1843	Audr	Prop
Jesse	William	M	1838	Audr	DTL
Jetson	John	E	1839	Plat	Prop
Jewell	William		1824	Boon	Deed
Jewell	William		1828	Boon	Lisc
Jewell	Wm		1828	Boon	Lisc
Jewitt	Walter		1830	Jeff	DTL
Jiller	Jas		1840	Call	Poll
Jinkins	Solomon		1836	StC	Prop
Jinnings	George	W	1840	Call	Poll
Jinson	Abraham		1840	Call	Poll
Jinson	Harrison		1840	Call	Poll
Jirar	Joseph		1780	StL	Mil
Job	William		1817	How	Prop
John	Arnaziah		1836	Carr	PrpPt
Johns	William		1836	Char	DTL

Last Name	First Name	Int	Year	County	Type
Johnson	Lewis		1839	Plat	Prop
Johnson	Benjamin		1839	Plat	Prop
Johnson	Edward		1839	Plat	Prop
Johnson	Beremore		1839	Plat	Prop
Johnson	Barbara		1839	Plat	Prop
Johnson	John	H	1839	Plat	Prop
Johnson	James		1839	Plat	Prop
Johnson	John	R	1831	Jack	DTL
Johnson	William	M	1836	Carr	Prop
Johnson	Amaziah		1836	Carr	Prop
Johnson	James		1836	Carr	Prop
Johnson	Alexander		1836	Carr	Prop
Johnson	Samuel		1836	Carr	Prop
Johnson	William		1836	Carr	PrpPt
Johnson	Amaziah		1836	Carr	PrpPt
Johnson	James		1836	Carr	PrpPt
Johnson	Alexander		1836	Carr	PrpPt
Johnson	Samuel		1836	Carr	PrpPt
Johnson	James		1836	Carr	Prop
Johnson	Alexander		1836	Carr	Prop
Johnson	Samuel		1836	Carr	PrpPt
Johnson	James		1836	Carr	PrpPt
Johnson	Alexander		1836	Carr	PrpPt
Johnson	John		1836	Carr	PrpPt
Johnson	George	T	1840	Call	Poll
Johnson	A	H	1840	Call	Poll
Johnson	Thomas	T	1840	Call	Poll
Johnson	James		1821	StC	CtS
Johnson	Saml		1830	Coop	CtS
Johnson	William		1834	Pett	Prop
Johnson	William		1834	Pett	PrpPt
Johnson	Alfred		1830	Howa	DTL
Johnson	William		1867	Reyn	DTL
Johnson	John		1836	StC	Prop
Johnson	Easter		1836	StC	Prop
Johnson	Evans		1836	StC	Prop
Johnson	John		1836	StC	Prop
Johnson	Charles	M	1836	StC	Prop
Johnson	George	B	1836	StC	Prop
Johnson	John	H	1836	StC	Prop
Johnson	Baker		1836	StC	Prop
Johnson	Bayly	W	1836	StC	Prop

Last Name	First Name	Int	Year	County	Type
Johnson	Jarvis		1836	StC	Prop
Johnson	Matthew		1830	Linc	DTL
Johnson	James		1810	Ark	Prop
Johnson	Greenbury		1838	Audr	DTL
Johnson	Miles		1838	Audr	DTL
Johnson	Phillip		1838	Audr	DTL
Johnson	Isaac		1838	Audr	DTL
Johnson	Josiah		1820	StL	Prop
Johnson	Sabrette		1825	Char	DTL
Johnson	Amasiah		1830	Ray	Prop
Johnson	James		1815	Ark	Prop
Johnson	Harrison		1839	Lew	DTL
Johnson	Thomas	J	1844	Osag	Real
Johnson	Richard		1838	Ripl	DTL
Johnson	Jesse	R	1837	Mill	DTL
Johnson	Thomas		1837	Mill	DTL
Johnson	Samuel		1831	Craw	DTL
Johnson	Richard		1831	Craw	DTL
Johnson	Moric		1829	NMad	DTL
Johnson (1)	Andrew		1817	How	Prop
Johnson (1)	William		1817	How	Prop
Johnson (2)	Andrew		1817	How	Prop
Johnson (2)	William		1817	How	Prop
Johnson's Heirs	Levi		1836	StC	Prop
Johnson, Jr	William		1844	Osag	Real
Johnston	Albert		1843	Audr	Prop
Johnston	Isaac		1843	Audr	Prop
Johnston	Stephen		1839	Plat	Prop
Johnston	David		1839	Plat	Prop
Johnston	William		1828	Boon	Lisc
Johnston	Robert		1830	Coop	CtS
Johnston	Charles		1867	Reyn	DTL
Johnston	Thomas		1820	StL	Prop
Jolliff	James		1838	Ripl	DTL
Jolly	Joseph	W	1840	Call	Poll
Jonathan	Mitchell		1839	Plat	Prop
Jonca	Pedro		1780	StL	Mil
Jones	Jas		1843	Audr	Prop
Jones	Jefferson		1839	Plat	Prop
Jones	F	B	1839	Plat	Prop
Jones	Stephen		1839	Plat	Prop
Jones	Henry		1839	Plat	Prop

Last Name	First Name	Int	Year	County	Type
Jones	William	S	1839	Plat	Prop
Jones	Gregoire	V	1838	Steg	DTL
Jones	John		1836	Carr	PrpPt
Jones	John		1836	Carr	Prop
Jones	John		1836	Carr	PrpPt
Jones	Horatio		1840	Call	Poll
Jones	B	F	1840	Call	Poll
Jones	James	G	1840	Call	Poll
Jones	Henry		1840	Call	Poll
Jones	Jefferson	F	1840	Call	Poll
Jones	John		1840	Call	Poll
Jones	Thomas	G	1840	Call	Poll
Jones	William		1840	Call	Poll
Jones	James		1821	StC	Ct
Jones	J	J	1867	Reyn	DTL
Jones	Jas	J	1867	Reyn	DTL
Jones	Jonathan		1836	StC	Prop
Jones	William		1829	Char	DTL
Jones	John		1810	Ark	Prop
Jones	John		1818	StL	Real
Jones	John		1820	StL	Prop
Jones	Dr Thomas		1820	StL	Prop
Jones	Jas	S	1829	Mari	DTL
Jones	Levi		1817	How	Prop
Jones	Richard	W	1827	Mari	Prop
Jones	John		1830	Ray	Prop
Jones	Robert		1815	Ark	Prop
Jones	Fountain		1839	Lew	DTL
Jones	Randolf		1835	Barr	DTL
Jones	Ransom	P	1844	Osag	Real
Jones	Russel		1844	Osag	Real
Jones	Elijah		1844	Osag	Real
Jones	Benjamin		1834	Lew	DTL
Jones (1)	David		1817	How	Prop
Jones (2)	David		1817	How	Prop
Jones, Jr	Thomas		1834	Call	DTL
Jonial	Joseph		1818	StL	Real
Joplin	Thomas	M	1838	Audr	DTL
Jordan	James	C	1839	Plat	Prop
Jordan	F Labrosse		1818	StL	Real
Jordan	Jefferson		1834	Lew	DTL
Jorden	Elisha		1836	StC	Prop

Last Name	First Name	Int	Year	County	Type
Jordon	James		1837	Lew	DTL
Josef	Hebert		1791	StL	Span
Joseph	Peter		1836	Carr	Prop
Joseph	Peter		1836	Carr	PrpPt
Joseph	Peter		1836	Carr	Prop
Joseph	Peter		1836	Carr	PrpPt
Joseph	Teabo		1836	StC	Prop
Joseph	James		1818	StL	Real
Jossling	Thomas		1834	Pett	Prop
Jott	Joseph		1836	StC	Prop
Jovial	Joseph		1820	StL	Prop
Jurney	Joseph		1836	StC	Prop
Justus	Peter		1829	Char	DTL
Kackel	Arnold		1836	StC	Prop
Kase	John		1836	StC	Prop
Kasgrith	Thomas		1867	Reyn	DTL
Kassel	Godried		1836	StC	Prop
Kauffman	Christopher		1815	Ark	Prop
Kavanaugh	A		1828	Boon	Lisc
Kavanaugh	John		1867	Reyn	DTL
Kavianan	William		1839	Plat	Prop
Kay's Heirs	John		1830	Ray	Prop
Kaye	James	C	1839	Plat	Prop
Kaye	Abner		1839	Plat	Prop
Kays	Peyer		1836	Carr	Prop
Kays	Peyer		1836	Carr	PrpPt
Kayser	Frederick		1836	StC	Prop
Kayser	Earnest		1836	StC	Prop
Keany	Thomas		1817	How	Prop
Keashler	Leonhard		1836	StC	Prop
Keathley	Samuel		1836	StC	Prop
Keathley	Simon		1836	StC	Prop
Keathley	Obedia		1836	StC	Prop
Keathley	Daniel		1836	StC	Prop
Keathley	Isaac		1836	StC	Prop
Keathley	Nathaniel		1836	StC	Prop
Keathley	William	R	1836	StC	Prop
Keathley	Frederich		1836	StC	Prop
Keathley	Absalom		1836	StC	Prop
Kecton	Thomas	I	1838	Audr	DTL
Kecton	Henry	R	1838	Audr	DTL
Kee	George	T	1840	Call	Poll

Last Name	First Name	Int	Year	County	Type
Keeney	Harden		1844	Osag	Real
Keeny	John		1821	Ray	Prop
Keeper	JOhn		1859	Reyn	DTL
Keer	William		1838	Ripl	DTL
Keese	Absalom		1818	StL	Real
Keeton	Thos	I	1843	Audr	Prop
Keeton	Josiah		1843	Audr	Prop
Keeton	Henry		1843	Audr	Prop
Keetor	John		1828	Boon	Lisc
Keiser	Christopher		1827	Mari	Prop
Keiser	Henry		1829	NMad	DTL
Keith	Saul		1830	Ray	Prop
Keizer	John	W	1827	Boon	Lisc
Keller	Baltaser		1859	Reyn	DTL
Keller	David		1836	StC	Prop
Keller	James		1836	StC	Prop
Keller, Jr	John		1836	StC	Prop
Keller, Sr	John		1836	StC	Prop
Kelley	John	S	1867	Reyn	DTL
Kelley	Conner		1836	StC	Prop
Kellum, Sr	Jas		1867	Reyn	DTL
Kelly	John		1859	Reyn	DTL
Kelly	Richard		1859	Reyn	DTL
Kelly	William		1867	Reyn	DTL
Kelly	Thomas	H	1836	StC	Prop
Kelly	Marshal		1827	Mari	Prop
Kelly	Richard		1835	Barr	DTL
Kelly	James	T	1837	Mill	DTL
Kelsoe	Harrison	R	1840	Call	Poll
Kemp	Jordan		1840	Call	Poll
Kemp	William		1840	Call	Poll
Kemp	Andrew	L	1840	Call	Poll
Kemp	George	W	1840	Call	Poll
Kemp	Michal		1840	Call	Poll
Kemp	Nathan		1840	Call	Poll
Kemp	Robert		1840	Call	Poll
Kemp	Walter		1840	Call	Poll
Kemp	William		1840	Call	Poll
Kemp	Thomas	A	1834	Pett	Prop
Kemp	William	R	1834	Pett	Prop
Kemp, Sr	Jordon		1840	Call	Poll
Kemper	Abselom		1840	Call	Poll

Last Name	First Name	Int	Year	County	Type
Kendrick	Lydia		1810	Ark	Prop
Kendrick	James		1827	Mari	Prop
Keneday	William	P	1836	Perr	Poll
Kenedy	James	B	1844	Osag	Real
Kennedy	George	W	1859	Reyn	DTL
Kennedy	D	H	1867	Reyn	DTL
Kennedy	John		1820	StL	Prop
Kennedy	William		1820	StL	Prop
Kennerly	James		1820	StL	Prop
Kennerly	Jas		1820	StL	Prop
Kennerly	George	H	1820	StL	Prop
Kennison's Heirs	Thomas		1836	Carr	Prop
Kennison's Heirs	Thomas		1836	Carr	PrpPt
Kenny	Moses		1830	Linc	DTL
Kensail	G	G	1867	Reyn	DTL
Kensley	John	B	1818	StL	Real
Kenton	James		1828	Boon	Lisc
Kerag	Daniel		1867	Reyn	DTL
Kerby	Daniel		1867	Reyn	DTL
Kern	Samuel	P	1859	Reyn	DTL
Kern	Daniel	S	1859	Reyn	DTL
Kern	S	J	1867	Reyn	DTL
Kern	Simeon	J	1867	Reyn	DTL
Kerney	Peter		1827	Boon	Lisc
Kerney	Peter		1828	Boon	Lisc
Kerr	Mathew		1820	StL	Prop
Kessler	Madam		1810	Ark	Prop
Kettenhouse	E	T	1822	NMad	Lisc
Key	James	C	1839	Plat	Prop
Key	Thomas	A	1839	Plat	Prop
Key	Adomjah		1840	Call	Poll
Key	Martin		1840	Call	Poll
Keykendall	J		1837	Boon	PM
Keykendall	W		1837	Boon	PM
Keyte	James		1829	Char	DTL
Keyton	Miles		1839	Plat	Prop
Kibble	Richard	B	1836	StC	Prop
Kibler	Geoorge		1840	Call	Poll
Kibler	Jacob		1836	StC	Prop
Kidwell	Randolph	W	1840	Call	Poll
Kidwell	James		1836	StC	Prop
Kidwell	Henry		1829	Mari	DTL

Last Name	First Name	Int	Year	County	Type
Kidwell	Mathew		1839	Lew	DTL
Kieffer	John		1843	Audr	Prop
Kier	John		1867	Reyn	DTL
Kiger	Lewis		1840	Call	Poll
Kilgore	Thomas		1843	Audr	Prop
Kilgore	Thomas	D	1843	Audr	Prop
Kilgore	Jas	W	1843	Audr	Prop
Kilgore	Washington		1843	Audr	Prop
Kilgore	Saml		1843	Audr	Prop
Kilgore	Pheby		1843	Audr	Prop
Kilgore	John	H	1843	Audr	Prop
Kilgore	Isham	R	1843	Audr	Prop
Kilgore	Balus		1843	Audr	Prop
Kilgore	Jakcson		1843	Audr	Prop
Kilgore	Thos		1843	Audr	Prop
Kilgore	J	B	1843	Audr	Prop
Kilgore	J	C	1843	Audr	Prop
Kilgore	Isam	T W	1838	Audr	DTL
Kilgore	Johnson		1838	Audr	DTL
Kilgore	John	H	1838	Audr	DTL
Kilgore	Thomas		1838	Audr	DTL
Kilgore	G	W	1838	Audr	DTL
Kilgore	Balez		1838	Audr	DTL
Kilgore	Hugh		1838	Audr	DTL
Kilgore	John	B	1838	Audr	DTL
Kilgore	Anderson		1834	Lew	DTL
Kill	John		1828	Sali	DTL
Killiam	Jesse		1810	Ark	Prop
Kimmel	Singleton	H	1836	Perr	Poll
Kimsey	James		1839	Plat	Prop
Kimsey	John	F	1839	Plat	Prop
Kimsey	John		1839	Plat	Prop
Kimsey	Alois		1839	Plat	Prop
Kincaid	James		1839	Plat	Prop
Kincheloe (1)	William		1817	How	Prop
Kincheloe (2)	William		1817	How	Prop
King	Daniel		1839	Plat	Prop
King	James		1828	Boon	Lisc
King	Stephen	N	1840	Call	Poll
King	George		1840	Call	Poll
King	Jessey	E	1840	Call	Poll
King	John	B	1840	Call	Poll

Last Name	First Name	Int	Year	County	Type
King	Silas		1840	Call	Poll
King	John		1836	StC	Prop
King	John		1823	Call	NRP
King	John		1810	Ark	Prop
King	Samuel	M	1827	Mari	Prop
King	William		1831	Cole	DTL
King	William		1833	Wayn	DTL
King	Elisha		1834	Call	DTL
King	H	F	1837	Mill	DTL
King	William		1831	Craw	DTL
King	Samuel	C	1829	NMad	DTL
King's Heirs	William		1836	StC	Prop
Kingsberry	Jere		1829	Char	DTL
Kinion	Jos	M	1827	Jack	DTL
Kinkead	David		1817	How	Prop
Kinnard	William		1836	StC	Prop
Kinner	John	H	1844	Osag	Real
Kinneson	Joel		1836	Perr	Poll
Kinneson	Stephen		1836	Perr	Poll
Kinnon	John		1840	Call	Poll
Kipler	Barbary		1815	Ark	Prop
Kirbin	James		1836	StC	Prop
Kirkandall	Joseph		1815	Ark	Prop
Kirkandall	Dempsey		1815	Ark	Prop
Kirkendall	Benjn		1815	Ark	Prop
Kirkendall	Robert		1815	Ark	Prop
Kirkpatrick	Wallace		1821	StC	CtS
Kirkpatrick	Wallace		1836	StC	Prop
Kirpatrick	Hugh		1836	Carr	Prop
Kirpatrick	Hugh		1836	Carr	PrpPt
Kirtley	Sinclair		1827	Boon	Lisc
Kirtley	Sinclair		1828	Boon	Lisc
Kisenhoover	Joseph		1838	Ripl	DTL
Kiser	John		1843	Audr	Prop
Kiser	Fleming		1836	Carr	Prop
Kiser	Fleming		1836	Carr	PrpPt
Kitchen	Thomas		1840	Call	Poll
Kline	Philip		1843	Audr	Prop
Knave	James		1836	Char	DTL
Knight	James		1840	Call	Poll
Knight	William		1840	Call	Poll
Knight	Jonathan		1838	Ripl	DTL

128

Last Name	First Name	Int	Year	County	Type
Knott	David		1836	StC	Prop
Knott	William		1836	StC	Prop
Knott's Heirs	Osbern		1836	StC	Prop
Knox	Ezekiel		1836	Perr	Poll
Knox	George		1827	Boon	Lisc
Koons	Jacob		1843	Char	DTL
Kormes	Mde		1805	Steg	Prop
Kosk	John		1836	StC	Prop
Kosk	Ferdinand		1836	StC	Prop
Kouns	Nathan		1836	Carr	Prop
Kouns	Nathan		1840	Call	Poll
Krag	Peter		1836	StC	Prop
Krasny	Jacob		1867	Reyn	DTL
Kray	Andrew		1836	StC	Prop
Kray	Lewis		1836	StC	Prop
Kray	Edward		1836	StC	Prop
Kray	Paul		1836	StC	Prop
Krentz	Fred		1859	Reyn	DTL
Krettzer	Charles		1836	StC	Prop
Krichbam	Henry		1836	StC	Prop
Kruise	Frederich		1836	StC	Prop
Kruise	Julien		1836	StC	Prop
Krumkey	John	H	1836	StC	Prop
Krust	Abrech		1836	StC	Prop
Kunze	Jonathan		1836	StC	Prop
Kuykendall	Benjamin		1839	Plat	Prop
Kuykendall	Jos		1810	Ark	Prop
Kyde	Mary		1843	Audr	Prop
Kyle	Larkin		1863	Jeff	Ass
Kyle	Joseph		1863	Jeff	Ass
Kyle	Simeon		1863	Jeff	Ass
Kyle	Danl		1863	Jeff	Ass
Labadia	Silvestre		1780	StL	Mil
Labadia	Dn. Silvestre		1791	StL	Span
labadie	Jos		1818	StL	Real
Labarge	Joseph		1820	StL	Prop
Labbaddie	Joseph St. Pierre		1820	StL	Prop
Labbadie	Joseph		1818	StL	Real
Labbadie	Julie (Free Mullato)		1818	StL	Real
Labbadie	Silvestre		1820	StL	Prop
Labbadie	Julie (Free Mullato)		1820	StL	Prop
Labbe	Wid Jacques		1818	StL	Real

Last Name	First Name	Int	Year	County	Type
Labe	Jacobo		1780	StL	Mil
Labeau	Jacque		1805	Steg	Prop
Labeau	Louis		1830	Linc	DTL
Labeau	Francois		1818	StL	Real
Labeaume	Louis		1818	StL	Real
Laberge	Joseph		1818	StL	Real
Labo	Ambrose		1836	StC	Prop
Labouche	Francois		1820	StL	Prop
Labourboard	Peter		1830	How	DTL
Labourn	Pierre		1818	StL	Real
Labreche	Juan Baptiste		1780	StL	Mil
Labrose	Joseph		1780	StL	Mil
Labrosse	Francois	J	1818	StL	Real
Labroza	Josef		1791	StL	Span
Labuche	Francis		1818	StL	Real
Labuciera	Jos		1780	StL	Mil
Labucke	Francois		1818	StL	Real
Lachance	Joseph		1805	Steg	Prop
Lachance	Madame		1805	Steg	Prop
Lachance	Gabriel		1805	Steg	Prop
Lachance	Jacob		1815	Ark	Prop
Lachance	John Bte		1815	Ark	Prop
Lachance	Michael		1838	Ripl	DTL
Lachassa	Juan Bapt		1791	StL	Span
Lackland	J	C	1836	StC	Prop
Laclear	Francis		1836	StC	Prop
Laclear	Antwine		1836	StC	Prop
Laclere	Louis		1805	Steg	Prop
Lacombie	Nicolas		1780	StL	Mil
Lacomte	Nicolas		1780	StL	Mil
Lacomte	Guillermo		1780	StL	Mil
Lacroia	Juan Louis		1780	StL	Mil
Lacroia	Juan Luis		1780	StL	Mil
Lacroix	Bapt		1791	StL	Span
Lacroix	Louis		1836	StC	Prop
Lacroix	Joseph		1818	StL	Real
Lacroix	Joseph		1820	StL	Prop
Laderruta	Pablo		1780	StL	Mil
Laduque	Ant		1836	StC	Prop
Ladusor	Antonio		1780	StL	Mil
Lafan, Jr	Alex		1836	StC	Prop
Lafarge	Andrew		1836	StC	Prop

Last Name	First Name	Int	Year	County	Type
Lafavere	Alxa		1836	StC	Prop
Laflanbuesa	Juan Bapt		1780	StL	Mil
Lafleur	J	W	1805	Steg	Prop
Laflor	Luis		1780	StL	Mil
Laflor	Luis		1791	StL	Span
Lafluer	Madame		1805	Steg	Prop
Lafluer	Francis		1805	Steg	Prop
Lafluer	Joseph		1805	Steg	Prop
Lafluexe	Sally		1844	Osag	Real
Laforge	Stephen	V	1836	Carr	Prop
Laforge	Stephen		1836	Carr	PrpPt
Laganern	Chavalier		1810	Ark	Prop
Lagenes	John	B	1836	StC	Prop
Laguie	Polly		1818	StL	Real
Lahe	Antonio		1780	StL	Mil
Laird	William		1836	Carr	Prop
Laird	William		1836	Carr	PrpPt
Lajeunesse	Jacques		1820	StL	Prop
Lajor	Pierre		1838	Steg	DTL
Lajoy	Antonio		1780	StL	Mil
Lake	Charles		1827	Mari	Prop
Lake	Burgess		1827	Mari	Prop
Lake	Ballard		1827	Mari	Prop
Lakin	Maryan	E	1843	Audr	Prop
Lakin	Elizabeth	A	1843	Audr	Prop
Lakin	Thos		1843	Audr	Prop
Lalande	Alexo		1791	StL	Span
Lalande	Alexis		1818	StL	Real
Lalande	Wid Mary		1820	StL	Prop
Lalaype	Peleigree		1818	StL	Real
Lamarch	Joseph		1836	StC	Prop
Lamarina	Juan Bapt		1780	StL	Mil
LaMarque	E		1839	Wash	Lisc
Lamaster	David		1821	StC	Ct
Lamaster	David		1821	StC	CtS
Lamasters	Evens		1836	StC	Prop
Lamasters	Benjamin		1836	StC	Prop
Lamb	Jas		1843	Audr	Prop
Lamb	John		1836	Carr	PrpPt
Lamb	Thomas		1834	Craw	DTL
Lambert	Jesse		1820	StL	Prop
Lamere	Jose		1791	StL	Span

131

Last Name	First Name	Int	Year	County	Type
Lamm	Richard		1821	Ray	Prop
Lamm	Joshua		1821	Ray	Prop
Lamm	James		1817	How	Prop
Lamm	William		1817	How	Prop
Lamme	William		1821	StC	Ct
Lamme	William		1830	How	DTL
Lamme	William	T	1823	Call	NRP
Lamme	Joshua		1823	How	DTL
Lampkins	Justin		1835	Barr	DTL
Lamy	Miguel		1780	StL	Mil
Lamy	Wid Madam		1791	StL	Span
Lamy	Genevieve		1820	StL	Prop
Lancaster	William		1836	Carr	Prop
Lancaster	William		1836	Carr	PrpPt
Lance	Isaac	B	1821	Ray	Prop
Lancisieus	God		1836	Carr	Prop
Lancisieus	God		1836	Carr	PrpPt
Lancy	Patrick		1822	Clay	Poll
Landers	William		1827	Mari	Prop
Landidge	Seland		1836	Char	DTL
Landley	Thomas		1839	Plat	Prop
Landley	Thomas		1839	Plat	Prop
Landrum	Greenvil		1831	Cole	DTL
Landrum	John		1831	Cole	DTL
Lane	Daniel		1836	Carr	Prop
Lane	William	I	1836	Carr	Prop
Lane	Isaac		1836	Carr	Prop
Lane	Daniel		1836	Carr	PrpPt
Lane	William		1836	Carr	PrpPt
Lane	Isaac		1836	Carr	PrpPt
Lane	Daniel		1836	Carr	PrpPt
Lane	W	C	1818	StL	Real
Lane	Wm Carr		1820	StL	Prop
Lane	Henry		1827	Mari	Prop
Lane	Thornton		1839	Lew	DTL
Lane	Lunford	L	1844	Osag	Real
Lanehart	William		1821	Ray	Prop
Lanford	Garrat		1836	StC	Prop
Langford	Thomas		1836	StC	Prop
Langford	Cambel		1836	StC	Prop
Langford	Berry		1830	Ray	Prop
Langham	August		1823	Call	NRP

Last Name	First Name	Int	Year	County	Type
Langham	Elias	S	1823	Call	NRP
Langham	Angus	L	1820	StL	Prop
Langley	Coley		1840	Call	Poll
Langley	Moses		1840	Call	Poll
Langley	Isaac		1840	Call	Poll
Langley	William	R	1840	Call	Poll
Langley	Cornelius		1840	Call	Poll
Langley	James		1840	Call	Poll
Langley	William		1840	Call	Poll
Langley	Moses		1817	How	Prop
Langley	Thomas		1834	Call	DTL
Langley, Sr	James		1840	Call	Poll
Langley, Sr	John		1840	Call	Poll
Langlois	Francois		1830	How	DTL
Langtree	Arbuckle		1840	Call	Poll
Lanodiere	????		1820	StL	Prop
Lanton	John		1821	StC	Ct
Lany	Patrick		1821	Ray	Prop
Laphsen	Jphn		1836	StC	Prop
Lapierre	Jn Bapt		1780	StL	Mil
Lapierre	Joseph		1780	StL	Mil
Lapierre	Jose		1791	StL	Span
Laplant	Nicholas		1805	Steg	Prop
LaPlant	Lewis		1840	Call	Poll
Laprise	Marie		1818	StL	Real
Laprise	Mary		1820	StL	Prop
Lapslry	Samuel		1830	Coop	Ct
Laquesse	Wid Marguerite		1818	StL	Real
Laquier	John		1815	Ark	Prop
Larabe	Russell		1836	Carr	Prop
Larabe	Russell		1836	Carr	PrpPt
Laramore	Henry		1840	Call	Poll
Larduera	Joseph		1780	StL	Mil
Larduera	Jacobo		1780	StL	Mil
Larduera	Antonio		1780	StL	Mil
Larduera	Luis		1780	StL	Mil
Laret	Luis		1780	StL	Mil
Lariviere	Pierre		1820	StL	Prop
Larker	John		1839	Plat	Prop
Larkin	James		1836	Carr	Prop
Larkin	Moses	M	1836	Carr	Prop
Larkin	James		1836	Carr	PrpPt

Last Name	First Name	Int	Year	County	Type
Larkin	Moses		1836	Carr	PrpPt
Laroux	Louis Petit		1820	StL	Prop
Larue	Francis		1810	Ark	Prop
Larver's Heirs	Joseph		1836	StC	Prop
Lasablonera	Jacobo		1780	StL	Mil
Lasarge	John		1836	StC	Prop
Lasier	Naopleion	P	1836	StC	Prop
Lasslry	Saml		1830	Coop	CtS
Lasudray	Luis		1780	StL	Mil
Lataup	Pelagie		1820	StL	Prop
Latham	Isaac		1827	Boon	Lisc
Laton	H	M	1867	Reyn	DTL
Latresse	Jean		1820	StL	Prop
Lattrail	Antwine		1836	StC	Prop
Lature	Joseph		1836	StC	Prop
Laughlin	Polly		1828	Boon	Lisc
Laughlin	John		1828	Boon	Lisc
Laughlin	William		1844	Osag	Real
Laughlin	John		1844	Osag	Real
Laughlin	Samuel		1844	Osag	Real
Laughlin	Bolin		1844	Osag	Real
Laughlin	Benjamin		1844	Osag	Real
Laughlin, Sr	John	M	1844	Osag	Real
Laughman	Angus	L	1828	Sali	DTL
Laurence	Thos		1843	Audr	Prop
Laurent	Lenandire		1818	StL	Real
Lauther's Heirs	James		1836	Carr	Prop
Lauther's Heirs	James		1836	Carr	PrpPt
Lavac	John		1836	StC	Prop
Lavergo	John		1815	Ark	Prop
Laves	Francis		1815	Ark	Prop
Lavin???	John		1810	Ark	Prop
Law	James		1840	Call	Poll
Law	Robet		1834	Craw	DTL
Lawerence	James		1836	Carr	Prop
Lawerence	James		1836	Carr	PrpPt
Lawler	Jesse	P	1844	Osag	Real
Lawless	Luke		1830	Jeff	DTL
Lawless	Burton		1829	Sali	DTL
Lawless	Burton		1828	Sali	DTL
Lawson	Robert		1840	Call	Poll
Lawson	Peter		1828	Sali	DTL

Last Name	First Name	Int	Year	County	Type
Lawyer	P	C	1867	Reyn	DTL
Laytham	James		1827	Mari	Prop
Layton	Ignatius		1836	Perr	Poll
Layton	James		1836	Perr	Poll
Layton	John		1836	Perr	Poll
Layton	John	B	1836	Perr	Poll
Layton	Joseph		1836	Perr	Poll
Layton	Lewis		1836	Perr	Poll
Layton	Walter		1836	Perr	Poll
Layton	Wilford		1836	Perr	Poll
Layton	Edwin		1839	Lew	DTL
Lea	John		1836	Carr	Prop
Lea	John		1836	Carr	PrpPt
Leach	David		1843	Audr	Prop
Leach	William		1836	Carr	Prop
Leach	William		1836	Carr	PrpPt
Leach	David		1838	Audr	DTL
Leach	William		1830	Ray	Prop
Leaky	Jeremiah		1817	How	Prop
Leapard	John		1840	Call	Poll
Lear	John		1827	Mari	Prop
Learnet	Lewis		1818	StL	Real
Leary	Dennis		1859	Reyn	DTL
Leavening	W	H	1867	Reyn	DTL
Leavitt	Michael		1836	Carr	Prop
Leavitt	Michael		1836	Carr	PrpPt
Leavitt	Michael		1830	Ray	Prop
Lebeau	Francois		1820	StL	Prop
Lebetter	Lewis		1834	Craw	DTL
Leblond	Joseph		1820	StL	Prop
Lebo	Isaac		1839	Plat	Prop
Lecompte	Nicolas		1791	StL	Span
Lecompte	Guillermo		1791	StL	Span
Lecompte	Wid Magaresse		1820	StL	Prop
Leconte	Guillermo		1780	StL	Mil
Leconte	Joseph		1780	StL	Mil
Lecourt	Hyacinthe		1818	StL	Real
Ledgewood	John		1821	Ray	Prop
Ledgewood	John		1822	Clay	Poll
Ledlie	John		1867	Reyn	DTL
Leduc	????		1821	StC	Ct
Leduc	Mary Phillip		1820	StL	Prop

Last Name	First Name	Int	Year	County	Type
Lee	R	R	1843	Audr	Prop
Lee	Jackson	W	1839	Plat	Prop
Lee	Oliver	H	1863	Jeff	Ass
Lee	O	F	1863	Jeff	Ass
Lee	William		1863	Jeff	Ass
Lee	Josiah		1863	Jeff	Ass
Lee	Medley		1863	Jeff	Ass
Lee	Wid Mary Ann		1818	StL	Real
Lee	Wid Mary Ann		1820	StL	Prop
Lee	Daniel		1844	Osag	Real
Lee	Giles		1844	Osag	Real
Lee	John		1838	Ripl	DTL
Lee	Samuel		1838	Ripl	DTL
Lee	Francis	T	1829	NMad	DTL
Lee's Heirs	George		1836	Carr	Prop
Lee's Heirs	George		1836	Carr	PrpPt
Leebo	Louis		1836	StC	Prop
Leech	Isaac		1839	Plat	Prop
Leeman	John		1830	Ray	Prop
Leeper	William	T	1859	Reyn	DTL
Leeper, Jr	John	B	1840	Call	Poll
Leets	Benjamin		1810	Ark	Prop
Lefress	Charles		1836	StC	Prop
Leguerrier	Charles		1818	StL	Real
Leguerrier	Charles		1820	StL	Prop
Lelande	Alexis		1818	StL	Real
Lemieu	Pierre		1815	Ark	Prop
Lemmons	Silas		1838	Ripl	DTL
Lemon	R		1827	Boon	Lisc
Lemon	William	S	1827	Boon	Lisc
Lemonde	Louis		1818	StL	Real
Lemonde	Louis		1820	StL	Prop
Lemonder	Louis		1818	StL	Real
Lemonie	Jose		1791	StL	Span
Lendrim	Joshua		1831	Cole	DTL
Lendy	William		1838	Ripl	DTL
Lenell	Reuben		1844	Osag	Real
Lengo	Elijah		1836	Carr	Prop
Lengo	Elijah		1836	Carr	PrpPt
Lenhart	William		1822	Clay	Poll
Lentz	William		1828	Boon	Lisc
Lenzo	Elijah		1830	Ray	Prop

Last Name	First Name	Int	Year	County	Type
Leonard	L	L	1839	Plat	Prop
Leonard	Henry		1836	Perr	Poll
Leonard	Nathiel		1836	Carr	PrpPt
Leonard	Nathaniel		1830	Ray	Prop
Leone	Robert		1810	Ark	Prop
Lepir	Juan		1780	StL	Mil
Lepper	Jacob		1836	Carr	Prop
Lepper	Jacob		1836	Carr	PrpPt
Leroy	Isaac		1840	Call	Poll
Lerru	Pedro		1780	StL	Mil
Lessame	Madame		1805	Steg	Prop
Lessieur	Raphael		1830	How	DTL
Letcher	W	S	1840	Call	Poll
Letcher	Rob	F	1863	Jeff	Ass
Letcher	A	K	1834	Call	DTL
Levaugh	Wm		1843	Audr	Prop
Levaugh	Jason		1843	Audr	Prop
Levaugh	William		1843	Audr	Prop
Levaugh	J	W	1843	Audr	Prop
Leveal	Pierre		1805	Steg	Prop
Leveall	Zebilan		1837	Mill	DTL
Leveille	Francoise	V	1820	StL	Prop
Levendy	Simon	W	1839	Plat	Prop
Levi	Hannah	M	1867	Reyn	DTL
Levielle	Carlos		1791	StL	Span
Levins	Bazabell		1830	Coop	Ct
Levit	John		1840	Call	Poll
Lewis	Isaac		1839	Plat	Prop
Lewis	Slone		1839	Plat	Prop
Lewis	Jesse		1839	Plat	Prop
Lewis	John		1839	Plat	Prop
Lewis	Bryan		1839	Plat	Prop
Lewis	John		1839	Plat	Prop
Lewis	Isaac	F	1839	Plat	Prop
Lewis	Isaac		1839	Plat	Prop
Lewis	Jesse		1839	Plat	Prop
Lewis	John		1839	Plat	Prop
Lewis	Thomas		1836	Carr	Prop
Lewis	Thomas		1836	Carr	PrpPt
Lewis	John	N	1840	Call	Poll
Lewis	Thomas		1867	Reyn	DTL
Lewis	G	W	1867	Reyn	DTL

Last Name	First Name	Int	Year	County	Type
Lewis	Geo	W	1867	Reyn	DTL
Lewis	William		1836	StC	Prop
Lewis	Milton		1836	StC	Prop
Lewis	James		1836	StC	Prop
Lewis	V	M	1836	StC	Prop
Lewis	John		1818	StL	Real
Lewis	Victor	M	1827	Mari	Prop
Lewis	William	W	1827	Mari	Prop
Lewis	Benjamin	J	1827	Mari	Prop
Lewis	Thomas		1827	Mari	Prop
Lewis	Jasper	W	1827	Mari	Prop
Lewis	Barlow		1839	Lew	DTL
Lewis	John		1834	Craw	DTL
Lewis	Sally		1834	Craw	DTL
Lewis	Thomas		1831	Craw	DTL
Lewis, Jr	Valentine	S	1827	Mari	Prop
Lewis, Sr	William		1839	Plat	Prop
Liberge	Josef		1791	StL	Span
Liby	John		1859	Reyn	DTL
Lifern, Jr	Pierre		1810	Ark	Prop
Lifern, Sr	Pierre		1810	Ark	Prop
Ligget	Jonathan		1821	Ray	Prop
Liggett	John		1839	Plat	Prop
Liggett	John		1839	Plat	Prop
Lightener	Jeremiah		1838	John	DTL
Lightfoot	Henry		1817	How	Prop
Lile	Henry		1834	Lew	DTL
Liles	Hughs		1830	Linc	DTL
Liles	Malaci		1821	Ray	Prop
Liles	David		1821	Ray	Prop
Liles	William		1821	Ray	Prop
Lilley	Taylor	P	1821	StC	Ct
Lilley	John		1836	StC	Prop
Linch	John		1859	Reyn	DTL
Linch	Michael		1859	Reyn	DTL
Lincoln	Daniel		1836	Carr	Prop
Lincoln	Daniel		1836	Carr	PrpPt
Lincoln	John		1821	Ray	Prop
Lincoln's Heirs	Thomas		1836	Carr	Prop
Lincoln's Heirs	Thomas		1836	Carr	PrpPt
Lincorn	John		1822	Clay	Poll
Lindell	Peter		1829	Char	DTL

Last Name	First Name	Int	Year	County	Type
Lindell	????		1820	StL	Prop
Lindell	Peter		1830	Ray	Prop
Lindenbooth	Benchard		1844	Osag	Real
Lindley	John		1835	Barr	DTL
Lindsay	James		1839	Plat	Prop
Lindsey	Noah		1836	Bent	DTL
Lindsey	Noah		1837	Bent	DTL
Lingard	Noah		1836	Carr	Prop
Lingard	Noah		1836	Carr	PrpPt
Link	John		1830	How	DTL
Linsey	Alpheus		1836	Carr	Prop
Linsey	Alpheus		1836	Carr	PrpPt
Linvell	William		1827	Boon	Lisc
Linville	Harrison		1839	Plat	Prop
Linville	Granville		1839	Plat	Prop
Linville	John		1839	Plat	Prop
Linville	Abraham		1839	Plat	Prop
Linville	Richard		1839	Plat	Prop
Linville	Richard		1821	Ray	Prop
Linville	Abraham		1821	Ray	Prop
Linville	Aaron		1821	Ray	Prop
Linville	John		1822	Clay	Poll
Lipcomb	Marcus		1839	Plat	Prop
Lisa	Manuel		1820	StL	Prop
Literal	George		1838	Audr	DTL
Literell	Garrot		1843	Audr	Prop
Litrell	George		1843	Audr	Prop
Little	William		1839	Plat	Prop
Little	Henry		1836	Perr	Poll
Little	Ransom	A	1836	Perr	Poll
Little	William		1840	Call	Poll
Little	John		1820	StL	Prop
Lively	James		1839	Plat	Prop
Livingston	John		1821	Ray	Prop
Livingston	Samuel		1821	Ray	Prop
Livingston	William		1817	How	Prop
Livingston	John		1822	Clay	Poll
Livingston	William		1822	Clay	Poll
Lochbridge	John		1838	Audr	DTL
Lochbridge	Jas		1838	Audr	DTL
Lockhart	William		1839	Plat	Prop
Lockhart	John		1836	Carr	Prop

Last Name	First Name	Int	Year	County	Type
Lockhart	John		1836	Carr	PrpPt
Lockie	Andrew		1836	Carr	Prop
Lockie	Andrew		1836	Carr	PrpPt
Lockridge	Elihu		1843	Audr	Prop
Lockridge	Jno		1843	Audr	Prop
Lockridge	Martha		1843	Audr	Prop
Lockridge, Jr	Jas		1843	Audr	Prop
Lockstone	Ebenezer		1836	Carr	Prop
Lockstone	Ebenezer		1836	Carr	PrpPt
Loclor	Henry		1836	StC	Prop
Lodie	Francis		1836	StC	Prop
Loels	Madame		1805	Steg	Prop
Loferry	George		1836	Carr	Prop
Loferry	George		1836	Carr	PrpPt
Logan	Robert	P	1839	Plat	Prop
Logan	Alexander		1859	Reyn	DTL
Logan	Philip		1836	Carr	PrtPt
Logan	James		1840	Call	Poll
Logan	S	M	1867	Reyn	DTL
Logan	Thomas		1867	Reyn	DTL
Logan	William	C	1836	StC	Prop
Logan	William		1839	Lew	DTL
Logan	Charles		1833	Wayn	DTL
Logan's Heirs	Green		1836	StC	Prop
Logmyer	Henrie		1836	StC	Prop
Loisa	Paul		1820	StL	Prop
Loisel	Victoria		1820	StL	Prop
Loiselle	Santiago		1791	StL	Span
Lollar	Jeramice		1836	StC	Prop
Loller	Thomas		1867	Reyn	DTL
Lomax	Asa		1834	Call	DTL
Long	Willis		1839	Plat	Prop
Long	E		1859	Reyn	DTL
Long	John		1836	Carr	Prop
Long	John		1836	Carr	PrpPt
Long	Samuel	B	1840	Call	Poll
Long	R	P	1840	Call	Poll
Long	James		1830	Coop	Ct
Long	C	J	1867	Reyn	DTL
Long	H	N	1867	Reyn	DTL
Long	????		1836	StC	Prop
Long	James	W	1836	StC	Prop

Last Name	First Name	Int	Year	County	Type
Long	John	T	1836	StC	Prop
Long	Joseph		1836	StC	Prop
Long	James		1817	How	Prop
Long	Gabriel		1820	StL	Prop
Longail	Timothy		1836	Carr	Prop
Longail	Timothy		1836	Carr	PrpPt
Longear	Thomas		1836	Carr	Prop
Longear	Thomas		1836	Carr	PrpPt
Longley	T	W	1840	Call	Poll
Longmire	John		1827	Mari	Prop
Longsdorf	Neri		1867	Reyn	DTL
Longwith	James		1836	Carr	Prop
Longwith	James		1836	Carr	PrpPt
Lony	George		1863	Jeff	Ass
Loomis' Heirs	Daniel		1836	Carr	Prop
Loomis' Heirs	Daniel		1836	Carr	PrpPt
Looney	T	D	1825	Char	DTL
Loper	James		1820	StL	Prop
Lora	Pier		1836	StC	Prop
Lorce	Louis		1836	StC	Prop
Lord	William		1836	StC	Prop
Lorens	Juan Bapt		1791	StL	Span
Lorenzo	Baptista		1780	StL	Mil
Loring	John		1829	Mari	DTL
Lorroese	Todos Santos		1780	StL	Mil
Lorton	John	J	1843	Audr	Prop
Lorton	John		1843	Audr	Prop
Lorton	J	J	1843	Audr	Prop
Lorton	Thomas		1838	Audr	DTL
Louis	Thomas	R	1835	Barr	DTL
Louise	Paul		1818	StL	Real
Louiso	Thirrese		1836	StC	Prop
Love	John		1836	Carr	Prop
Love	John		1836	Carr	PrpPt
Lovelace	Eli		1836	Carr	Prop
Lovelace	Eli		1836	Carr	PrpPt
Lovelady	Moses		1839	Plat	Prop
Lovelady	F	J	1843	Char	DTL
Loveless	E	N	1840	Call	Poll
Lovell	John		1830	How	DTL
Lovely	William	J J	1815	Ark	Prop
Lovering	Babary		1836	StC	Prop

Last Name	First Name	Int	Year	County	Type
Low	William		1836	StC	Prop
Lowe	Thomas	B	1867	Reyn	DTL
Lowery	James	T	1828	Boon	Lisc
Lowin	Hamilton		1837	Lew	DTL
Lowns	Caleb		1839	Plat	Prop
Lowthian	Isaac		1821	Ray	Prop
Loyd	Isaac		1840	Call	Poll
Lucas	Alexander		1816	How	Lic
Lucas	C		1826	Coop	DTL
Lucas	Timothy		1836	Carr	Prop
Lucas	Timothy		1836	Carr	PrpPt
Lucas	Charles		1818	StL	Real
Lucas	Andrien		1818	StL	Real
Lucas	Charles		1829	Sali	DTL
Lucas	John	B C	1820	StL	Prop
Lucas	Adrian		1820	StL	Prop
Lucas	C		1826	Coop	DTL
Lucas' Heirs	C		1827	Coop	DTL
Lucas, dec	Charles		1823	Call	NRP
Luch	Joseph		1836	Carr	Prop
Luch	Joseph		1836	Carr	PrpPt
Luck	John		1844	Osag	Real
Luckett	William		1836	StC	Prop
Luckey	David		1836	Perr	Poll
Lucus	Adam	J	1839	Plat	Prop
Lucus	Allen	B	1836	StC	Prop
Lucy	Elizabeth		1838	Ripl	DTL
Lucy	John		1838	Ripl	DTL
Ludolf	Charles		1836	StC	Prop
Luese	Alexandro		1780	StL	Mil
Lumden	Charles	D	1836	Carr	Prop
Lumden	Charles		1836	Carr	PrpPt
Lunceford	Robert	W	1839	John	DTL
Luper	David	H	1843	Audr	Prop
Lurton	Charles		1836	StC	Prop
Lusby	Eliett		1836	StC	Prop
Lusere	Antonio		1780	StL	Mil
Lusney	Benjamin		1836	Carr	PrtPt
Luster	Robert		1831	Cole	DTL
Lutting	Andrew		1810	Ark	Prop
Luzoeder	Abraham		1840	Call	Poll
Lydy	????		1867	Reyn	DTL

Last Name	First Name	Int	Year	County	Type
Lynch	H		1843	Audr	Prop
Lynch	John		1839	Plat	Prop
Lynch	Joseph		1839	Plat	Prop
Lynch	James		1839	Plat	Prop
Lynch	Cornelius		1828	Boon	Lisc
Lynch	William	A	1821	StC	Ct
Lynch	Nathaniel		1821	StC	CtS
Lynch	Charles		1836	StC	Prop
Lynch	David		1836	StC	Prop
Lynch	Bryan		1810	Ark	Prop
Lynch	David		1839	John	DTL
Lynch	Aaron		1839	John	DTL
Lyndsay	William	C	1836	StC	Prop
Lyndsay	Henry	C	1836	StC	Prop
Lyndsay	Landen		1836	StC	Prop
Lyndsay, Jr	Thomas		1836	StC	Prop
Lyndsay, Sr	James		1836	StC	Prop
Lyndsay, Sr	Thomas		1836	StC	Prop
Lynsdon	William		1833	Lew	DTL
Lynville	Thomas		1830	Coop	Ct
Lyon	James		1821	Ray	Prop
Lyons	J	W	1840	Call	Poll
Lyons	Washington		1840	Call	Poll
Lytle	Robert		1836	Carr	PrpPt
Lytle	Robert		1830	Ray	Prop
M'Caferty	Thomas		1823	How	DTL
M'Call	John		1818	Lawr	DTL
M'Call	Dugald		1837	Bent	DTL
M'Carty	John		1837	Cass	DTL
M'Clendon	Frc?????		1810	Ark	Prop
M'Clendon	John		1810	Ark	Prop
M'Clendon	Jas		1810	Ark	Prop
M'Cormack	William		1838	Audr	DTL
M'Elmurry	John		1815	Ark	Prop
M'Glocklin	Thomas		1818	Lawr	DTL
M'Guire	Thomas		1818	StL	Real
M'Haque	James		1843	Char	DTL
M'Klew	John		1831	Craw	DTL
M'Lain	Walter		1838	Steg	DTL
M'Laughlin	Daniel		1834	Craw	DTL
M'Millan	Simeon		1815	Ark	Prop
M'Pike	James		1838	Audr	DTL

Last Name	First Name	Int	Year	County	Type
Mabe	John		1836	StC	Prop
Maberry	Andrew		1859	Reyn	DTL
Mabin	William	P	1844	Osag	Real
Mace	John		1820	StL	Prop
Mackey	James		1817	How	Prop
Macky	James		1818	StL	Real
Macky	James		1820	StL	Prop
Macom	Anthony		1838	Ripl	DTL
Maddock	Richard		1836	Perr	Poll
Maddon	William		1836	Carr	PrpPt
Maddox	Nathaniel		1836	Carr	PrpPt
Maddox	Larkin		1840	Call	Poll
Maddox	Sherwood		1840	Call	Poll
Maden	John		1810	Ark	Prop
Magagnus	Joseph		1829	Char	DTL
Magard	Isaac		1840	Call	Poll
Magard	Jacob		1817	How	Prop
Magee	Patrick		1827	Mari	Prop
Magill	Samuel		1821	Ray	Prop
Magill	David		1821	Ray	Prop
Mahan	John	A	1843	Audr	Prop
Mahan	Jas	A	1843	Audr	Prop
Mahan	Anthony		1839	Plat	Prop
Mahan	Pat	M	1859	Reyn	DTL
Mahan	Peyton		1838	Audr	DTL
Mahan	James		1817	How	Prop
Mahan	James	F	1827	Mari	Prop
Mahaney	David		1838	Audr	DTL
Mahar	Joseph		1840	Call	Poll
Mahony	John		1859	Reyn	DTL
Maimes	James		1840	Call	Poll
Major	Weden		1840	Call	Poll
Major	Wm		1840	Call	Poll
Majores	James		1836	StC	Prop
Malenkott	Julies		1836	StC	Prop
Malett	William		1831	Jack	DTL
Mallerson	Elija		1836	StC	Prop
Mallery	Thomas	W	1839	Lew	DTL
Mallett	William	M	1859	Reyn	DTL
Mallory	Elvington		1838	Audr	DTL
Mallote	William		1839	Plat	Prop
Malone	Simon		1837	Cass	DTL

144

Last Name	First Name	Int	Year	County	Type
Malone	John		1840	Call	Poll
Malony	Jeremiah		1867	Reyn	DTL
Malott	John	S	1839	Plat	Prop
Malott	Thomas		1839	Plat	Prop
Malott	John	S	1821	Ray	Prop
Malotte	William		1821	Ray	Prop
Malrey	Joseph	R	1843	Audr	Prop
Malsey	Elvinton		1843	Audr	Prop
Man	Stephen		1829	Char	DTL
Manasseth	Beth		1839	Plat	Prop
Manchester	Abell		1836	Carr	Prop
Manchester	Abell		1836	Carr	PrpPt
Mandell	Samuel		1836	Carr	PrpPt
Maney	James	W	1830	Coop	Ct
Maney	Joseph	B	1844	Osag	Real
Manger	A		1844	Osag	Real
Mangford	Alfred		1840	Call	Poll
Mangrum	Arnold		1844	Osag	Real
Manian	William		1839	Plat	Prop
Manian	Woodson		1839	Plat	Prop
Manley	John		1836	StC	Prop
Mann	Nathaniel		1839	Plat	Prop
Mann	Mashal		1821	StC	Ct
Mann	Jesse		1821	Ray	Prop
Mann	Charles		1830	Ray	Prop
Mann	Joseph		1844	Osag	Real
Manning	James		1836	Perr	Poll
Manser	A		1867	Reyn	DTL
Mansfield	Robt	C	1843	Audr	Prop
Mansfield	R	C	1843	Audr	Prop
Mansfield	R	C	1838	Audr	DTL
Mantle	B		1867	Reyn	DTL
Manuel	Bazelle		1805	Steg	Prop
Manyard	Thomas		1844	Osag	Real
Marable	John		1836	Carr	Prop
Marable	John		1836	Carr	PrpPt
March	randolph		1817	How	Prop
Marchael	Thomas		1839	Plat	Prop
Marchael	J	M	1839	Plat	Prop
Marchoteau	Joseph		1780	StL	Mil
Marcil	Luis		1780	StL	Mil
Marice	Acan		1836	StC	Prop

145

Last Name	First Name	Int	Year	County	Type
Marichar	Joseph		1780	StL	Mil
Marichar	Antonio		1780	StL	Mil
Marichar	Jacobo		1780	StL	Mil
Marichar	Francisco		1780	StL	Mil
Marie	Alexo		1791	StL	Span
Mariscal	Antonio		1791	StL	Span
Markle, dec	Charles		1827	Mari	Prop
Markwell	A	J	1839	Plat	Prop
Marlin	Thomas	C	1834	Pett	Prop
Marlin	James		1834	Pett	Prop
Marlin	Thomas	C	1834	Pett	PrpPt
Marlin	Thomas		1827	Mari	Prop
Marlow	Gabriel		1836	StC	Prop
Marly	Lucas		1791	StL	Span
Marly	Wid Felicite		1820	StL	Prop
Marly	Luke		1820	StL	Prop
Marly	Michel		1820	StL	Prop
Marmon	Henry		1830	Coop	Ct
Marney	A		1828	Boon	Lisc
Marquis	Robert		1817	How	Prop
Marr	Joseph		1836	StC	Prop
Marrasse	Pierre		1820	StL	Prop
Marrow	A	M	1833	Lew	DTL
Marrs	James		1823	Call	NRP
Marscroff	Samuel		1867	Reyn	DTL
Marscroff	Samuel		1867	Reyn	DTL
Marscroft	Samuel		1867	Reyn	DTL
Marsh	John		1839	Plat	Prop
Marsh	Eiphus		1836	Char	DTL
Marshal	William		1836	Perr	Poll
Marshall	Frederick		1839	Plat	Prop
Marshall	Henry		1836	StC	Prop
Marshall	Thomas	J	1836	StC	Prop
Martan	Jn Baptiste		1805	Steg	Prop
Martigny	Marguerite		1818	StL	Real
Martigny	Margarete		1820	StL	Prop
Martilo	Custavus		1836	StC	Prop
Martilo	Frederick		1836	StC	Prop
Martin	John	A	1843	Audr	Prop
Martin	John	C	1843	Audr	Prop
Martin	Peter		1830	Wash	DTL
Martin	George		1839	Plat	Prop

Last Name	First Name	Int	Year	County	Type
Martin	John		1839	Plat	Prop
Martin	Joseph		1839	Plat	Prop
Martin	George		1839	Plat	Prop
Martin	William		1839	Plat	Prop
Martin	Franklin		1839	Plat	Prop
Martin	Harden		1839	Plat	Prop
Martin	Zadock		1839	Plat	Prop
Martin	Joseph		1839	Plat	Prop
Martin	Bright		1839	Plat	Prop
Martin	Gilleston		1836	Perr	Poll
Martin	David		1836	Carr	Prop
Martin	Sherwood		1836	Carr	Prop
Martin	William		1836	Carr	Prop
Martin	John		1836	Carr	Prop
Martin	Elijah		1836	Carr	Prop
Martin	David		1836	Carr	PrpPt
Martin	Sherwood		1836	Carr	PrpPt
Martin	William		1836	Carr	PrpPt
Martin	John		1836	Carr	PrpPt
Martin	Elijah		1836	Carr	PrpPt
Martin	James		1840	Call	Poll
Martin	Robert		1840	Call	Poll
Martin	Noah		1840	Call	Poll
Martin	John	W	1840	Call	Poll
Martin	John		1840	Call	Poll
Martin	Russell		1840	Call	Poll
Martin	Robert	H	1840	Call	Poll
Martin	S	D	1863	Jeff	Ass
Martin	Phillip		1836	StC	Prop
Martin	James	L	1836	StC	Prop
Martin	Abner		1829	Char	DTL
Martin	John	L	1829	Char	DTL
Martin	William	B	1821	Ray	Prop
Martin	William		1821	Ray	Prop
Martin	Isaac		1821	Ray	Prop
Martin	Henry		1821	Ray	Prop
Martin	I	C	1838	Audr	DTL
Martin	J	A	1838	Audr	DTL
Martin	Nily		1823	How	DTL
Martin	Elijah		1830	Ray	Prop
Martin	John		1830	Ray	Prop
Martin	William		1822	Clay	Poll

Last Name	First Name	Int	Year	County	Type
Martin, dec	John		1843	Audr	Prop
Martin, Jr	Zadoc		1821	Ray	Prop
Martin, Sr	Zadoc		1821	Ray	Prop
Martinno	Joseph		1836	StC	Prop
Martinno	Peter		1836	StC	Prop
Martinno	Francis		1836	StC	Prop
Martinno's Heirs	Charles		1836	StC	Prop
Martiny	Juan		1780	StL	Mil
Mary	L	P	1867	Reyn	DTL
Masar	Thomas	G	1867	Reyn	DTL
Maschaney	G	B	1836	StC	Prop
Mascheda	Francis		1836	StC	Prop
Mashe	????		1820	StL	Prop
Masingill	Blake		1821	Ray	Prop
Mason	Albert	W	1839	Plat	Prop
Mason	Samuel	T	1839	Plat	Prop
Mason	William		1836	Carr	Prop
Mason	William		1836	Carr	PrpPt
Mason	Samuel		1840	Call	Poll
Mason	Thos	G	1867	Reyn	DTL
Mason	Mary		1836	StC	Prop
Mason	Ann		1818	StL	Real
Mason	Ann		1820	StL	Prop
Mason	John		1830	Ray	Prop
Mason's Heirs	Nathan		1836	StC	Prop
Mason, Jr	James		1823	How	DTL
Masse	Jesse		1839	Plat	Prop
Masse	Jesse		1839	Plat	Prop
Masse	William		1839	Plat	Prop
Massey	Joseph	A	1836	Perr	Poll
Massey	R	D	1863	Jeff	Ass
Massey	William		1844	Osag	Real
Massie	William		1827	Mari	Prop
Massing	George	W	1844	Osag	Real
Masten	John		1810	Ark	Prop
Masters	Jesse		1823	Call	NRP
Masters	William		1830	Call	DTL
Masters	Richard		1828	Sali	DTL
Masterson	Robert		1827	Mari	Prop
Masthena	Stephen		1838	Audr	DTL
Mastin	Pheby		1843	Audr	Prop
Mastin	David		1843	Audr	Prop

Last Name	First Name	Int	Year	County	Type
Mastin	Wm	H	1843	Audr	Prop
Mastin	Thos	J	1843	Audr	Prop
Mastin	David		1838	Audr	DTL
Maston	Matthias		1839	Plat	Prop
Matheney	Henry		1839	Plat	Prop
Mathery	Stephen		1843	Audr	Prop
Mathew	Watson		1867	Reyn	DTL
Mathews	Britain		1840	Call	Poll
Mathews	Willia,		1867	Reyn	DTL
Mathews	Edward	P	1836	StC	Prop
Mathews	John		1836	StC	Prop
Mathews	James		1836	StC	Prop
Mathews	Phineas		1836	StC	Prop
Mathias	William		1867	Reyn	DTL
Mathis	William		1859	Reyn	DTL
Mathurin	Baptiste		1820	StL	Prop
Matson	Peton		1827	Mari	Prop
Matthew	John		1828	Boon	Lisc
Matthew	Willis		1828	Boon	Lisc
Matthews	Greefield		1839	Plat	Prop
Matthews	Drury		1836	Carr	Prop
Matthews	John		1836	Carr	Prop
Matthews	Drury		1836	Carr	PrpPt
Matthews	John		1836	Carr	PrpPt
Matthews	John		1830	Howa	DTL
Matthews	Lazarus	P	1839	John	DTL
Matthews	Henry		1827	Mari	Prop
Matthews	Daniels		1829	NMad	DTL
Mattingly	Joseph	B	1837	Perr	Lisc
Mattingly	Joseph		1837	Perr	Adv
Mattingly	James	B	1836	Perr	Poll
Mattingly	Joseph		1836	Perr	Poll
Mattingly	William		1836	Perr	Poll
Maupin	Thomas	R	1828	Boon	Lisc
Maupin	George		1840	Call	Poll
Maupin	William		1830	Howa	DTL
Maupin	Waller	C	1836	StC	Prop
Maupin	Gabriel		1829	Char	DTL
Mawry	Evariste		1818	StL	Real
Maxwell	Mn	J	1805	Steg	Prop
Maxwell	John		1829	Char	DTL
Maxwell	Joseph		1829	Mari	DTL

Last Name	First Name	Int	Year	County	Type
Maxwell	John		1827	Mari	Prop
May	W	S	1839	Plat	Prop
May	Silas		1839	Plat	Prop
May	James	R	1838	Cass	DTL
May	Gabriel		1840	Call	Poll
May	Henry	H	1840	Call	Poll
May	Charles	D	1836	StC	Prop
May	Pinkney	M	1836	StC	Prop
May	Charles	P	1836	StC	Prop
Mayberry	Theoderick		1821	Ray	Prop
Maychett	James		1836	StC	Prop
Mayes	John		1817	How	Prop
Mayfield	Elisha		1863	Jeff	Ass
Mays	Drury	D	1843	Audr	Prop
Mays	Bever;y	S	1843	Audr	Prop
Mays	W	W	1843	Audr	Prop
Mays	James		1827	Boon	Lisc
Mays	B	S	1838	Audr	DTL
Mayse	Drusa	D	1838	Audr	DTL
Mayse	William	W	1838	Audr	DTL
Mazingoe	Wesley		1840	Call	Poll
McAdow	Samuel		1839	Plat	Prop
McAdow	George	B	1839	Plat	Prop
McAfee	George		1839	Plat	Prop
McAfee	Peter		1828	Boon	Lisc
McAferty	L	H	1839	Lew	DTL
McAllister	Garrett		1838	Steg	DTL
McAllister	William		1836	Char	DTL
McAnnabsy	Jesse		1836	Carr	PrpPt
McArlin	Charles		1840	Call	Poll
McAslin	Charles		1840	Call	Poll
McAuley	Benj		1836	Perr	Poll
McAuley	James		1836	Perr	Poll
McAustin	Henry		1836	Perr	Poll
McBride	William		1839	Plat	Prop
McBride	Patrick		1836	Perr	Poll
McBride	P	H	1828	Boon	Lisc
McCabe	Orvil		1839	Wash	Lisc
McCafferty	Hugh		1839	Plat	Prop
McCafferty	Samuel		1839	Plat	Prop
McCalister	Frances		1838	Ripl	DTL
McCall	Jesse		1839	Plat	Prop

Last Name	First Name	Int	Year	County	Type
McCall	Dugald		1836	Bent	DTL
McCall	James	E	1840	Call	Poll
McCall	Peter	H	1840	Call	Poll
McCall	William	S	1840	Call	Poll
McCampbell	John		1840	Call	Poll
McCarty	Calvin		1843	Audr	Prop
McCarty	Benjamin		1843	Audr	Prop
McCarty	John		1839	Plat	Prop
McCarty	Michael		1859	Reyn	DTL
McCarty	William		1840	Call	Poll
McCarty	J	F L	1863	Jeff	Ass
McCarty	Benjamin		1838	Audr	DTL
McCarty	William		1844	Osag	Real
McCarven	William		1840	Call	Poll
McCatee	Stephen		1836	StC	Prop
McCauslin	David		1836	StC	Prop
McClain	J	T	1863	Jeff	Ass
McClain	David		1817	How	Prop
McClain	David		1817	How	Prop
McClain	Robert		1839	Lew	DTL
McClair	Thomas		1839	Plat	Prop
McClair	George		1839	Plat	Prop
McClair	James		1839	Plat	Prop
McClair	William		1839	Plat	Prop
McClair	John		1839	Plat	Prop
McClamee	Laurence		1836	StC	Prop
McClanahan	John		1840	Call	Poll
McClanahan	James		1840	Call	Poll
McClanahan	Job		1830	Coop	CtS
McClane	John		1836	StC	Prop
McClanis	Peter		1828	Boon	Lisc
McClarey	John		1839	Plat	Prop
McClausland	J		1829	Char	DTL
McClay	William		1836	StC	Prop
McClearney	William	S	1836	StC	Prop
McClelland	John		1840	Call	Poll
McClelland	Jas		1840	Call	Poll
McClelland	Robert		1840	Call	Poll
McClelland	Thomas		1840	Call	Poll
McClenilland	Elisha		1836	StC	Prop
McClenney	Micaja		1836	StC	Prop
McClenney	James		1836	StC	Prop

Last Name	First Name	Int	Year	County	Type
McCloud	Absalom		1829	NMad	DTL
McClure	John		1840	Call	Poll
McClure	I	H	1840	Call	Poll
McClure	Samuel		1840	Call	Poll
McClure	Thomas		1840	Call	Poll
McClure	William		1840	Call	Poll
McClure	Robert		1836	StC	Prop
McClure	Sophia		1836	StC	Prop
McClure	John		1817	How	Prop
McClure's Heirs	Robert		1836	StC	Prop
McCollom	Wesley		1839	Plat	Prop
McCollom	Jackson		1839	Plat	Prop
McCollum	David		1839	Plat	Prop
McCome	William	P	1867	Reyn	DTL
McConnel	Joel		1840	Call	Poll
McConnel	John		1836	StC	Prop
McConnel	James		1836	StC	Prop
McCord	John		1839	Plat	Prop
McCormack	Seth		1859	Reyn	DTL
McCormack	George		1863	Jeff	Ass
McCormack	Wats		1863	Jeff	Ass
McCormack	Wm	F	1863	Jeff	Ass
McCormack	Wm	S	1863	Jeff	Ass
McCormack	P	A	1863	Jeff	Ass
McCormack	Hardy		1863	Jeff	Ass
McCormack	George	W	1863	Jeff	Ass
McCormack	Jno		1863	Jeff	Ass
McCormack	David		1838	Audr	DTL
McCormack	John		1834	Call	DTL
McCormick	Jas		1843	Audr	Prop
McCormick	Patrick		1867	Reyn	DTL
McCormick	Charles		1838	Ripl	DTL
McCoskey	Archibald		1836	StC	Prop
McCourt	James		1836	StC	Prop
McCoy	John		1836	Carr	Prop
McCoy	John		1836	Carr	PrpPt
McCoy	Timothy		1836	StC	Prop
McCoy	William		1836	StC	Prop
McCoy	Jacob		1821	Ray	Prop
McCoy	Robert		1822	Clay	Poll
McCoy	Jacob		1822	Clay	Poll
McCracken	Nimrod		1839	Plat	Prop

Last Name	First Name	Int	Year	County	Type
McCracken	Robert		1839	Plat	Prop
McCracken	William		1839	Wash	Lisc
McCracken	Otho		1840	Call	Poll
McCray	William		1839	Plat	Prop
McCray	Daniel		1821	Ray	Prop
McCroscay	Isaac		1822	Clay	Poll
McCroskie	John		1821	Ray	Prop
McCroskie	Andrew		1821	Ray	Prop
McCroskie	Isaac		1821	Ray	Prop
McCubbins	William		1837	Mill	DTL
McCulloch	William	H	1840	Call	Poll
McCulloch	Aus		1863	Jeff	Ass
McCulloch	Levi		1863	Jeff	Ass
McCullough	????		1818	StL	Real
McCulough	J	C	1859	Reyn	DTL
McCulough	Joseph		1840	Call	Poll
McCurdy	James		1867	Reyn	DTL
McCutchen	Thomas		1840	Call	Poll
McCutchen	Zerelda		1836	StC	Prop
McCutchen's Heirs	J	L	1836	StC	Prop
McCutcheon	Walter	T	1836	StC	Prop
McDaniel	????		1845	Sali	Lisc
McDaniel	Silas		1810	Ark	Prop
McDaniel	Cashus		1838	Audr	DTL
McDaniel	Thomas		1838	Audr	DTL
McDaniel	Jos		1838	Audr	DTL
McDaniel	Edward		1817	How	Prop
McDaniel	George		1827	Mari	Prop
McDaniel	John		1839	Lew	DTL
McDaniel, Sr	Joseph		1838	Audr	DTL
McDermont	James	R	1836	StC	Prop
McDode	John		1836	Carr	Prop
McDode	John		1836	Carr	PrpPt
McDonald	Thomas		1843	Audr	Prop
McDonald	Wm		1843	Audr	Prop
McDonald	Arthur		1843	Audr	Prop
McDonald	John		1843	Audr	Prop
McDonald	Barnet		1843	Audr	Prop
McDonald	Alexander		1839	Plat	Prop
McDonald	Pat		1859	Reyn	DTL
McDonald	John		1840	Call	Poll
McDonald	Edward		1840	Call	Poll

Last Name	First Name	Int	Year	County	Type
McDonald	Matthew		1823	Call	NRP
McDonald	Patrick		1820	StL	Prop
McDonnel	Alexander		1836	StC	Prop
McDonnel	Baptist		1836	StC	Prop
McDormott	John		1867	Reyn	DTL
McDow	B		1828	Boon	Lisc
McDowell	J		1829	Char	DTL
McDowell	John		1829	Sali	DTL
McDowell	John		1817	How	Prop
McElroy	William	J	1827	Mari	Prop
McElwee	David		1821	Ray	Prop
McEwens	Samuel		1836	Carr	PrtPt
McEwin	Samuel		1830	Ray	Prop
McFadden	Jas	M	1843	Audr	Prop
McFadden	Mathew		1867	Reyn	DTL
McFadden	Mathew		1867	Reyn	DTL
McFadden	Alexander		1830	Ray	Prop
Mcfaddin	Wyatt		1836	Char	DTL
McFadon	Alexander		1836	Carr	Prop
McFadon	Alexander		1836	Carr	PrpPt
McFall	Anderson		1839	Plat	Prop
McFall	Lasarez		1836	StC	Prop
McFall	John		1827	Mari	Prop
McFarland	Houston		1839	Plat	Prop
McFarland	George		1840	Call	Poll
Mcfarland	Isaac		1867	Reyn	DTL
McFarland	John		1817	How	Prop
Mcfarlin	John		1839	John	DTL
McFarris	Charles		1836	StC	Prop
McFee	James		1836	Carr	Prop
McFee	James		1836	Carr	PrpPt
McFerson	Edward		1839	Plat	Prop
McFerson	Nicholas		1839	Plat	Prop
McGarry	H	H	1840	Call	Poll
McGarvey	G	W A	1859	Reyn	DTL
McGary	James	D	1840	Call	Poll
McGary	William	D	1840	Call	Poll
McGary	James		1829	NMad	DTL
McGaugh	John		1821	Ray	Prop
McGee	Harvy		1843	Audr	Prop
McGee	Benjamin		1843	Audr	Prop
McGee	David		1839	Plat	Prop

Last Name	First Name	Int	Year	County	Type
McGee	David		1838	Cass	DTL
McGee	Benjamin		1840	Call	Poll
McGee	William		1840	Call	Poll
McGee	Charles		1821	Ray	Prop
McGee	Benjamin		1838	Audr	DTL
McGee	David		1817	How	Prop
McGee	Henry		1844	Osag	Real
McGinnis	John		1859	Reyn	DTL
McGinnis	Edward		1836	Perr	Poll
McGirk	Mathias		1830	Jeff	DTL
McGirk	Mathias		1820	StL	Prop
McGowin	David		1836	StC	Prop
McGown	Samuel		1839	Plat	Prop
McGown	John		1840	Call	Poll
McGrath	Owen		1859	Reyn	DTL
McGriffin	Charles		1830	Ray	Prop
McGrow	Madison		1867	Reyn	DTL
McGuire	William		1839	Plat	Prop
McGuire	Robert		1836	Carr	PrpPt
McGuire	Patrick		1867	Reyn	DTL
McGuire	Patrick		1867	Reyn	DTL
McGuire	Thomas		1820	StL	Prop
McGuire's Heirs	Robert		1836	Carr	Prop
McGuire's Heirs	Robert		1836	Carr	PrpPt
McGumegle	James		1820	StL	Prop
McGunnigle	Geo		1829	Char	DTL
McGunnigle	George		1830	Ray	Prop
McHahlan	Hinson		1837	Lew	DTL
McHenry	David		1836	Perr	Poll
McIntire	Robert		1836	Carr	Prop
McIntire	Robert		1836	Carr	PrpPt
McIntire	John		1840	Call	Poll
McIntosh	David		1836	Carr	Prop
McIntosh	David		1836	Carr	PrpPt
McIntosh	George		1840	Call	Poll
McIntush	George		1843	Audr	Prop
McIntyre	C	W	1843	Audr	Prop
McIntyre	Roland		1838	Audr	DTL
McIntyre	Charles		1838	Audr	DTL
McKamey	James		1840	Call	Poll
McKamey	James	I	1840	Call	Poll
McKamey	Robert		1840	Call	Poll

155

Last Name	First Name	Int	Year	County	Type
McKamey	William	H	1840	Call	Poll
McKane	James		1836	Carr	Prop
McKane	James		1836	Carr	PrpPt
McKay	John		1821	StC	Ct
McKay	Gartern	H	1867	Reyn	DTL
McKay	James	M	1836	StC	Prop
McKay	John	G	1836	StC	Prop
McKeever	Thomas		1863	Jeff	Ass
McKey	Caton	H	1867	Reyn	DTL
McKine	Elisha		1840	Call	Poll
McKine	Joseph	M	1840	Call	Poll
McKinney	James		1840	Call	Poll
McKinney	John		1840	Call	Poll
McKinney	Jonathan		1840	Call	Poll
McKinney	William		1840	Call	Poll
McKinney	William		1840	Call	Poll
McKinney	A	W	1836	StC	Prop
McKinney	Stephen		1837	Lew	DTL
McKinsee	Solomon		1836	Carr	Prop
McKinsee	Solomon		1836	Carr	PrpPt
McKissick	Jacob		1839	Plat	Prop
McKnight	John	F	1821	StC	Ct
McKnight	Jno		1820	StL	Prop
McKnight	Thomas		1820	StL	Prop
McLaughlin	Michael		1836	Perr	Poll
McLaughlin	Andrew		1840	Call	Poll
McLaughlin	James		1840	Call	Poll
McLean	John		1836	Perr	Poll
McLean	Robert		1830	Ray	Prop
McLeare	William	R	1845	Sali	Lisc
McLester	John		1830	Ray	Prop
McLin, Jr	Henry		1839	John	DTL
McLoan	John		1836	Carr	Prop
McLoan	John		1836	Carr	PrpPt
McMahan	Richard		1840	Call	Poll
McMahan	Jesse		1840	Call	Poll
McMahan	Isham		1840	Call	Poll
McMahan	Jesse		1845	Sali	Lisc
McMahan	Etienne		1815	Ark	Prop
McMahan (1)	Thomas		1817	How	Prop
McMahan (2)	Thomas		1817	How	Prop
McMahon	Richard		1839	Plat	Prop

Last Name	First Name	Int	Year	County	Type
McMahon	James		1839	Plat	Prop
McManus	L	W	1839	Plat	Prop
McMillen	John	M	1836	StC	Prop
McMullin	Madison		1843	Audr	Prop
McMullin	John		1836	Carr	Prop
McMullin	John		1836	Carr	PrpPt
McNair	Alexander		1820	StL	Prop
McNairy	John		1829	Char	DTL
McNally	Willis		1838	Steg	DTL
McNamee	George		1863	Jeff	Ass
McNennoy	Robert		1829	Char	DTL
McNight	Joseph	A	1836	StC	Prop
McNight	J	F	1836	StC	Prop
McNight	D	G	1836	StC	Prop
McNight	John	F	1836	StC	Prop
McNight	Thomas		1844	Osag	Real
McNutt	Alexander		1836	Carr	PrtPt
McNutt	John		1836	StC	Prop
MCoy	Joseph		1820	StL	Prop
McPhael	A		1839	Wash	Lisc
McPike	Mathey		1830	Wash	DTL
McQuitty	David		1817	How	Prop
McRae	William		1827	Mari	Prop
McReynolds	William		1827	Mari	Prop
McRobaras	Harvey		1840	Call	Poll
McRoberts	J	D	1843	Audr	Prop
McRoberts	John		1843	Audr	Prop
McRoberts	Preston		1836	StC	Prop
McRoberts	John		1836	StC	Prop
McRoberts	Milton		1836	StC	Prop
McRoberts	Sarah		1836	StC	Prop
McRoberts	Harrison		1836	StC	Prop
McRoy	Samuel		1831	Craw	DTL
McSwain	Neal		1843	Audr	Prop
McSwain	Jas	E	1843	Audr	Prop
McSwain	Daniel		1843	Audr	Prop
McSwain	Daniel		1838	Audr	DTL
McUrvine	Robert		1836	StC	Prop
McWaters	Aaron		1836	StC	Prop
McWaters	Edward		1836	StC	Prop
McWaters	Wilford		1836	StC	Prop
McWaters	Hugh		1836	StC	Prop

Last Name	First Name	Int	Year	County	Type
McWhirter	John	F	1839	Plat	Prop
McWilliam	John		1836	Carr	Prop
McWilliam	John		1836	Carr	PrpPt
McWilliams	David	S	1839	Plat	Prop
McWilliams	John	A	1867	Reyn	DTL
McWilliams	John		1827	Mari	Prop
Meacham	Berry		1818	StL	Real
Mead	August		1867	Reyn	DTL
Meador	John	H	1839	Plat	Prop
Meadows	Moses	G	1840	Call	Poll
Means	Andrew		1822	Clay	Poll
Meard, Sr	John		1837	Cass	DTL
Mecho	Mich		1819	Steg	Lic
Medcalf	Garner	J	1836	StC	Prop
Meddendorf	Henry		1836	StC	Prop
Meddlin	Dan		1839	Plat	Prop
Medley	Bazil		1836	Carr	PrpPt
Medley	James		1863	Jeff	Ass
Medley	H	W H	1863	Jeff	Ass
Medlin	Handy		1831	Cole	DTL
Meeker	John		1830	Ray	Prop
Meeks	Jeremiah		1829	NMad	DTL
Meeks	Jacob		1829	NMad	DTL
Meens	James	C	1839	Plat	Prop
Megibbes	EloinisElonis	S	1836	StC	Prop
Meguire	Francis		1821	Ray	Prop
Melling	Samuel		1859	Reyn	DTL
Mellon	William		1843	Audr	Prop
Mellon	Arthur		1828	Sali	DTL
Memville	Josef		1791	StL	Span
Menar	Pedro		1791	StL	Span
Menard	John	B	1810	Ark	Prop
Menard	John Bte		1815	Ark	Prop
Mercasmith	Rozanah		1844	Osag	Real
Merchand	Dedier		1830	Linc	DTL
Mercie	Luis		1780	StL	Mil
Merrawine	William		1843	Audr	Prop
Merrill	Eli		1827	Mari	Prop
Merry	Stephen		1838	Ripl	DTL
Messersmith	Royal		1831	Cole	DTL
Metcalf	William		1843	Audr	Prop
Metcalf	William	F	1838	Audr	DTL

Last Name	First Name	Int	Year	County	Type
Meyer	Ludwig		1836	StC	Prop
Meyer	Charles		1836	StC	Prop
Miacal	Gaspar		1836	StC	Prop
Michael	James		1837	Perr	Lisc
Michael	James		1836	Perr	Poll
Micham	Berry		1820	StL	Prop
Michel	Francis		1810	Ark	Prop
Michel	Francis		1815	Ark	Prop
Michon	Lorenzo		1780	StL	Mil
Michon	Alexandro		1780	StL	Mil
Mickel	Archibald		1836	Perr	Poll
Micker	Isaac		1820	StL	Prop
Middleburger	John	C	1836	StC	Prop
Middleton	Robt	C	1843	Audr	Prop
Middleton	William		1843	Audr	Prop
Middleton	W	B	1843	Audr	Prop
Middleton	William	B	1838	Audr	DTL
Migeron	Solomon		1820	StL	Prop
Migren	Jos	W	1838	Steg	DTL
Milan	William		1839	Wash	Lisc
Mildrow, Sr	John		1827	Mari	Prop
Miles	Francis		1836	Perr	Poll
Miles	Joseph		1836	Perr	Poll
Mileu	William		1836	StC	Prop
Milihan	Jacob		1839	Plat	Prop
Milikin	J	H	1843	Audr	Prop
Milikin	Oliver		1867	Reyn	DTL
Miller	John	T	1843	Audr	Prop
Miller	Bailey		1843	Audr	Prop
Miller	David	A	1843	Audr	Prop
Miller	Christian		1843	Audr	Prop
Miller	Joseph	H	1843	Audr	Prop
Miller	William	G	1843	Audr	Prop
Miller	Jas	H	1843	Audr	Prop
Miller	J		1827	Coop	DTL
Miller	Isaac		1839	Plat	Prop
Miller	James		1839	Plat	Prop
Miller	John		1839	Plat	Prop
Miller	Abraham		1839	Plat	Prop
Miller	JOhn		1839	Plat	Prop
Miller	Joseph	B	1836	Perr	Poll
Miller	John		1836	Carr	Prop

Last Name	First Name	Int	Year	County	Type
Miller	John		1836	Carr	PrpPt
Miller	William	B	1840	Call	Poll
Miller	William		1840	Call	Poll
Miller	Abram		1840	Call	Poll
Miller	Moses	T	1840	Call	Poll
Miller	Allen	D	1840	Call	Poll
Miller	Daniel		1840	Call	Poll
Miller	Martin		1840	Call	Poll
Miller	Robert	W	1840	Call	Poll
Miller	Samuel		1840	Call	Poll
Miller	Samuel		1834	Pett	Prop
Miller	William	A	1834	Pett	PrpPt
Miller	Henry		1867	Reyn	DTL
Miller	George	W	1836	StC	Prop
Miller	Jacob		1836	StC	Prop
Miller	Robert		1836	StC	Prop
Miller	Fleming		1836	StC	Prop
Miller	Christian	R	1836	StC	Prop
Miller	Philip		1823	Call	NRP
Miller	John		1823	Call	NRP
Miller	Sebron	J	1821	Ray	Prop
Miller	William		1821	Ray	Prop
Miller	Barly		1838	Audr	DTL
Miller	William		1828	Sali	DTL
Miller	John		1828	Sali	DTL
Miller	J		1827	Coop	DTL
Miller	James		1827	Mari	Prop
Miller	Jesse		1844	Osag	Real
Miller	Michael		1844	Osag	Real
Miller	Thomas		1844	Osag	Real
Miller	Adam		1844	Osag	Real
Miller, Jr	Simon		1815	Ark	Prop
Milles	Ignatus		1836	StC	Prop
Milliams	Bird		1840	Call	Poll
Milligan	William		1838	Ripl	DTL
Millikin	Ezekiel		1836	Carr	Prop
Millikin	Ezekiel		1836	Carr	PrpPt
Millington	J		1821	StC	CtS
Millington	Jerem		1821	StC	CtS
Millington	Jeremia		1836	StC	Prop
Millington's Heirs	Seth		1836	StC	Prop
Mills	H	S	1845	Sali	Lisc

160

Last Name	First Name	Int	Year	County	Type
Mills	Natahn		1818	StL	Real
Mills	Nathan		1820	StL	Prop
Mills	James		1844	Osag	Real
Millsaps	William		1821	Ray	Prop
Milmurry	John		1810	Ark	Prop
Milton	James		1836	Carr	Prop
Milton	James		1836	Carr	PrpPt
Milton	George	W	1837	Lew	DTL
Milton	Milton		1837	Lew	DTL
Miner	John		1843	Audr	Prop
Miner	Elizabeth		1867	Reyn	DTL
Ming	Thomas	N	1840	Call	Poll
Minkirs	James		1821	Ray	Prop
Minor	Garry		1839	Lew	DTL
Minot	Robert		1836	Carr	Prop
Minot	Robert		1836	Carr	PrpPt
Minrs	John		1830	Coop	Ct
Minton	John		1835	Barr	DTL
Minton	Laura		1844	Osag	Real
Minton, dec	John		1844	Osag	Real
Miron	Solomon		1818	StL	Real
Mirra	Jaque		1805	Steg	Prop
Missaha	Lydua		1810	Ark	Prop
Missla	Perran		1805	Steg	Prop
Missplay	John		1838	Steg	DTL
Mitchel	Stephen		1827	Sali	DTL
Mitchell	John	J	1843	Audr	Prop
Mitchell	Robert	B	1839	Plat	Prop
Mitchell	Henry		1840	Call	Poll
Mitchell	Joseph		1830	How	DTL
Mitchell	Danl		1810	Ark	Prop
Mitchell	Richard		1823	How	DTL
Mitchell	Thomas		1817	How	Prop
Mixon	Solomon		1818	StL	Real
Mobidou	Josef		1791	StL	Span
Mobley	John		1839	Plat	Prop
Mockbee	R	E	1863	Jeff	Ass
Molntardy	Pedro		1791	StL	Span
Molaire	Baptist		1818	StL	Real
Moletoe	Francis		1836	StC	Prop
Mollaire	Baptiste		1820	StL	Prop
Molls	William		1863	Jeff	Ass

Last Name	First Name	Int	Year	County	Type
Moloney	????		1820	StL	Prop
Monatesse	David		1818	StL	Real
Monatress	David		1820	StL	Prop
Moncus	Benjamin		1839	Plat	Prop
Mongrain	Noel		1820	StL	Prop
Mongrin	Noel		1818	StL	Real
Monicle	Christo		1823	Call	NRP
Monkey	David		1867	Reyn	DTL
Monneyham	Ervin		1839	Plat	Prop
Monneyham	William		1839	Plat	Prop
Monneyham	Joseph		1839	Plat	Prop
Monplier	Joseph		1844	Osag	Real
Monro	William		1817	How	Prop
Monroe	William		1830	Howa	DTL
Monroe	William		1821	Ray	Prop
Monroe	William		1817	How	Prop
Monroe	Thomas		1821	Ray	Prop
Monsett	Batiste		1818	StL	Real
Montagne	Joseph		1820	StL	Prop
Montanime	Jean		1828	Sali	DTL
Montaque	Frances		1818	StL	Real
Montardy	Pedro		1780	StL	Mil
Montgomery	David		1821	Ray	Prop
Montgomery	Ruth		1810	Ark	Prop
Montgomery	Thomas		1838	Ripl	DTL
Moody	Isaac		1839	Plat	Prop
Moon	Newton		1840	Call	Poll
Mooney	G	O	1867	Reyn	DTL
Mooney	Danl		1810	Ark	Prop
Mooney	Daniel		1815	Ark	Prop
Moor	Thos		1843	Audr	Prop
Moor	John	B	1840	Call	Poll
Moor	Ira		1836	StC	Prop
Moor	Andrew		1821	Ray	Prop
Moordock	Mary		1836	StC	Prop
Moordock	George		1836	StC	Prop
Moordock	James		1836	StC	Prop
Moordock	John		1836	StC	Prop
Moordock	Robert		1836	StC	Prop
Moordock's Heirs	Alexander		1836	StC	Prop
Moore	Moses		1818	Lawr	DTL
Moore	Jesse		1839	Plat	Prop

Last Name	First Name	Int	Year	County	Type
Moore	William		1839	Plat	Prop
Moore	Joseph		1839	Plat	Prop
Moore	Robert		1838	Perr	Lisc
Moore	John		1838	Perr	Lisc
Moore	Robert		1838	Perr	Adv
Moore	John		1838	Perr	Adv
Moore	John		1859	Reyn	DTL
Moore	Ignatus		1836	Perr	Poll
Moore	James	C	1836	Perr	Poll
Moore	James	N	1836	Perr	Poll
Moore	Levi		1836	Perr	Poll
Moore	Lewis		1836	Perr	Poll
Moore	Martin	L	1836	Perr	Poll
Moore	Sylvester		1836	Perr	Poll
Moore	Hugh	A	1836	Carr	Prop
Moore	Augustus		1836	Carr	Prop
Moore	Alfred		1836	Carr	Prop
Moore	John	B	1836	Carr	Prop
Moore	Hugh		1836	Carr	PrpPt
Moore	Augustus		1836	Carr	PrpPt
Moore	Alfred		1836	Carr	PrpPt
Moore	John		1836	Carr	PrpPt
Moore	John	R	1836	Carr	PrpPt
Moore	James	W	1840	Call	Poll
Moore	John	B	1840	Call	Poll
Moore	Goke		1840	Call	Poll
Moore	William		1840	Call	Poll
Moore	Jas	B	1840	Call	Poll
Moore	James	W	1840	Call	Poll
Moore	William		1840	Call	Poll
Moore	John		1836	StC	Prop
Moore	John	C	1836	StC	Prop
Moore	Zacaria		1836	StC	Prop
Moore	James	D	1836	StC	Prop
Moore	John		1829	Char	DTL
Moore	Quinton		1830	Linc	DTL
Moore	Vincent		1838	Audr	DTL
Moore	Jas		1818	StL	Real
Moore	????		1820	StL	Prop
Moore	Hugh		1830	Ray	Prop
Moore	Elijah		1839	Lew	DTL
Moore	A	J	1843	Char	DTL

Last Name	First Name	Int	Year	County	Type
Moore	Alfred	J	1844	Osag	Real
Moore	Robert		1844	Osag	Real
Moore	Ephraim		1836	Char	DTL
Moore	Elizabeth		1836	Char	DTL
Moorehead	John	H	1831	Jack	DTL
Moorey	W	C	1859	Reyn	DTL
Moran	William		1836	Carr	Prop
Moran	William		1836	Carr	PrpPt
Moran	James		1867	Reyn	DTL
Moran	John		1867	Reyn	DTL
Morasse	Peter		1818	StL	Real
Mordica	Soloman		1817	How	Prop
More	Wharton	H	1840	Call	Poll
Moreau	Franco		1791	StL	Span
Morehead	John	H	1839	Lew	DTL
Moreland	Sandy	H	1839	Plat	Prop
Moreland	Daniel		1839	Plat	Prop
Moren	Antonio		1791	StL	Span
Moren	Thos		1863	Jeff	Ass
Moren	Edw		1863	Jeff	Ass
Morey	L	P	1867	Reyn	DTL
Morgan	Elisha		1839	Plat	Prop
Morgan	Phelix		1859	Reyn	DTL
Morgan	Thomas		1859	Reyn	DTL
Morgan	Thomas		1859	Reyn	DTL
Morgan	Charles		1836	Carr	Prop
Morgan	James		1836	Carr	Prop
Morgan	Charles		1836	Carr	PrpPt
Morgan	James		1836	Carr	PrpPt
Morgan	William		1840	Call	Poll
Morgan	James		1867	Reyn	DTL
Morgan	Jacques		1818	StL	Real
Morgan	Thompson		1839	John	DTL
Morgan	Asa		1817	How	Prop
Morgan	Eneas		1817	How	Prop
Morgan, Jr	Joseph		1823	How	DTL
Morin	John		1839	Plat	Prop
Morin	Jesse		1839	Plat	Prop
Morin	Joseph		1818	StL	Real
Morin	Joseph		1820	StL	Prop
Morin	Wid Pelagie		1820	StL	Prop
Morisitte	John	B	1818	StL	Real

164

Last Name	First Name	Int	Year	County	Type
Moro	Madame		1805	Steg	Prop
Moro	Baptiste		1805	Steg	Prop
Moro	Bapt		1780	StL	Mil
Moro	William		1817	How	Prop
Morras	Jesse		1839	Plat	Prop
Morrell	Francis		1805	Steg	Prop
Morris	John	B	1843	Audr	Prop
Morris	John		1843	Audr	Prop
Morris	Harry		1805	Steg	Prop
Morris	Ephraim		1836	Carr	Prop
Morris	Ephraim		1836	Carr	PrpPt
Morris	Robert	M	1830	How	DTL
Morris	????		1867	Reyn	DTL
Morris	William		1836	StC	Prop
Morris	Benjamin		1836	StC	Prop
Morris	William		1836	StC	Prop
Morris	Edward		1821	Ray	Prop
Morris	Joshua		1827	Mari	Prop
Morris	Joshua		1838	Ripl	DTL
Morris	George		1837	Mill	DTL
Morris' Heirs	Mayberry		1830	Ray	Prop
Morrison	William	P	1818	Lawr	DTL
Morrison	Jesse		1821	StC	Ct
Morrison	J	S	1867	Reyn	DTL
Morrison	James		1836	StC	Prop
Morrison	Jas		1836	StC	Prop
Morrison	Jesse		1836	StC	Prop
Morrison	James		1830	Linc	DTL
Morrison	William		1810	Ark	Prop
Morrison	William		1818	StL	Real
Morrison	William		1818	StL	Real
Morrison	William		1815	Ark	Prop
Morrow	David		1836	Carr	PrpPt
Morrow	David		1830	Ray	Prop
Morrow	John		1844	Osag	Real
Morrow	John	W	1838	Ripl	DTL
Morrow	David		1838	Ripl	DTL
Morsee	Pierre		1818	StL	Real
Morton	Hugh		1859	Reyn	DTL
Morton	Patrick		1836	Carr	Prop
Morton	Patrick		1836	Carr	PrpPt
Morton	????		1820	StL	Prop

165

Last Name	First Name	Int	Year	County	Type
Morton	Samuel		1827	Mari	Prop
Mosby	William		1844	Osag	Real
Moseley	John		1840	Call	Poll
Mosely	Sharrach		1823	Call	NRP
Moses	A	E	1859	Reyn	DTL
Moses	Adaline		1867	Reyn	DTL
Moses	Ran		1844	Osag	Real
Moses	Micajah		1831	Craw	DTL
Mosley	Benj	L	1840	Call	Poll
Mosley	Samuel		1815	Ark	Prop
Moss	James	W	1828	Boon	Lisc
Moss	John		1840	Call	Poll
Moss	Mathew		1810	Ark	Prop
Moss	Carrol		1827	Mari	Prop
Moss	Matthew		1827	Mari	Prop
Moss	Edward		1844	Osag	Real
Moss	John		1844	Osag	Real
Moss	William		1844	Osag	Real
Mosses	J	B	1838	Audr	DTL
Moster	Williard		1836	Carr	Prop
Moster	Williard		1836	Carr	PrpPt
Mosure	Jonathan		1839	Plat	Prop
Mott	William		1825		DTL
Mount	Samuel		1820	StL	Prop
Mousette	Baptist		1820	StL	Prop
Mozee	Thomas	W	1836	StC	Prop
Msterson	Edward		1829	Mari	DTL
Mucey	Charles		1839	Plat	Prop
Muhnnn	Justice		1836	StC	Prop
Muir	Jerrimah		1840	Call	Poll
Muker	John		1836	Carr	Prop
Muker	John		1836	Carr	PrpPt
Muldro	James		1827	Mari	Prop
Muldroe	Geo	F	1843	Audr	Prop
Muldroe	Margaret		1843	Audr	Prop
Muldroe	John	G	1843	Audr	Prop
Muldroe	G	F	1843	Audr	Prop
Muldrow	Margaret		1843	Audr	Prop
Muldrow	Samuel		1827	Mari	Prop
Mulford	Thomas	D	1836	Carr	Prop
Mulford	Thomas		1836	Carr	PrpPt
Mulkey	Zachariah		1839	John	DTL

166

Last Name	First Name	Int	Year	County	Type
Mullanphy	John		1820	StL	Prop
Mullens	Susanna		1817	How	Prop
Mullet	Frederick		1820	StL	Prop
Mullet	Joseph		1820	StL	Prop
Mulligan	Felix	G	1839	Plat	Prop
Mullins	Charles		1839	Plat	Prop
Mullins	David		1836	Char	DTL
Mun	Eunice		1818	StL	Real
Muncus	John		1823	How	DTL
Munkers	Richard		1821	Ray	Prop
Munkirs	Redman		1821	Ray	Prop
Munkres	Berryman		1822	Clay	Poll
Munkres	Richard		1822	Clay	Poll
Munkres	William		1822	Clay	Poll
Munkres	James		1822	Clay	Poll
Munn	Charles		1836	Carr	PrpPt
Munro	John		1817	How	Prop
Munro, Sr	Daniel		1817	How	Prop
Murdock	James		1821	StC	Ct
Murphey	Patton		1839	Plat	Prop
Murphey	William	S	1839	Plat	Prop
Murphey	Thomas	C	1839	Wash	Lisc
Murphey	W	D	1839	Wash	Lisc
Murphey	Travis		1836	StC	Prop
Murphey	Maurice		1820	StL	Prop
Murphy	Martin		1859	Reyn	DTL
Murphy	Tarlton		1836	Carr	Prop
Murphy	Tarlton		1836	Carr	PrpPt
Murphy	Augustus	H	1840	Call	Poll
Murphy	Alfred	K	1830	Coop	Ct
Murphy	Darin		1830	Coop	CtS
Murphy	William		1830	Coop	CtS
Murphy	James		1810	Ark	Prop
Murphy	Talton		1830	Ray	Prop
Murphy	John		1844	Osag	Real
Murray	Joseph		1836	Perr	Poll
Murray	Andrew	R	1840	Call	Poll
Murray	Enoch		1840	Call	Poll
Murray	Edmond		1821	Ray	Prop
Murrell	John		1863	Jeff	Ass
Murry	Saml		1843	Audr	Prop
Murry	John		1867	Reyn	DTL

Last Name	First Name	Int	Year	County	Type
Musick	Lewis		1843	Audr	Prop
Musick	L	T	1843	Audr	Prop
Myass	David		1838	Audr	DTL
Myass	Prebly		1838	Audr	DTL
Myers	Meredeth		1843	Audr	Prop
Myers	D		1843	Audr	Prop
Myers	Mordecai		1836	Carr	Prop
Myers	Michael		1836	Carr	Prop
Myers	Mordecai		1836	Carr	PrpPt
Myers	Michael		1836	Carr	PrpPt
Myre	Louis		1836	StC	Prop
Myres	Lorenzo	D	1836	Perr	Poll
Myres	George		1836	StC	Prop
Myres	George		1836	StC	Prop
Myres	Frederick		1836	StC	Prop
Myres	John		1836	StC	Prop
Naper	Thomas		1844	Osag	Real
Narfleet	Abram		1840	Call	Poll
Nash	Alford		1840	Call	Poll
Nash	Allen		1840	Call	Poll
Nash	Wm		1840	Call	Poll
Nash	William		1817	How	Prop
Nash	Ira		1817	How	Prop
Nate's Heors	David		1836	Carr	Prop
Nate's Heors	David		1836	Carr	PrpPt
Nave	William		1839	Plat	Prop
Naylor	John		1836	StC	Prop
Naylor	Thomas		1836	StC	Prop
Neagle	????		1820	StL	Prop
Neal	William		1838	Steg	DTL
Neal	Thomas		1825	CGir	Lisc
Neal	Charles		1836	Carr	PrpPt
Neal	Arthur		1840	Call	Poll
Neal	John		1840	Call	Poll
Neal	William	H	1840	Call	Poll
Neal	Rueben		1818	StL	Real
Neal	Ruben		1820	StL	Prop
Neal	Harry	A	1844	Osag	Real
Neele	John	W	1838	Perr	Lisc
Neele	John		1838	Perr	Adv
Neely	John		1817	How	Prop
Neil	Benjamin		1840	Call	Poll

Last Name	First Name	Int	Year	County	Type
Neil	Joseph		1840	Call	Poll
Neiland	Martin		1867	Reyn	DTL
Neill	H	W	1840	Call	Poll
Neill	Stephen		1823	Call	NRP
Neiter	William		1830	Ray	Prop
Nelson	James		1840	Call	Poll
Nelson	Thomas		1840	Call	Poll
Nelson	James	R	1829	Mari	DTL
Nelson	Finnal		1834	Lew	DTL
Nelson	Ephraim		1834	Craw	DTL
Nelson	John		1834	Craw	DTL
Neotor	William		1836	Carr	PrpPt
Neptuno	(Free Negro)		1791	StL	Span
Nesbit	Thomas		1840	Call	Poll
Nesbit	Samuel		1840	Call	Poll
Nettle	William		1838	Ripl	DTL
Nettle	Shadrich		1834	Craw	DTL
Nevel	James	C	1815	Ark	Prop
Neville	Presley	I	1834	Call	DTL
Nevins	James		1840	Call	Poll
Nevins	Thomas		1840	Call	Poll
Nevins, Sr	John		1840	Call	Poll
Newberry	Thomas		1836	Perr	Poll
Newbill	Nathan		1834	Pett	Prop
Newbraugh	Joshua		1828	Boon	Lisc
Newell	George	S	1859	Reyn	DTL
Newell	Thomas		1829	Mari	DTL
Newell	Richard	W	1829	Mari	DTL
Newell	Thomas		1827	Mari	Prop
Newkirk	Barnet		1843	Audr	Prop
Newkirk	B	W	1843	Audr	Prop
Newkirk	Abraham		1867	Reyn	DTL
Newkirk	Abraham		1867	Reyn	DTL
Newland	Saml		1840	Call	Poll
Newlin	Peyton	W	1844	Osag	Real
Newman	William		1839	Plat	Prop
Newman	William	L	1867	Reyn	DTL
Newman	Alexander		1821	Ray	Prop
Newsom	Robert		1840	Call	Poll
Newsom	John		1830	Call	DTL
Newson	Alfred		1840	Call	Poll
Newton	James		1836	Carr	Prop

Last Name	First Name	Int	Year	County	Type
Newton	James		1836	Carr	PrpPt
Newton	John		1840	Call	Poll
Newton	James		1830	Ray	Prop
Nice	Geprge		1836	Carr	Prop
Nice	Geprge		1836	Carr	PrpPt
Nicholas	Ephraim		1836	Carr	Prop
Nicholas	Ephraim		1836	Carr	PrpPt
Nicholas	Robert		1867	Reyn	DTL
Nicholasgarden	John		1844	Osag	Real
Nichols	Samuel		1836	Carr	PrpPt
Nichols	William		1827	Boon	Lisc
Nichols	Bartet		1840	Call	Poll
Nichols	Daniel		1840	Call	Poll
Nichols	George		1840	Call	Poll
Nichols	Felix	G	1840	Call	Poll
Nichols	Jesse		1840	Call	Poll
Nichols	Frederick		1840	Call	Poll
Nichols	Garret		1840	Call	Poll
Nichols	William		1840	Call	Poll
Nichols	John		1821	Ray	Prop
Nichols	Danl	N	1834	Call	DTL
Nicholson	George	A	1840	Call	Poll
Nicholson	George		1834	Call	DTL
Nickel	James		1836	Perr	Poll
Nicolas	John	H	1836	Carr	Prop
Nicolas	John		1836	Carr	PrpPt
Nidever	John		1831	Cole	DTL
Night	Daniel		1839	Plat	Prop
Nilson	Gabriel		1839	Plat	Prop
Niovan	John		1867	Reyn	DTL
Nipp	John		1836	StC	Prop
Noarth	Martin		1836	StC	Prop
Noble	Thomas		1817	How	Prop
Nobles	Margaret		1844	Osag	Real
Nobles	Elizabeth		1844	Osag	Real
Noell	Chesley	M	1836	StC	Prop
Noise	J		1818	StL	Real
Noize	Tereze		1820	StL	Prop
Noland	Joshua		1839	Plat	Prop
Noland	Joel		1839	Plat	Prop
Noland	Nicholas		1839	Plat	Prop
Noland	Obed		1839	Plat	Prop

Last Name	First Name	Int	Year	County	Type
Noland	John		1839	Plat	Prop
Noland	Randolph		1836	Carr	Prop
Noland	Randolph		1836	Carr	PrpPt
Nolen	Randolph		1830	Ray	Prop
Nolen	Mordecai		1830	Ray	Prop
Nolley	Daniel		1840	Call	Poll
Norman	Elisha		1818	Lawr	DTL
Norman	Baranabas		1818	Lawr	DTL
Norman	Isaac		1839	Plat	Prop
Norris	Thomas		1843	Audr	Prop
Norris	Hosea		1839	Plat	Prop
Norris	Abner		1839	Plat	Prop
Norris	John	B	1836	Carr	PrpPt
North	James		1823	Call	NRP
Norton	David		1843	Audr	Prop
Norton	D		1843	Audr	Prop
Norton	R	J	1867	Reyn	DTL
Norvel	Harison		1843	Audr	Prop
Norvell	Thomason		1838	Audr	DTL
Norvell	J	M	1843	Char	DTL
Notrible	Edward		1815	Ark	Prop
Noval	Francis		1836	StC	Prop
Noval	Joseph		1836	StC	Prop
Nowell	James	C	1810	Ark	Prop
Null	John	W	1837	Perr	Lisc
Null	John		1837	Perr	Adv
Null	Thomas	A	1863	Jeff	Ass
Null	J	W	1863	Jeff	Ass
Nulls	W	J	1863	Jeff	Ass
Numan	Alex		1822	Clay	Poll
Nunley	Willis		1835	Barr	DTL
Nurchard	Samuel		1844	Osag	Real
Nutting	David		1821	Ray	Prop
O'Brien	Michael		1863	Jeff	Ass
O'Brien	Orren		1863	Jeff	Ass
O'Brien	Peter		1863	Jeff	Ass
O'Carrol	James	Y	1810	Ark	Prop
O'Connell	Dennis		1867	Reyn	DTL
O'Connell	Daniel		1867	Reyn	DTL
O'Conner	Patrick		1867	Reyn	DTL
O'Connor	Joseph	G	1831	Jack	DTL
O'Fallon	John		1818	StL	Real

Last Name	First Name	Int	Year	County	Type
O'Fallon	JOhn		1820	StL	Prop
O'Meara	Daniel		1836	Perr	Poll
O'Neal	Michael		1867	Reyn	DTL
O'Neil	Hugh		1820	StL	Prop
Oaks	William		1839	John	DTL
Oats	F	J	1867	Reyn	DTL
Obachon	Anthony		1805	Steg	Prop
Obachon	Augustus		1805	Steg	Prop
Obachon	Pierre		1805	Steg	Prop
Obannon	John		1834	Pett	Prop
Obannon	John		1834	Pett	PrpPt
Ober	J	R	1818	StL	Real
Ober	John	R	1820	StL	Prop
Obertson	W	H	1840	Call	Poll
Obeshon	Louis		1836	StC	Prop
Odana	John		1836	Carr	Prop
Odana	John		1836	Carr	PrpPt
Odd	William		1835	Barr	DTL
Odel	Abraham		1839	Lew	DTL
Odiniel	Levi		1830	Coop	Ct
Odnald	Martin		1843	Audr	Prop
Oearrel	James	Y	1815	Ark	Prop
Oeland	Henry		1867	Reyn	DTL
Offett	B	Z	1843	Audr	Prop
Officer	William		1821	Ray	Prop
Officer	James		1822	Clay	Poll
Officer	Thomas		1822	Clay	Poll
Offutt	John	E W	1840	Call	Poll
Ogden	John		1843	Audr	Prop
Ogden's Heirs	James		1836	Carr	Prop
Ogden's Heirs	James		1836	Carr	PrpPt
Ogle	Henry		1863	Jeff	Ass
Ogle	Joseph		1863	Jeff	Ass
Ogle	Jacob		1863	Jeff	Ass
Ogle	William		1834	Craw	DTL
Oldelier	Herman		1844	Osag	Real
Oldham	Jesse	D	1840	Call	Poll
Oldham	William		1840	Call	Poll
Olds	Bery		1840	Call	Poll
Olds	William		1840	Call	Poll
Olgie	Francis		1805	Steg	Prop
Oliphant	Samuel		1821	Ray	Prop

172

Last Name	First Name	Int	Year	County	Type
Oliver	Benjamin	A	1840	Call	Poll
Oliver	Thomas	H	1840	Call	Poll
Oliver	Isaac		1840	Call	Poll
Oliver	James		1840	Call	Poll
Oliver	John		1836	StC	Prop
Oliver, Sr	Isaac		1840	Call	Poll
Oltensinger	Stephen		1844	Osag	Real
Oneal	Michael		1867	Reyn	DTL
Oneal	Levi		1831	Cole	DTL
Ongee	Joseph		1836	StC	Prop
Orme	Robert		1840	Call	Poll
Orme	James	M	1840	Call	Poll
Ormen	Thomas		1822	NMad	Lisc
Orra	Annry		1780	StL	Mil
Orrich	Phillip		1836	StC	Prop
Orrick	????		1836	StC	Prop
Orrick	Cambel		1836	StC	Prop
Orrick	John		1836	StC	Prop
Orrick	Benj		1836	StC	Prop
Orrick	Benjamin		1836	StC	Prop
Orrick	W	D	1836	StC	Prop
Ortiz	Joseph		1780	StL	Mil
Osbanden	J	B	1859	Reyn	DTL
Osborn	John		1828	Boon	Lisc
Osburn's Heirs	Isaac		1836	Carr	Prop
Osburn's Heirs	Isaac		1836	Carr	PrpPt
Osgood	Aaron		1836	StC	Prop
Oslin	Martin		1843	Audr	Prop
Oslin	Jas		1843	Audr	Prop
Oslin	J		1843	Audr	Prop
Oslin	M		1843	Audr	Prop
Oslin	James		1838	Audr	DTL
Oslin	Martin		1838	Audr	DTL
Ostrander	Tunis		1836	Carr	Prop
Ostrander	Tunis		1836	Carr	PrpPt
Otonere, Sr	Luis		1780	StL	Mil
Ottin	John		1836	StC	Prop
Ovail	John		1836	Carr	Prop
Ovail	John		1836	Carr	PrpPt
Ovail	John		1830	Ray	Prop
Overall	Ezra		1836	StC	Prop
Overall	William	L	1836	StC	Prop

Last Name	First Name	Int	Year	County	Type
Overall's Heirs	Nathaniel		1836	StC	Prop
Overfelt (1)	Eli	M	1840	Call	Poll
Overfelt (2)	Eli	M	1840	Call	Poll
Overstreet	John		1836	StC	Prop
Overton	Benjamin	P	1836	Perr	Poll
Overton	Benjamin		1840	Call	Poll
Overton	James		1840	Call	Poll
Overton	Lewis		1840	Call	Poll
Overton	R	B	1840	Call	Poll
Overton	W	H	1839	Lew	DTL
Owen	N	P	1839	Plat	Prop
Owen	J	H	1839	Plat	Prop
Owen	Aaron		1839	Plat	Prop
Owen	Timothy		1839	Plat	Prop
Owen	Thomas		1827	Boon	Lisc
Owen	William	M	1867	Reyn	DTL
Owen	Lynch		1834	Call	DTL
Owens	Evan		1836	Carr	PrtPt
Owens	Robert		1829	Char	DTL
Owens	John		1821	Ray	Prop
Owens	Joel		1838	Ripl	DTL
Owings	Alvin		1843	Audr	Prop
Owings	Joshua		1843	Audr	Prop
Owings	B	H	1843	Audr	Prop
Owings	Preston		1843	Audr	Prop
Owings	Uriah		1843	Audr	Prop
Oxier	John		1840	Call	Poll
Pabels	Casy		1837	Boon	PM
Pace	James		1840	Call	Poll
Pace	John		1840	Call	Poll
Pace	W	H	1840	Call	Poll
Pack	Smith		1834	Call	DTL
Paesy	S		1843	Audr	Prop
Page	Joseph		1822	Clay	Poll
Page	Robert		1822	Clay	Poll
Page	Robert		1822	Clay	Poll
Pagel	Aken		1805	Steg	Prop
Paine	Robert		1840	Call	Poll
Pallarda	Peter		1836	StC	Prop
Pallarda	Bazel		1836	StC	Prop
Pallarda	Antwine		1836	StC	Prop
Pallarda, Jr	Peter		1836	StC	Prop

Last Name	First Name	Int	Year	County	Type
Pally	John	H	1844	Osag	Real
Palmer	James		1831	Jack	DTL
Palmer	Joel		1840	Call	Poll
Palmer	Mire		1867	Reyn	DTL
Palmer	Armstead		1844	Osag	Real
Panton	Claudio		1791	StL	Span
Papen	Joseph		1780	StL	Mil
Papin	Juan Maria		1780	StL	Mil
Papin	Jose Marie		1791	StL	Span
Papin	Pierre		1818	StL	Real
Papin	Pierre		1818	StL	Real
Papin	Joseph		1818	StL	Real
Papin	Alexander		1818	StL	Real
Papin	Joseph		1820	StL	Prop
Papin	Pierre Milicourt		1820	StL	Prop
Papin	Joseph		1820	StL	Prop
Paples	Alexander		1836	Carr	Prop
Paples	Alexander		1836	Carr	PrpPt
Par	Joseph		1780	StL	Mil
Paran	Todos Santos		1780	StL	Mil
Pardom	Breton		1838	Ripl	DTL
Parent	Todos Santos		1791	StL	Span
Parish	Samuel		1836	Carr	Prop
Parish	Samuel		1836	Carr	PrpPt
Parker	Nathan		1830	Wash	DTL
Parker	Wil		1859	Reyn	DTL
Parker	Louis		1836	Carr	Prop
Parker	Louis		1836	Carr	PrpPt
Parker	John		1828	Boon	Lisc
Parker	Oliver		1828	Boon	Lisc
Parker	Sidney		1840	Call	Poll
Parker	John		1810	Ark	Prop
Parker	John		1837	Boon	PM
Parkinson	William		1839	Wash	Lisc
Parks	Alfred	L	1836	Perr	Poll
Parks	Arthur		1820	StL	Prop
Parmer	John		1827	Mari	Prop
Parmer	Martin		1822	Clay	Poll
Parrish	Joseph		1837	Lew	DTL
Parrish	Ezekial		1827	Mari	Prop
Parry	Jos	G	1810	Ark	Prop
Parson	James		1844	Osag	Real

Last Name	First Name	Int	Year	County	Type
Parsons	John		1831	Jack	DTL
Parsons	I	M	1836	Carr	Prop
Parsons	I		1836	Carr	PrpPt
Parsons	Clark		1836	Carr	PrpPt
Parsons	Henry		1867	Reyn	DTL
Partnay	Eli		1863	Jeff	Ass
Parton	Edward		1859	Reyn	DTL
Pasont	Madam		1805	Steg	Prop
Pasquel	Joseph		1837	Lew	DTL
Pasquin	Noel		1829	NMad	DTL
Patchen	P	P	1836	StC	Prop
Pate	Thomas		1843	Audr	Prop
Pate	Miner		1843	Audr	Prop
Pate	Miner		1843	Audr	Prop
Pate	Minor		1838	Audr	DTL
Pate	Minor		1834	Call	DTL
Paterson	Michel		1810	Ark	Prop
Patri	Joseph		1836	StC	Prop
Patrick	James		1838	Steg	DTL
Patrick	George		1839	John	DTL
Patrick	Andrew		1839	John	DTL
Patrick	Luke		1817	How	Prop
Patten	James		1836	StC	Prop
Patterson	Jos		1837	Sali	DTL
Patterson	John		1836	Perr	Poll
Patterson	John		1838	Steg	DTL
Patterson	Joseph		1838	Steg	DTL
Patterson	John		1836	Carr	PrpPt
Patterson	Farris		1836	StC	Prop
Patterson	James		1836	StC	Prop
Patterson	Benjamin		1828	Sali	DTL
Patterson	Jesse		1823	How	DTL
Patterson	James		1838	Ripl	DTL
Patterson	John		1834	Call	DTL
Patterson	Jesse		1831	Craw	DTL
Pattibone	Rufus		1818	StL	Real
Patton	William		1840	Call	Poll
Patton	John		1840	Call	Poll
Patton	Thomas		1840	Call	Poll
Patton	Nath		1829	Char	DTL
Patton	Robert		1818	StL	Real
Patton	Robert		1818	StL	Real

Last Name	First Name	Int	Year	County	Type
Patton	Robert		1820	StL	Prop
Paty	Solomon		1780	StL	Mil
Paul	James		1867	Reyn	DTL
Paul	Rene		1820	StL	Prop
Paul	Gabriel		1820	StL	Prop
Pavey	Jesse	H	1828	Boon	Lisc
Pavsorvee	Thomas		1838	Ripl	DTL
Paxley	John		1836	Carr	Prop
Paxley	John		1836	Carr	PrpPt
Paxton	William		1836	Carr	Prop
Paxton	William		1836	Carr	PrpPt
Payne	M	M	1843	Audr	Prop
Payne	Archibald		1859	Reyn	DTL
Payne	William		1839	John	DTL
Pearce	William		1836	StC	Prop
Pearce, Jr	Thomas		1836	StC	Prop
Pearson	Richmond		1843	Audr	Prop
Pearson	Wm		1843	Audr	Prop
Pearson	Thomas	S	1843	Audr	Prop
Pearson	John	A	1843	Audr	Prop
Pearson	John	O P	1843	Audr	Prop
Pearson	Wm		1843	Audr	Prop
Pearson	J	O	1843	Audr	Prop
Pearson	Nathaniel		1838	Audr	DTL
Pearson	P	W	1838	Audr	DTL
Pearson	Richmond		1838	Audr	DTL
Pearson	William		1838	Audr	DTL
Pearson	J	A	1838	Audr	DTL
Pearson	Joseph		1838	Audr	DTL
Pearsons	Alfred		1867	Reyn	DTL
Peck	Ruduff		1821	StC	Ct
Peck	Ruduff		1821	StC	CtS
Peck	Horace	M	1867	Reyn	DTL
Peck	Charles		1836	StC	Prop
Pedlow	Jas	C	1867	Reyn	DTL
Peebley	Thomas		1822	Clay	Poll
Peebly	Hannah		1821	Ray	Prop
Peebly	Thomas		1821	Ray	Prop
Peeples	Alexander		1836	Carr	PrpPt
Peeples	Alex		1830	Ray	Prop
Peerce	William		1828	Boon	Lisc
Peery	John		1843	Audr	Prop

Last Name	First Name	Int	Year	County	Type
Peery	Thos		1843	Audr	Prop
Peery	Joseph	A	1843	Audr	Prop
Pelferson	E		1859	Reyn	DTL
Pelky	Joseph		1831	Jack	DTL
Pelky	Lewis		1831	Jack	DTL
Pelletier	Antonio		1791	StL	Span
Peltie	Pedro		1780	StL	Mil
Peltier	William		1830	Howa	DTL
Pemberton	John	C	1840	Call	Poll
Pemberton	Edmond		1840	Call	Poll
Pemberton	J	B	1840	Call	Poll
Pence, Sr	Thomas		1836	StC	Prop
Penington	William	A	1867	Reyn	DTL
Penison	Lud	C	1863	Jeff	Ass
Pepan	Pedro		1780	StL	Mil
Pepper	Saml		1863	Jeff	Ass
Peppers	James		1830	Jeff	DTL
Perciville	Michael		1867	Reyn	DTL
Peri	Pedro		1791	StL	Span
Perkins	Jesse		1843	Audr	Prop
Perkins	Jesse		1827	Boon	Lisc
Perkins	Jesse		1828	Boon	Lisc
Perkins	Benjamin		1840	Call	Poll
Perkins	Michael		1838	Audr	DTL
Perkins	Jesse		1838	Audr	DTL
Perkins	John		1838	Audr	DTL
Perkins	Levy		1844	Osag	Real
Peron	Joseph		1780	StL	Mil
Peronie	F	X	1818	StL	Real
Peronie	F	X	1818	StL	Real
Perrin	Caleb	H	1836	Perr	Poll
Perrin	George		1845	Sali	Lisc
Perrow	Joseph		1836	StC	Prop
Perrow	S	W	1836	StC	Prop
Perry	Solimon		1843	Audr	Prop
Perry	Miner		1843	Audr	Prop
Perry	Jon		1840	Call	Poll
Perry	Samuel		1817	How	Prop
Pertle	Cornelius		1836	Perr	Poll
Pertues	????		1815	Ark	Prop
Pescey	Widow		1820	StL	Prop
Peslay	Henry		1817	How	Prop

Last Name	First Name	Int	Year	County	Type
Peter	H	M	1859	Reyn	DTL
Peter	Harmon		1836	Carr	Prop
Peter	Harmon		1836	Carr	PrpPt
Peters	James		1836	Carr	Prop
Peters	Benjamin		1836	Carr	Prop
Peters	James		1836	Carr	PrpPt
Peters	Benjamin		1836	Carr	PrpPt
Peterson	David	K	1867	Reyn	DTL
Peterson	William		1810	Ark	Prop
Petrell	Michelle		1815	Ark	Prop
Petross	John		1840	Call	Poll
Pettibone	Rufus		1821	StC	Ct
Pettibone	Levi		1821	StC	Ct
Pettibone	Rufus		1821	StC	CtS
Pettigrew	John	W	1817	How	Prop
Pettis	Spencer		1829	Char	DTL
Pettitt	John		1810	Ark	Prop
Pettus	Mason		1836	Carr	Prop
Pettus	Mason		1836	Carr	PrpPt
Pettus	Thomas		1836	Carr	PrpPt
Petty	Alfred	M	1843	Audr	Prop
Petty	Jackson		1840	Call	Poll
Petty	Zachariah		1840	Call	Poll
Petty	William		1836	StC	Prop
Petty	Alfred		1838	Audr	DTL
Pety	Baptista		1780	StL	Mil
Peycott	William		1863	Jeff	Ass
Peyton	John		1840	Call	Poll
Peyton	Benjamin		1838	Ripl	DTL
Pharris	Thomas		1817	How	Prop
Pharris	John		1817	How	Prop
Phelpes	John		1836	StC	Prop
Phelps	Charles		1840	Call	Poll
Phelps	Robert		1844	Osag	Real
Phelps	James		1844	Osag	Real
Phelps	Holeman		1844	Osag	Real
Phelps	Pekien		1844	Osag	Real
Phelps	Charles		1844	Osag	Real
Philibert	Joseph		1820	StL	Prop
Philips	William		1859	Reyn	DTL
Philips	James		1836	Perr	Poll
Philips	Lewis		1867	Reyn	DTL

Last Name	First Name	Int	Year	County	Type
Philips	Henry		1867	Reyn	DTL
Philips	Zackeus		1810	Ark	Prop
Philips	Slyvanus		1810	Ark	Prop
Philipson	Joseph		1820	StL	Prop
Phillips	John		1836	Carr	PrtPt
Phillips	James		1844	Osag	Real
Phillips	Daniel		1844	Osag	Real
Phillips	Mary		1844	Osag	Real
Phillips	Moses		1844	Osag	Real
Piburn	Benjamin		1818	Lawr	DTL
Piburn	Edward		1821	Ray	Prop
Piburn	Edward		1822	Clay	Poll
Pica	Joseph		1840	Call	Poll
Pichet	Lester		1836	Carr	Prop
Pichet	Lester		1836	Carr	PrpPt
Pickam	Augustus		1844	Osag	Real
Pickamann	John		1844	Osag	Real
Pierce	Stephen		1836	Carr	PrpPt
Pierce	Samuel		1836	StC	Prop
Pierce	Robert		1821	Ray	Prop
Pierce	Stephen		1830	Ray	Prop
Pierce	James		1839	Lew	DTL
Pierce	Jonathan		1839	Lew	DTL
Pierce	Hugh		1835	Barr	DTL
Piget	Louis		1818	StL	Real
Pike	Dominick		1836	Carr	PrtPt
Pike	Dominike		1836	Carr	Prop
Pike	Dominike		1836	Carr	PrpPt
Pike	Dominick		1830	Ray	Prop
Piles	James	A	1838	Ripl	DTL
Pinconneau	Stephen		1820	StL	Prop
Pinkleton	David		1836	Perr	Poll
Pinnell	Acy		1844	Osag	Real
Piorer	Francois		1820	StL	Prop
Pipes	William		1830	Howa	DTL
Pipes	James		1817	How	Prop
Pitman	D	K	1836	StC	Prop
Pitman	Richard	B	1836	StC	Prop
Pitman	D	K	1836	StC	Prop
Pittis	George	R	1836	StC	Prop
Pitts	John		1827	Boon	Lisc
Pitzer	????		1820	StL	Prop

Last Name	First Name	Int	Year	County	Type
Pitzer	George		1820	StL	Prop
Pitzer's Heirs	George		1836	StC	Prop
Places	Louis		1810	Ark	Prop
Placet	Zeno		1838	Steg	DTL
Plancha	Pedro		1780	StL	Mil
Plank	John		1839	Lew	DTL
Plauo	Louis		1815	Ark	Prop
Poage	Robert		1817	How	Prop
Poe	Harden		1836	StC	Prop
Poes	William		1836	Carr	PrpPt
Pogue	Andrew		1821	Ray	Prop
Pogue	Andrew		1821	Ray	Prop
Pogur	Robert		1830	Coop	CtS
Poindexter	Oscar		1840	Call	Poll
Poindexter	Thomas		1840	Call	Poll
Poinsalate	Bazel		1836	StC	Prop
Poirier	Francois		1818	StL	Real
Poirier	Francis		1818	StL	Real
Pokern	Holmere	J	1836	StC	Prop
Polett	Paul		1805	Steg	Prop
Pollock	Andrew		1867	Reyn	DTL
Pollock	Hiram		1867	Reyn	DTL
Polly	John		1838	Ripl	DTL
Polo	Joseph		1780	StL	Mil
Pomroy	Oliver		1867	Reyn	DTL
Pomroy	Oliver		1867	Reyn	DTL
Poncen	Moses		1844	Osag	Real
Pool	Jas	L	1831	Cole	DTL
Pool	Asa		1835	Barr	DTL
Pool's Heirs	Hiram		1836	Carr	Prop
Pool's Heirs	Hiram		1836	Carr	PrpPt
Pool's Heirs	Hiram		1830	Ray	Prop
Poor	David		1838	Ripl	DTL
Porceline	Jean		1818	StL	Real
Porcelly	Wid Madam		1791	StL	Span
Porcelly	John		1820	StL	Prop
Porsley	Juan Pedro		1780	StL	Mil
Porten	Francisco		1780	StL	Mil
Porter	Stanfield		1843	Audr	Prop
Porter	Juan		1780	StL	Mil
Porter	Warner		1837	Cass	DTL
Porter	John		1838	Cass	DTL

Last Name	First Name	Int	Year	County	Type
Porter	Hugh		1836	Carr	Prop
Porter	Hugh		1836	Carr	PrpPt
Porter	William	C	1830	Coop	Ct
Porter	Jas	W	1863	Jeff	Ass
Porter	R	J	1863	Jeff	Ass
Porter	Henry		1836	StC	Prop
Porter	Hugh		1821	Ray	Prop
Porter	Joseph		1821	Ray	Prop
Porter	Hugh		1830	Ray	Prop
Porter	William		1844	Osag	Real
Portzey	William		1836	StC	Prop
Posey	Joseph	A	1838	Audr	DTL
Postal	William		1821	StC	Ct
Pothoff	Francis	M	1840	Call	Poll
Potie	Luis		1780	StL	Mil
Potter	John		1830	Coop	Ct
Potter	John		1830	Coop	CtS
Potter	John		1834	Pett	Prop
Potter	John		1834	Pett	PrpPt
Potter	Elridge		1821	Ray	Prop
Potter	Elijah		1837	Lew	DTL
Potter	William	C	1820	StL	Prop
Potter	John	C	1820	StL	Prop
Potter	David		1820	StL	Prop
Potts	John		1843	Audr	Prop
Pottz	John		1838	Audr	DTL
Poulton	T	W	1837	Lew	DTL
Powel	Robert		1843	Audr	Prop
Powel	Alford		1843	Audr	Prop
Powel	Monroe		1843	Audr	Prop
Powel	L	E	1836	StC	Prop
Powell	Richard		1836	Carr	Prop
Powell	Richard		1836	Carr	PrpPt
Powell	Thomas	L	1840	Call	Poll
Powell	James	H	1840	Call	Poll
Powell	Charles	L	1840	Call	Poll
Powell	James	H	1840	Call	Poll
Powell	John		1867	Reyn	DTL
Powell	P	H	1838	Audr	DTL
Powell	Nathaniel		1822	Clay	Poll
Powell	Thomas	L	1844	Osag	Real
Power	George		1836	StC	Prop

Last Name	First Name	Int	Year	County	Type
Powers	Clement		1836	Perr	Poll
Powers	Jeffery		1836	Perr	Poll
Powers	Alexander		1844	Osag	Real
Praer	Joel	F	1821	StC	Ct
Prange	Schrale		1859	Reyn	DTL
Pranz	Schrall		1859	Reyn	DTL
Pratee	Peter	R	1837	Perr	Lisc
Prater	Jn Baptiste		1805	Steg	Prop
Prather	John		1818	StL	Real
Pratt	Joseph		1805	Steg	Prop
Pratt	John		1859	Reyn	DTL
Pratt	Fk		1836	Perr	Poll
Pratt	Thomas	J	1840	Call	Poll
Pratt	William		1840	Call	Poll
Pratt	James		1810	Ark	Prop
Pratt	John		1810	Ark	Prop
Pratt	Joseph		1820	StL	Prop
Pratt	Bernard		1820	StL	Prop
Pratte	Joseph		1837	Perr	Lisc
Pratte	Peter	R	1837	Perr	Lisc
Pratte	Peter		1837	Perr	Adv
Pratte	P	R	1836	Perr	Poll
Pratte	Bernard		1820	StL	Prop
Preor	Noil Ant		1836	StC	Prop
Preston	George		1836	Perr	Poll
Preston	William		1836	StC	Prop
Prewett	Laburn		1863	Jeff	Ass
Prewett	George	M	1867	Reyn	DTL
Prewit	Samuel		1821	Ray	Prop
Prewitt	Galbreath		1828	Sali	DTL
Price	John	M	1843	Audr	Prop
Price	John		1805	Steg	Prop
Price	Columbus		1836	Perr	Poll
Price	William		1836	Perr	Poll
Price	William		1836	Carr	PrtPt
Price	Francis		1836	Carr	Prop
Price	Francis		1836	Carr	PrpPt
Price	Courtland	W	1836	Carr	PrpPt
Price	Jas		1840	Call	Poll
Price	William	M	1863	Jeff	Ass
Price	Frederick		1836	StC	Prop
Price	George		1836	StC	Prop

Last Name	First Name	Int	Year	County	Type
Price	Augustus		1836	StC	Prop
Price	Jacob		1836	StC	Prop
Price	Risdon	H	1823	Call	NRP
Price	Michael		1836	StC	Prop
Price	William		1836	StC	Prop
Price	Risdon	H	1820	StL	Prop
Price	Christoph	M	1820	StL	Prop
Price	????		1820	StL	Prop
Price	William		1830	Ray	Prop
Pricer	S	M	1859	Reyn	DTL
Pricer	Samuel	M	1867	Reyn	DTL
Prigamore	Benjn		1834	Pett	Prop
Prigamore	Benjn		1834	Pett	PrpPt
Primen, Sr	John		1820	StL	Prop
Primo	Paul		1830	Linc	DTL
Primo	Paul		1820	StL	Prop
Primor	Juan Bapt		1791	StL	Span
Prince	William	H	1836	StC	Prop
Prine	Willian		1821	Ray	Prop
Prine	Daniel		1831	Cole	DTL
Pringle	Christopher		1815	Ark	Prop
Pringle, Jr	Isaac		1829	NMad	DTL
Prior	Frederich		1836	StC	Prop
Prior	Norial John		1836	StC	Prop
Pritchard	Bird		1837	Lew	DTL
Pritchard	William		1827	Mari	Prop
Pritchard	P	B	1839	Lew	DTL
Pritchet	Henry		1836	StC	Prop
Pritchet	Robert		1821	Ray	Prop
Prite	Humphrey		1822	Clay	Poll
Probanche	Juan Bapt		1780	StL	Mil
Probo	Juan		1780	StL	Mil
Proctor	Edward		1810	Ark	Prop
Proctor	Nicholas		1817	How	Prop
Proffitt	John		1821	Ray	Prop
Provenche	Juan Bapt		1791	StL	Span
Provenchere	Pierre		1818	StL	Real
Provenchere	Peter		1820	StL	Prop
Provenchere	Jean Louis		1820	StL	Prop
Provenchire	Jean	S	1818	StL	Real
Pryor	Quales		1818	StL	Real
Puckett	A	H	1837	Perr	Lisc

Last Name	First Name	Int	Year	County	Type
Puckett	Alfred	H	1837	Perr	Lisc
Puckett	Alfred		1837	Perr	Adv
Puckett	Alfred	H	1838	Perr	Lisc
Puckett	Alfred		1838	Perr	Adv
Pugget	Lurent		1818	StL	Real
Pujet	Louis		1836	StC	Prop
Pujol	Louis		1836	StC	Prop
Puliam	Asa		1840	Call	Poll
Pulie	(Negro)		1818	StL	Real
Pullem	Samuel	G	1836	StC	Prop
Pulliam	John	S	1840	Call	Poll
Pulliam	Henry		1840	Call	Poll
Pulliam	Levi		1840	Call	Poll
Pulliam	John	W	1840	Call	Poll
Pullim	John		1836	Perr	Poll
Pullis	David		1829	Mari	DTL
Pulls	Ruebin		1838	Audr	DTL
Pulus	R		1843	Audr	Prop
Pume	Madam		1815	Ark	Prop
Purdon	Hezekiah		1817	How	Prop
Purnell	Sampson		1844	Osag	Real
Pursell	David		1836	Carr	Prop
Pursell	David		1836	Carr	PrpPt
Pursley	John		1817	How	Prop
Putman	Joseph		1867	Reyn	DTL
Quale	William		1838	Ripl	DTL
Quarles	Paschall		1836	Carr	Prop
Quarles	Paschall		1836	Carr	PrpPt
Quarles	Prior		1830	Call	DTL
Quarles	Prior		1818	StL	Real
Quarles	David		1820	StL	Prop
Quenal	Pedro		1791	StL	Span
Quick	Stephen		1840	Call	Poll
Quinn	John		1859	Reyn	DTL
Quinn	George		1867	Reyn	DTL
Quoenel	Pedro		1780	StL	Mil
Rabbs	George		1820	StL	Prop
Racine	Tana	B	1810	Ark	Prop
Racine	Jacko		1810	Ark	Prop
Ragland	N		1827	Coop	DTL
Ragland	Finess		1836	Carr	PrtPt
Ragland	N		1827	Coop	DTL

Last Name	First Name	Int	Year	County	Type
Ragland	French		1830	Ray	Prop
Raimen	Phillip		1815	Ark	Prop
Rain	Absalom		1830	Coop	Ct
Raine	Athanas		1815	Ark	Prop
Raine	Jacob		1815	Ark	Prop
Ralatathein	I		1825	CGir	Lisc
Ramey	James		1834	Pett	Prop
Ramey	James		1834	Pett	PrpPt
Ramey	William		1863	Jeff	Ass
Ramsay	Lambert		1829	Char	DTL
Ramsay	Jonathan		1829	Char	DTL
Ramsay	Jonatahn		1830	Call	DTL
Ramsey	Charles		1836	Carr	Prop
Ramsey	Charles		1836	Carr	PrpPt
Ramsey	Washington		1840	Call	Poll
Ramsey	L	L	1838	Audr	DTL
Ramsy	Euel	L	1840	Call	Poll
Ramsy	Jonithan		1840	Call	Poll
Rancombe	Antoine		1818	StL	Real
Randal	John		1827	Mari	Prop
Randolph	F	M	1839	Plat	Prop
Randolph	Payton		1836	Carr	Prop
Randolph	Payton		1836	Carr	PrpPt
Rangie	Pierre		1805	Steg	Prop
Rankeen	????		1820	StL	Prop
Rankin	Thomas	G	1840	Call	Poll
Rannebarger	Otho		1840	Call	Poll
Ranney	Allen	D	1840	Call	Poll
Rariddon	William		1836	Perr	Poll
Rashaw	John		1836	StC	Prop
Rassor	Joel		1836	StC	Prop
Rattan	Julien		1805	Steg	Prop
Rawley	John		1840	Call	Poll
Rawling	Hiram		1840	Call	Poll
Rawls	Daniel		1817	How	Prop
Ray	Sidney		1839	Plat	Prop
Ray	Aaron		1836	Carr	Prop
Ray	Alexdego	I	1836	Carr	Prop
Ray	Aaron		1836	Carr	PrpPt
Ray	Alexdego		1836	Carr	PrpPt
Ray	Saml		1839	Wash	Lisc
Ray	John		1830	Ray	Prop

Last Name	First Name	Int	Year	County	Type
Rayburn	Joseph		1830	Wash	DTL
Raymond	Gilbert		1836	Carr	Prop
Raymond	Gilbert		1836	Carr	PrpPt
Rayne	Robert		1830	Howa	DTL
Read	John	A	1843	Audr	Prop
Read	Granville		1843	Audr	Prop
Read	Israel	B	1826	Coop	DTL
Read	Israel	B	1827	Coop	DTL
Read	Solomon		1834	Pett	Prop
Read	Isreal	B	1829	Char	DTL
Read	John	A	1838	Audr	DTL
Read	Granville		1838	Audr	DTL
Read	Lewis		1837	Boon	PM
Read	Isreal	B	1827	Coop	DTL
Read	Isreal	B	1826	Coop	DTL
Read	John		1834	Call	DTL
Readhorst	John	D	1836	StC	Prop
Readman	John		1836	StC	Prop
Readman	Lucy		1836	StC	Prop
Readman's Heirs	George		1836	StC	Prop
Ready	W	H	1863	Jeff	Ass
Realie	Anthony	E	1821	StC	Ct
Reams	Unity		1834	Pett	Prop
Reams	Absalom		1834	Pett	PrpPt
Reaves	Samuel		1835	Barr	DTL
Recontre	Antoine		1820	StL	Prop
Rector	William		1823	Call	NRP
Rector	Elias		1823	Call	NRP
Rector	Stephen		1818	StL	Real
Rector	William		1820	StL	Prop
Rector	Elias		1817	How	Prop
Redcock	William		1825	Char	DTL
Redford	William		1836	Perr	Poll
Redman	Thomas		1836	StC	Prop
Redman	Daniel		1825	Char	DTL
Reece	Abrahm		1817	How	Prop
Reece	William		1817	How	Prop
Reed	Jas		1843	Audr	Prop
Reed	Garrison		1839	Plat	Prop
Reed	John	C	1839	Wash	Lisc
Reed	Jno	C	1839	Wash	Lisc
Reed	John		1840	Call	Poll

187

Last Name	First Name	Int	Year	County	Type
Reed	William		1830	Coop	Ct
Reed	William		1830	Coop	CtS
Reed	Ezrea		1867	Reyn	DTL
Reed	Absalom		1821	Ray	Prop
Reed	Jonathan		1821	Ray	Prop
Reed	John	H	1818	StL	Real
Reed	Jacob		1818	StL	Real
Reed	John	H	1820	StL	Prop
Reed	Jacob		1820	StL	Prop
Reed	Andrew		1833	Wayn	DTL
Reed	Jonathan		1822	Clay	Poll
Reed	Thomas	W	1838	Ripl	DTL
Reeder	H		1838	Steg	DTL
Reeder	Martin		1836	StC	Prop
Reeder	George		1836	StC	Prop
Reeder	Provelluven		1829	NMad	DTL
Reenes	Benj	H	1830	Howa	DTL
Reese	????		1820	StL	Prop
Reeves	Howard		1840	Call	Poll
Reeves	Burrel		1836	StC	Prop
Refelo	Charles		1810	Ark	Prop
Reid	Archibald		1834	Call	DTL
Reilhe	Antonio		1791	StL	Span
Reils	Anthony	E	1821	StC	Ct
Rellmer	Jacob		1867	Reyn	DTL
Remmons	John		1836	StC	Prop
Renard	Hyacinthe		1820	StL	Prop
Renau	Antoine		1820	StL	Prop
Rencomber, Jr	Antoine		1820	StL	Prop
Rendfro	Wade		1838	Ripl	DTL
Renfro	Calvin		1840	Call	Poll
Renfro	William		1840	Call	Poll
Renfro	Ratio		1838	Ripl	DTL
Renfro	Bluford		1838	Ripl	DTL
Renfro	Mark		1834	Call	DTL
Renick	Leonard	H	1838	John	DTL
Renjstoft	Louis		1836	StC	Prop
Renn	James		1836	Carr	Prop
Renn	James		1836	Carr	PrpPt
Rennard	Daniel		1836	StC	Prop
Renner	Roden		1836	StC	Prop
Rennick	Phelix		1827	Sali	DTL

Last Name	First Name	Int	Year	County	Type
Rennick	William		1827	Sali	DTL
Renolontete	Antoine		1818	StL	Real
Renshaw	William		1820	StL	Prop
Rensome	John	H	1840	Call	Poll
Renty	John	J	1822	NMad	Lisc
Reusau	Nicholas		1805	Steg	Prop
Reusau	N		1805	Steg	Prop
Revierre	Wid Marianne		1820	StL	Prop
Revis	G	W	1844	Osag	Real
Rexroad	Frederick	A	1836	StC	Prop
Reynal	Antonio		1791	StL	Span
Reynold	Antoine		1821	StC	CtS
Reynold	Antwine		1836	StC	Prop
Reynold	Thomas	C	1834	Call	DTL
Reynolds	Allen	C	1843	Audr	Prop
Reynolds	Oston		1843	Audr	Prop
Reynolds	J	G	1843	Audr	Prop
Reynolds	Edward		1859	Reyn	DTL
Reynolds	James	P	1840	Call	Poll
Reynolds	John		1840	Call	Poll
Reynolds	Bedford		1840	Call	Poll
Reynolds	James		1840	Call	Poll
Reynolds	H	T	1867	Reyn	DTL
Reynolds	Francis		1836	StC	Prop
Reynolds	Russell		1821	Ray	Prop
Reynolds	James		1821	Ray	Prop
Reynolds	James		1810	Ark	Prop
Reynolds	William		1838	Audr	DTL
Reynolds	Obediah		1820	StL	Prop
Rhea	William		1838	Cass	DTL
Rhea	Lund		1836	Carr	Prop
Rhea	Lund		1836	Carr	PrpPt
Rhoadcriss	William		1844	Osag	Real
Rhoadcriss	Lewis		1844	Osag	Real
Rhoads	Charles		1844	Osag	Real
Rhodes	Corns.		1838	Steg	DTL
Riam	Abasalom		1830	Coop	CtS
Ribar	Joseph		1780	StL	Mil
Ribet	Joseph		1780	StL	Mil
Ricard	Pedro		1791	StL	Span
Rice	John		1836	Perr	Poll
Rice	David		1836	Carr	Prop

Last Name	First Name	Int	Year	County	Type
Rice	David		1836	Carr	PrpPt
Rice	Hollem		1836	StC	Prop
Rice	S	W	1836	StC	Prop
Rice	Simeon		1836	StC	Prop
Rice	Hollen		1836	StC	Prop
Rice	Nathaniel		1836	StC	Prop
Rice	George	A	1839	John	DTL
Rice	Elijah		1827	Mari	Prop
Richard	Meavet		1836	Carr	Prop
Richard	Meavet	B	1836	Carr	PrpPt
Richards	Joel		1836	StC	Prop
Richards	William		1821	Ray	Prop
Richards	Lewis		1821	Ray	Prop
Richards	Lewis		1817	How	Prop
Richards	Lewis		1822	Clay	Poll
Richardson	Zacheus		1836	Carr	Prop
Richardson	Zacheus		1836	Carr	PrpPt
Richardson	B	F	1867	Reyn	DTL
Richardson	T	D	1867	Reyn	DTL
Richardson	D	p	1867	Reyn	DTL
Richardson	Jesse		1817	How	Prop
Richardson	Silas		1817	How	Prop
Richardson	Samuel		1831	Cole	DTL
Richardson	Zacheus		1830	Ray	Prop
Richardson	Benjamin		1834	Craw	DTL
Richardson	Abram		1837	Mill	DTL
Richey	Cinthia		1836	StC	Prop
Richmond	Henry		1836	Carr	PrpPt
Ride	Lorenzo		1780	StL	Mil
Ride	Luis		1780	StL	Mil
Riden	Joseph		1834	Craw	DTL
Ridgeway	Ninian		1840	Call	Poll
Ridgeway	Thomas		1840	Call	Poll
Ridgeway	William		1817	How	Prop
Ridgway	Reason		1843	Audr	Prop
Riffe	Jacob		1821	Ray	Prop
Riffe	John		1821	Ray	Prop
Riggs	James	B	1839	Plat	Prop
Riggs	William		1836	Carr	Prop
Riggs	William		1836	Carr	PrpPt
Riggs	Timothy		1821	Ray	Prop
Riggs	James		1831	Cole	DTL

Last Name	First Name	Int	Year	County	Type
Riggs	Isaac		1839	Lew	DTL
Riggs	James		1837	Mill	DTL
Right	F	M	1859	Reyn	DTL
Rightsman	John		1821	Ray	Prop
Riley	James		1834	Craw	DTL
Riney	Thomas		1836	Perr	Poll
Ringer	William		1839	Lew	DTL
Ringo	Henry		1836	StC	Prop
Rinz	Josef		1791	StL	Span
Rissinger	Adam		1819	Steg	Lic
Ritchey	William		1827	Mari	Prop
Rittson	William		1867	Reyn	DTL
River	Antonio		1791	StL	Span
Rivera	Estevan		1780	StL	Mil
Rivera	Antonio		1780	StL	Mil
Rivera	Baptista		1780	StL	Mil
Rivera	Phelipe		1780	StL	Mil
Rivera	Antonio		1791	StL	Span
Riviera	Felipe		1791	StL	Span
Rivire	Wid M		1818	StL	Real
Roach	T	J	1867	Reyn	DTL
Roach	Thomas		1867	Reyn	DTL
Robbins	Welcome	A	1836	StC	Prop
Robbins	Thomas	J	1836	StC	Prop
Robbins	Frederick		1836	StC	Prop
Robbins	Thadeus	E	1836	StC	Prop
Robbns	Moses	B	1836	StC	Prop
Roben	Mesami	P	1805	Steg	Prop
Roberson	Henry		1867	Reyn	DTL
Robert	Pierre		1805	Steg	Prop
Roberts	Michael		1843	Audr	Prop
Roberts	Jesse		1843	Audr	Prop
Roberts	Richard		1859	Reyn	DTL
Roberts	Richard		1859	Reyn	DTL
Roberts	Abraham		1836	Perr	Poll
Roberts	Thomas		1836	Carr	PrpPt
Roberts	William		1836	Carr	Prop
Roberts	Thomas		1836	Carr	Prop
Roberts	William		1836	Carr	PrpPt
Roberts	Thomas		1836	Carr	PrpPt
Roberts	Jacob		1836	Carr	PrpPt
Roberts	John		1827	Boon	Lisc

Last Name	First Name	Int	Year	County	Type
Roberts	Edward		1821	Ray	Prop
Roberts	Nicholas		1821	Ray	Prop
Roberts	Aaron		1821	Ray	Prop
Roberts	Samuel		1821	Ray	Prop
Roberts	Tilman		1829	Mari	DTL
Roberts	Thomas		1829	Mari	DTL
Roberts	John		1817	How	Prop
Roberts	Ligelman		1839	Lew	DTL
Roberts	Jonathan		1822	Clay	Poll
Roberts	Jonas		1822	Clay	Poll
Roberts	Edmond		1822	Clay	Poll
Roberts	Nicholas		1822	Clay	Poll
Roberts	John		1822	Clay	Poll
Roberts	James		1837	Bent	DTL
Roberts	Asa		1829	NMad	DTL
Roberts	John		1829	NMad	DTL
Robertson	William		1839	Plat	Prop
Robertson	Charles		1839	Plat	Prop
Robertson	William		1836	Carr	Prop
Robertson	William		1836	Carr	PrpPt
Robertson	William		1817	How	Prop
Robertson	John		1835	Barr	DTL
Robertson	William		1843	Char	DTL
Robertson	Adolphus		1834	Call	DTL
Robertson	George		1834	Call	DTL
Robertson's Heirs	Isaac		1836	StC	Prop
Robey	Hezekiah		1829	Mari	DTL
Robideaux	Joasdose		1821	StC	Ct
Robidoux	Joseph		1820	StL	Prop
Robidoux	Francis		1820	StL	Prop
Robieu	Gasper		1791	StL	Span
Robinette	Moses		1828	Boon	Lisc
Robinette	I		1828	Boon	Lisc
Robinson	Baldwin		1818	Lawr	DTL
Robinson	William		1836	Carr	PrpPt
Robinson	Mathias		1836	Carr	PrpPt
Robinson	Willis		1836	Carr	PrpPt
Robinson	John		1836	Carr	Prop
Robinson	Hugh		1836	Carr	Prop
Robinson	John		1836	Carr	PrpPt
Robinson	Hugh		1836	Carr	PrpPt
Robinson	G		1828	Boon	Lisc

Last Name	First Name	Int	Year	County	Type
Robinson	Jas		1828	Boon	Lisc
Robinson	John		1823	Call	NRP
Robinson	Geo		1829	Char	DTL
Robinson	Andrew		1810	Ark	Prop
Robinson	Hugh		1830	Ray	Prop
Robinson	F		1844	Osag	Real
Robinson	Ryston		1844	Osag	Real
Robinson	Drusilla		1844	Osag	Real
Robnet	Zepheniah		1827	Mari	Prop
Rochester	John		1821	StC	CtS
Rochester	John	C	1830	Coop	Ct
Rochester	John	C	1830	Coop	Ct
Rochester	John		1836	StC	Prop
Rockeblave	????		1820	StL	Prop
Rockford	Francis		1820	StL	Prop
Rodes	Joseph		1836	Perr	Poll
Rodgers	G	W	1867	Reyn	DTL
Rodman	W	E H	1837	Lew	DTL
Roe	William		1835	Barr	DTL
Roger	John		1836	Carr	Prop
Roger	John		1836	Carr	PrpPt
Rogers	Russell		1839	Plat	Prop
Rogers	John		1839	Plat	Prop
Rogers	James	M	1839	Plat	Prop
Rogers	Anderson		1839	Plat	Prop
Rogers	John	P	1839	Plat	Prop
Rogers	William		1836	Carr	PrpPt
Rogers	Thomas		1836	Carr	Prop
Rogers	Thomas		1836	Carr	PrpPt
Rogers	Thomas		1830	Coop	Ct
Rogers	Derick		1810	Ark	Prop
Rogers	William	R	1839	John	DTL
Rogers	William		1831	Cole	DTL
Rogers	Thomas	F	1830	Ray	Prop
Rogerson	Abell		1836	Carr	Prop
Rogerson	Abell		1836	Carr	PrpPt
Roggers	George	W	1867	Reyn	DTL
Rogoche	Wid. Mada.		1791	StL	Span
Rogues	Joseph		1863	Jeff	Ass
Rogus	Jeremiah	S	1836	Carr	Prop
Rogus	John		1836	Carr	Prop
Rogus	Jeremiah	S	1836	Carr	PrpPt

193

Last Name	First Name	Int	Year	County	Type
Rogus	John		1836	Carr	PrpPt
Rollet dit Laderout	Michae;		1818	StL	Real
Rollett's Heirs	William		1836	Carr	Prop
Rollett's Heirs	William		1836	Carr	PrpPt
Rollins	John		1838	Cass	DTL
Rollins	William		1821	Ray	Prop
Rolls	Silas		1815	Ark	Prop
Rolls	Daniel		1815	Ark	Prop
Rolls, Jr	Silas		1815	Ark	Prop
Rolston	William		1839	Plat	Prop
Romain	John		1830	Ray	Prop
Romine	John		1836	Carr	PrpPt
Roney	John	M	1834	Call	DTL
Roobatham	William		1867	Reyn	DTL
Roobathem	William		1867	Reyn	DTL
Roque	Thomas	T	1836	Carr	PrpPt
Roque	Augustin		1791	StL	Span
Rose	Jeremiah		1839	Plat	Prop
Rose	Thomas		1836	Carr	PrpPt
Rose	Jeremiah		1822	Clay	Poll
Roseassboum	Joseph		1867	Reyn	DTL
Roseberry	William		1830	Ray	Prop
Rosebury	William		1836	Carr	PrpPt
Rosenberger	Martin		1867	Reyn	DTL
Ross	Samuel		1839	Plat	Prop
Ross	Robert		1839	Plat	Prop
Ross	John		1836	Perr	Poll
Ross	John		1836	Perr	Poll
Ross	William		1830	Coop	Ct
Ross	Churchill	B	1830	Coop	Ct
Ross	William		1830	Coop	CtS
Ross	Churchill	B	1830	Coop	CtS
Ross	Stephen		1843	Char	DTL
Ross' Heirs	Lawrence		1836	StC	Prop
Rosseau	John		1836	StC	Prop
Rosseau	Joseph		1836	StC	Prop
Rosseau, Sr's Heirs	Francis		1836	StC	Prop
Rotard	Josef		1791	StL	Span
Rouce	Jacob		1836	StC	Prop
Rouels	William		1836	Carr	Prop
Rouels	William		1836	Carr	PrpPt
Rouo	John		1839	Plat	Prop

Last Name	First Name	Int	Year	County	Type
Roup	David		1839	Plat	Prop
Roup	William		1839	Plat	Prop
Roup	James		1839	Plat	Prop
Roussin	E		1839	Wash	Lisc
Rouvenbergach	Frederick		1836	StC	Prop
Rover	Luis		1780	StL	Mil
Rowan	John		1835	Barr	DTL
Rowan	William		1835	Barr	DTL
Rowe	John		1863	Jeff	Ass
Rowe	Riley		1863	Jeff	Ass
Rowland	Dowdle		1821	Ray	Prop
Rowland	George		1821	Ray	Prop
Rowland	Mathew		1821	Ray	Prop
Rowland	John		1833	Lew	DTL
Rowland	Thomas		1834	Lew	DTL
Rowley	Russel	B	1836	Carr	Prop
Rowley	Russel		1836	Carr	PrpPt
Roy	Nicolas		1780	StL	Mil
Roy	Carlos		1780	StL	Mil
Roy	Pedro		1780	StL	Mil
Roy	Joachim		1780	StL	Mil
Roy	Louis		1837	Cass	DTL
Roy	Charles		1836	Perr	Poll
Roy	Pedro		1791	StL	Span
Roy	Julian		1791	StL	Span
Roy	Joaquin		1791	StL	Span
Roy	Josef		1791	StL	Span
Roy	Pattrice		1836	StC	Prop
Roy	Julien		1836	StC	Prop
Roylance	John		1831	Jack	DTL
Rozier	Ferdinand		1823	Steg	Lisc
Rozier	Ferdinand		1836	Perr	Lisc
Rozier	Ferdinand		1837	Perr	Lisc
Rozier	Ferdinand		1837	Perr	Adv
Rozier, Jr	Ferdinand		1838	Perr	Lisc
Rozier, Jr	Ferdinand		1838	Perr	Adv
Rpgan	Zededoah		1867	Reyn	DTL
Rubbles' Heirs	Jacob		1836	Carr	PrpPt
Rubidu	Joseph		1780	StL	Mil
Rubio	Joseph		1780	StL	Mil
Ruby	Henry		1830	Coop	Ct
Ruby	Thomas		1830	Coop	CtS

Last Name	First Name	Int	Year	County	Type
Ruchester	I		1810	Ark	Prop
Rucker	George	W	1840	Call	Poll
Ruckey	Thomson		1836	Perr	Poll
Rudal	Polly		1829	NMad	DTL
Rudder	Jacob		1818	Lawr	DTL
Rudder	Epaphrodites		1836	Carr	Prop
Rudder	Epaphrodites		1836	Carr	PrpPt
Ruddy	Jas		1843	Char	DTL
Rudy	Peter		1840	Call	Poll
Rueben	Wilson		1844	Osag	Real
Ruggels	Michael		1836	Carr	PrpPt
Ruggles	Benjamin		1839	Wash	Lisc
Ruland	John		1830	Linc	DTL
Rummons	John		1839	Plat	Prop
Runkle	Matthew	M	1843	Audr	Prop
Rupard	Erasmus		1836	StC	Prop
Rupe	Gillead		1817	How	Prop
Rush	John		1827	Mari	Prop
Rush	Susannah		1827	Mari	Prop
Rush	Gabriel		1827	Mari	Prop
Russal	James		1820	StL	Prop
Russel	Lewis		1843	Audr	Prop
Russel	Andrew		1821	Ray	Prop
Russel	Alexander		1835	Barr	DTL
Russell	Alexander		1839	Plat	Prop
Russell	W		1836	Carr	Prop
Russell	Philip		1836	Carr	Prop
Russell	Philip		1836	Carr	PrpPt
Russell	William		1830	Jeff	DTL
Russell	William		1830	Linc	DTL
Russell	William		1830	Ray	Prop
Russell, Jr	Robert	S	1840	Call	Poll
Rutherford	Samuel		1829	Char	DTL
Rutherford	Saul		1829	Char	DTL
Ruthey	John	P	1833	Wayn	DTL
Rutledge	David		1839	Plat	Prop
Rutledge	James		1839	Plat	Prop
Rutledge	J	A	1837	Perr	Lisc
Rutledge	Jonas	A	1837	Perr	Adv
Rutledge	Jonas	A	1837	Perr	Lisc
Rutledge	Charles	C	1838	Perr	Lisc
Rutledge	Charles		1838	Perr	Adv

Last Name	First Name	Int	Year	County	Type
Rutledge	George		1836	Perr	Poll
Rutledge	William		1836	Perr	Poll
Rutter	E		1828	Boon	Lisc
Rutter	Edmund		1827	Mari	Prop
Rutter	Fleix	G	1827	Mari	Prop
Ryan	John		1859	Reyn	DTL
Ryan	Jas		1840	Call	Poll
Ryon	Elisha		1836	Carr	Prop
Ryon	Elisha		1836	Carr	PrpPt
Sabourin	Pierre		1820	StL	Prop
Sabourn	Peter		1818	StL	Real
Sack	Ferdinand		1836	StC	Prop
Sack	John		1836	StC	Prop
Saddler	Alfred		1836	Perr	Poll
Saddler	Fedeston		1836	Perr	Poll
Saddler	Joseph		1836	Perr	Poll
Saddler	James		1836	Perr	Poll
Saddler	John		1836	Perr	Poll
Sage	David		1840	Call	Poll
Sailing	John		1843	Audr	Prop
Sailor	George		1843	Audr	Prop
Sailor	Johnathan		1837	Lew	DTL
Sale	Juan Bapt		1791	StL	Span
Sale	Joseph		1863	Jeff	Ass
Salisbury	Samuel		1831	Cole	DTL
Sallion	John		1810	Ark	Prop
Sally	Isaac		1840	Call	Poll
Saloir	Joseph		1818	StL	Real
Salvis	Joseph		1818	StL	Real
Samms	William		1830	Coop	CtS
Sampson	William	J	1836	StC	Prop
Sampson, Sr	Benjamin		1821	Ray	Prop
Sams	Burdit		1827	Mari	Prop
Sams	Green Lee		1827	Mari	Prop
Samuel	Richd		1824	Boon	Deed
Samuels	Robert		1836	StC	Prop
San Francisco	Antonio		1780	StL	Mil
Sanders	Stephen		1836	Perr	Poll
Sanders	Thomas		1836	Perr	Poll
Sanders	Mark		1867	Reyn	DTL
Sangerman	Josef		1791	StL	Span
Sanguinet	Carlos		1791	StL	Span

197

Last Name	First Name	Int	Year	County	Type
Sanguinete	Carlos		1780	StL	Mil
Sanquinet	Simon		1818	StL	Real
Sanquinet	Wid Marianne		1820	StL	Prop
Sanquinet	Charles		1820	StL	Prop
Sanquinet	Simon		1820	StL	Prop
Sanselier	Luis		1780	StL	Mil
Sansir	Jacinto		1791	StL	Span
Sansy	Antonio		1780	StL	Mil
Saquinet	????		1820	StL	Prop
Sarpy	Gregorio		1791	StL	Span
Sarters	George		1836	Carr	PrpPt
Saugrain	Antoine		1818	StL	Real
Saugrain	Antoine	F	1820	StL	Prop
Saunders	John		1836	Carr	Prop
Saunders	John		1836	Carr	PrpPt
Saunders	James		1840	Call	Poll
Saunders	James		1840	Call	Poll
Saunders	Frederick		1840	Call	Poll
Saunders	William	B	1840	Call	Poll
Saupe	Christopher		1836	StC	Prop
Savacove	William		1836	Carr	PrpPt
Savage	William		1830	Coop	Ct
Savage	William		1830	Coop	CtS
Savage	Thomas		1863	Jeff	Ass
Savage	John		1817	How	Prop
Savage	William		1817	How	Prop
Savercool	William		1836	Carr	Prop
Savercool	William		1836	Carr	PrpPt
Sayle's Heirs	Ezekiel		1836	Carr	Prop
Sayle's Heirs	Ezekiel		1836	Carr	PrpPt
Schinder	John		1867	Reyn	DTL
Schinler	Adolfe		1844	Osag	Real
Schleueboch	Hubert		1844	Osag	Real
Schofield	Ellis		1827	Mari	Prop
Schooler	William		1843	Audr	Prop
Schooler	Whorton		1843	Audr	Prop
Schooler	Elizabeth		1843	Audr	Prop
Schooling	R		1828	Boon	Lisc
Schoval	Joseph		1829	Char	DTL
Schroeder	Julius		1844	Osag	Real
Schultz	Frederick		1836	StC	Prop
Schultz	Louis		1836	StC	Prop

Last Name	First Name	Int	Year	County	Type
Schultz	Andrew		1836	StC	Prop
Schwatz	Gertrude		1844	Osag	Real
Scidmore	Reuben		1836	StC	Prop
Scoff	Henry	D	1836	Carr	PrpPt
Scoff	John	D	1830	Ray	Prop
Scoobark	Vicenot		1836	StC	Prop
Scools	Francis		1836	Perr	Poll
Scott	George		1836	Perr	Poll
Scott	Samuel		1836	Carr	PrpPt
Scott	John	M	1836	Carr	PrpPt
Scott	William	A	1840	Call	Poll
Scott	Allen		1840	Call	Poll
Scott	James		1840	Call	Poll
Scott	William	A	1840	Call	Poll
Scott	Alexander	D	1840	Call	Poll
Scott	????		1845	Sali	Lisc
Scott	William		1830	Howa	DTL
Scott	John		1830	Howa	DTL
Scott	John		1830	Call	DTL
Scott	Joseph		1836	StC	Prop
Scott	Felix		1836	StC	Prop
Scott	George		1836	StC	Prop
Scott	Presely		1836	StC	Prop
Scott	Elizabeth		1836	StC	Prop
Scott	Thomas	P	1836	StC	Prop
Scott	John		1821	Ray	Prop
Scott	Moses		1818	StL	Real
Scott	Moses		1820	StL	Prop
Scott	Alexander		1820	StL	Prop
Scott	Labert		1817	How	Prop
Scott	Lewis		1817	How	Prop
Scott	John		1844	Osag	Real
Scott's Heirs	David		1836	StC	Prop
Scough's Heirs	Noiles		1836	StC	Prop
Scudder	John		1838	Perr	Lisc
Scudder	John		1838	Perr	Adv
Scull	James		1810	Ark	Prop
Scull	Hewes		1810	Ark	Prop
Scull	James	H	1815	Ark	Prop
Scull	Herves		1815	Ark	Prop
Seadford	Daniel		1839	Lew	DTL
Seagg	Henry		1844	Osag	Real

Last Name	First Name	Int	Year	County	Type
Seagraves	Robert		1836	StC	Prop
Seale	John	K	1840	Call	Poll
Seals	J	C	1863	Jeff	Ass
Seals	Jerry		1844	Osag	Real
Sealy	Calvin		1844	Osag	Real
Searcy	William		1836	Perr	Poll
Seay	Cain		1844	Osag	Real
Sebven	Allfred		1838	Ripl	DTL
Secil	Charles		1844	Osag	Real
Seipes	John	G	1836	StC	Prop
Selby	Cephas		1840	Call	Poll
Selby	Jas		1840	Call	Poll
Selby	John		1840	Call	Poll
Selby	Joshua		1840	Call	Poll
Selby	Lewis	V	1840	Call	Poll
Selby's Heirs	Henry		1836	Carr	PrpPt
Senetchfield	Nicholas		1830	Coop	Ct
Serre	Gabriel		1780	StL	Mil
Sessions	Isaac		1836	Carr	Prop
Sessions	Isaac		1836	Carr	PrpPt
Settles	Henry		1827	Mari	Prop
Severds	James		1820	StL	Prop
Seward	Benjamin	J	1820	StL	Prop
Sexton	George		1823	Call	NRP
Sexton	J	B	1829	Char	DTL
Shackford	John		1820	StL	Prop
Shackleford	Richard	B	1830	Coop	CtS
Shacleford	Richard		1840	Call	Poll
Shanks	Jacob		1844	Osag	Real
Shanner	John		1834	Craw	DTL
Shannon	James		1840	Call	Poll
Shannon	John		1830	Jeff	DTL
Shannon	George		1836	StC	Prop
Shannon	Mary		1820	StL	Prop
Shannon	Hugh	W	1827	Mari	Prop
Shannon	Alexander		1827	Mari	Prop
Sharp	Benjamin		1823	Call	NRP
Sharpe	William		1836	Carr	Prop
Sharpe	William		1836	Carr	PrpPt
Shater	John		1810	Ark	Prop
Shaver	Frederich		1836	StC	Prop
Shaw	Jonathan		1836	Carr	Prop

Last Name	First Name	Int	Year	County	Type
Shaw	Jonathan		1836	Carr	PrpPt
Shaw	Lewis		1867	Reyn	DTL
Shaw	Joel		1817	How	Prop
Shaw	William		1835	Barr	DTL
Shaw's Heirs	Samuel		1836	StC	Prop
Sheets	Benj		1840	Call	Poll
Sheets	Thos		1867	Reyn	DTL
Shelby	Reuben		1837	Perr	Lisc
Shelby	Rueben		1836	Perr	Poll
Shelby	Ely		1830	How	DTL
Sheley	Benjon		1840	Call	Poll
Sheley	Benjamin		1840	Call	Poll
Sheley	Horace		1840	Call	Poll
Sheley	Reason		1840	Call	Poll
Sheley	Van		1840	Call	Poll
Shell	D	V	1825	CGir	Lisc
Shell	Isham	M	1836	Carr	PrpPt
Sheller	Addam		1836	StC	Prop
Shelly	Abraham		1817	How	Prop
Shelton	Gabriel	N	1834	Pett	PrpPt
Shelton	James	N	1836	StC	Prop
Shelton	Pines	H	1836	StC	Prop
Shelton	William		1822	Clay	Poll
Shepard	Chauncey		1821	StC	Ct
Shepard	William		1838	Audr	DTL
Shepard	Benjamin		1834	Call	DTL
Shepherd	Soliman		1843	Audr	Prop
Shepherd	Jeramiah		1843	Audr	Prop
Shepherd	S		1843	Audr	Prop
Shepherd	Abram		1836	Carr	Prop
Shepherd	Abram		1836	Carr	PrpPt
Shepherd	Chauncey		1821	StC	CtS
Shepherd	Chancey		1836	StC	Prop
Sheridan	William		1867	Reyn	DTL
Sherman	William		1836	StC	Prop
Shevil	Daniel		1836	StC	Prop
Shickley	William		1844	Osag	Real
Shields	Jeptha	D	1843	Audr	Prop
Shinn	Josie	C	1836	StC	Prop
Shird	David		1820	StL	Prop
Shirley	Robert		1836	Carr	Prop
Shirley	Robert		1836	Carr	PrpPt

Last Name	First Name	Int	Year	County	Type
Shirliff	Benjamin		1829	Char	DTL
Shirtliff	Benjamin		1830	Ray	Prop
Shobe	A	J	1840	Call	Poll
Shobe	John		1840	Call	Poll
Shobe	Abraham		1836	StC	Prop
Shobe	Joseph		1844	Osag	Real
Shobe	Mary		1844	Osag	Real
Shobe	Benjamin		1844	Osag	Real
Shock	Henry		1843	Audr	Prop
Shock	H	P L	1843	Audr	Prop
Shock	H	P L	1838	Audr	DTL
Shock	Flinny		1838	Audr	DTL
Shockley	Josiah		1823	How	DTL
Shockley	John		1844	Osag	Real
Shockley	Thomas	V	1844	Osag	Real
Shoemaker's Heirs	Peter		1836	StC	Prop
Sholar	W		1831	Craw	DTL
Shook	Amos		1830	Wash	DTL
Shorrs	Gilbert		1830	Coop	CtS
Shoults	Philip		1863	Jeff	Ass
Shoultz	Christa		1863	Jeff	Ass
Shoutts	Joseph		1837	Perr	Lisc
Shoutts	Joseph		1837	Perr	Lisc
Shoutts	Joseph		1837	Perr	Adv
Shroer	John	H	1836	StC	Prop
Shults	Joseph		1836	Perr	Poll
Shupback	Fred		1859	Reyn	DTL
Shurtliff	Benjamin		1836	Carr	Prop
Sibert	Charles		1838	Steg	DTL
Sibley	George		1836	StC	Prop
Siburt	George		1836	Perr	Poll
Siburt	Henry		1836	Perr	Poll
Sidner	Barnhart		1844	Osag	Real
Sientz	William		1823	Call	NRP
Silas	Oliver		1836	Carr	PrpPt
Silvers	John		1817	How	Prop
Silvers	William		1817	How	Prop
Silvestre	Hypolet		1820	StL	Prop
Simeons	Cary		1829	NMad	DTL
Simmon's Heirs	Samuel		1836	Carr	Prop
Simmon's Heirs	Samuel		1836	Carr	PrpPt
Simmons	Jethro		1836	Carr	PrpPt

Last Name	First Name	Int	Year	County	Type
Simmons	Charles		1830	How	DTL
Simmons	Ann		1867	Reyn	DTL
Simmons	Charles		1817	How	Prop
Simonds	Nathaniel		1830	Linc	DTL
Simoneau	Carlos		1791	StL	Span
Simono	Carlos		1780	StL	Mil
Simpkins	Jeremiah		1830	Linc	DTL
Simpson	Joseph	D	1836	Perr	Poll
Simpson	Samuel		1836	Carr	Prop
Simpson	Samuel		1836	Carr	PrpPt
Simpson	James	A	1840	Call	Poll
Simpson	Moses	L	1840	Call	Poll
Simpson	Joseph		1867	Reyn	DTL
Simpson	Erasmus		1836	StC	Prop
Simpson	William	H H	1836	StC	Prop
Simpson	James	W	1836	StC	Prop
Simpson	Foster	B	1836	StC	Prop
Simpson	Robert		1818	StL	Real
Simpson	Robert		1818	StL	Real
Simpson	Robert		1820	StL	Prop
Simpson	Samuel		1830	Ray	Prop
Simpson	Benjamin		1844	Osag	Real
Simpson	Samuel		1844	Osag	Real
Simpson, Jr	Moses		1844	Osag	Real
Simpson, Sr	Moses		1844	Osag	Real
Sims	William		1843	Audr	Prop
Sims	William	R	1843	Audr	Prop
Sims	Jas		1843	Audr	Prop
Sims	J		1843	Audr	Prop
Sims	James	S	1859	Reyn	DTL
Sims	Felix		1836	Perr	Poll
Sims	Thomas	A	1837	Boon	PM
Since	(Free Colored) F		1836	StC	Prop
Sinclair	Samuel		1834	Craw	DTL
Singleton	Jaconias		1823	Call	NRP
Siperon	Ellis		1837	Lew	DTL
Sipple	James		1829	Char	DTL
Sitton	Joseph	T	1840	Call	Poll
Skaggs	John		1834	Craw	DTL
Skidmore	James		1836	Perr	Poll
Skillon	William		1836	Char	DTL
Skinner	Richard		1843	Audr	Prop

Last Name	First Name	Int	Year	County	Type
Sladden	Sidney	P	1867	Reyn	DTL
Sladen	Alfred		1838	Ripl	DTL
Slater	John		1867	Reyn	DTL
Slater	Samuel		1836	StC	Prop
Slater	????		1818	StL	Real
Slaughter	Robert	P	1825	CGir	Lisc
Slaughter	James		1840	Call	Poll
Sliver	John		1836	Carr	Prop
Sliver	John		1836	Carr	PrpPt
Sloan	Bryan		1836	Carr	Prop
Sloan	Bryan		1836	Carr	PrpPt
Sloan	Thomas		1830	Ray	Prop
Sloane	Robert		1834	Pett	PrpPt
Sloane	Thomas		1834	Call	DTL
Sloly	John		1836	Carr	Prop
Sloly	John		1836	Carr	PrpPt
Sloten	William		1834	Craw	DTL
Small	George		1834	Pett	Prop
Small	Henry		1834	Pett	PrpPt
Small, Sr	Henry		1834	Pett	Prop
Smallet	William		1867	Reyn	DTL
Smart	James	A	1840	Call	Poll
Smart	Susannah		1818	StL	Real
Smart	John	C	1829	Mari	DTL
Smelser	John		1836	StC	Prop
Smelser's Heirs	George		1836	StC	Prop
Smelsor	David		1817	How	Prop
Smemure	John	F	1836	StC	Prop
Smiley	Jas		1843	Audr	Prop
Smiley	William		1834	Pett	Prop
Smiley	George	W	1834	Pett	Prop
Smiley	George		1834	Pett	PrpPt
Smiley	George	W	1834	Pett	PrpPt
Smiley	James		1834	Pett	PrpPt
Smit	William		1817	How	Prop
Smith	Eli		1843	Audr	Prop
Smith	Joseph		1843	Audr	Prop
Smith	Kitty		1843	Audr	Prop
Smith	Jas		1843	Audr	Prop
Smith	Abraham		1843	Audr	Prop
Smith	Matthew	H	1843	Audr	Prop
Smith	E		1826	Coop	DTL

Last Name	First Name	Int	Year	County	Type
Smith	Richd		1859	Reyn	DTL
Smith	John	S	1859	Reyn	DTL
Smith	Richard		1837	Cass	DTL
Smith	Thomas		1838	Cass	DTL
Smith	Sampson		1831	Jack	DTL
Smith	Christian		1836	Carr	PrpPt
Smith	John		1836	Carr	PrpPt
Smith	William	S	1836	Carr	Prop
Smith	William		1836	Carr	Prop
Smith	Eli		1836	Carr	Prop
Smith	William		1836	Carr	PrpPt
Smith	William	S	1836	Carr	PrpPt
Smith	Eli		1836	Carr	PrpPt
Smith	Jeremiah	R	1836	Carr	Prop
Smith	Curtis		1836	Carr	Prop
Smith	Hiram		1836	Carr	Prop
Smith	John		1836	Carr	Prop
Smith	Christian	B	1836	Carr	Prop
Smith	John		1836	Carr	Prop
Smith	Jeremiah	R	1836	Carr	PrpPt
Smith	Curtis		1836	Carr	PrpPt
Smith	Hiram		1836	Carr	PrpPt
Smith	John		1836	Carr	PrpPt
Smith	Christian	B	1836	Carr	PrpPt
Smith	John		1836	Carr	PrpPt
Smith	James		1836	Carr	PrpPt
Smith	R		1839	Wash	Lisc
Smith	Nancy		1828	Boon	Lisc
Smith	George		1828	Boon	Lisc
Smith	John		1840	Call	Poll
Smith	Peter	S	1840	Call	Poll
Smith	Richard		1840	Call	Poll
Smith	William	H	1840	Call	Poll
Smith	William		1840	Call	Poll
Smith	Jonathan		1830	How	DTL
Smith	James		1867	Reyn	DTL
Smith	William	H	1867	Reyn	DTL
Smith	Charles		1867	Reyn	DTL
Smith	William	H	1867	Reyn	DTL
Smith	Joseph	S	1867	Reyn	DTL
Smith	C	W	1867	Reyn	DTL
Smith	Glass		1867	Reyn	DTL

Last Name	First Name	Int	Year	County	Type
Smith	W	C	1867	Reyn	DTL
Smith	John		1823	Call	NRP
Smith	Thomas	A	1823	Call	NRP
Smith	N		1829	Char	DTL
Smith	Thomas	A	1829	Char	DTL
Smith	Daniel		1836	StC	Prop
Smith	Volentine		1836	StC	Prop
Smith	Randolph	B	1836	StC	Prop
Smith	Nancy		1836	StC	Prop
Smith	John		1836	StC	Prop
Smith	Ahi		1821	Ray	Prop
Smith	William	L	1821	Ray	Prop
Smith	Humphrey		1821	Ray	Prop
Smith	William		1810	Ark	Prop
Smith	John		1838	Audr	DTL
Smith	Abraham		1838	Audr	DTL
Smith	Eli		1838	Audr	DTL
Smith	George	B	1838	Audr	DTL
Smith	Jas	H	1838	Audr	DTL
Smith	John	B N	1818	StL	Real
Smith	Oliver	C	1820	StL	Prop
Smith	Christian		1820	StL	Prop
Smith	E		1826	Coop	DTL
Smith	John	B N	1817	How	Prop
Smith	Peter		1817	How	Prop
Smith	Joseph		1817	How	Prop
Smith	Andrew		1817	How	Prop
Smith	John		1827	Mari	Prop
Smith	Charles		1827	Mari	Prop
Smith	Thomas		1831	Cole	DTL
Smith	James		1830	Ray	Prop
Smith	Thomas	A	1830	Ray	Prop
Smith	James	A	1839	Lew	DTL
Smith	William		1839	Lew	DTL
Smith	Tilman		1833	Wayn	DTL
Smith	Teral		1822	Clay	Poll
Smith	A		1822	Clay	Poll
Smith	Leroy		1835	Barr	DTL
Smith	James	A	1844	Osag	Real
Smith	Wyatt		1844	Osag	Real
Smith	Benjamin		1844	Osag	Real
Smith	David		1844	Osag	Real

Last Name	First Name	Int	Year	County	Type
Smith	William		1836	Char	DTL
Smith	Eli		1834	Call	DTL
Smith	James	W	1834	Lew	DTL
Smith	Charles		1834	Craw	DTL
Smith	Deliley		1837	Mill	DTL
Smith	Nathaniel		1837	Mill	DTL
Smith's Heirs	John		1836	StC	Prop
Smith, Jr	Hawkins		1829	Mari	DTL
Smith, Sr	Hawkins		1827	Mari	Prop
Smith., dec	William		1820	StL	Prop
Smithe	John	A	1836	StC	Prop
Smithe	James		1836	StC	Prop
Smithey	John		1840	Call	Poll
Smoot	John		1839	Lew	DTL
Snead	Harrison		1836	Carr	PrpPt
Snead	Harrison		1836	Carr	Prop
Snead	Harrison		1836	Carr	PrpPt
Snell	Lueden		1827	Boon	Lisc
Snider	James		1859	Reyn	DTL
Snodgrass	William		1836	Carr	Prop
Snodgrass	William		1836	Carr	PrpPt
Snodgrass	George		1834	Craw	DTL
Snow	Chas	B	1859	Reyn	DTL
Snow	Henry		1859	Reyn	DTL
Snow	Henry		1836	Carr	Prop
Snow	Henry		1836	Carr	PrpPt
Snow	Leve		1836	Char	DTL
Snow's Heirs	Paul		1836	Carr	Prop
Snow's Heirs	Paul		1836	Carr	PrpPt
Snow's Heirs	Paul		1830	Ray	Prop
Snowden	Jas		1830	Call	DTL
Snquiney	C		1818	StL	Real
Snyder	Daniel		1859	Reyn	DTL
Snyder	Chas		1863	Jeff	Ass
Snyder	William		1867	Reyn	DTL
Snyder	Joseph		1836	StC	Prop
Snyder	Phillip		1836	StC	Prop
Soane	Michael		1831	Cole	DTL
Socier	Battist		1836	StC	Prop
Socier	Francis		1836	StC	Prop
Sollars	Thomas		1821	Ray	Prop
Soloman	Samuel		1818	StL	Real

Last Name	First Name	Int	Year	County	Type
Solomon	Samuel		1818	StL	Real
Son	John	T	1830	Coop	Ct
Songan	Austin	K	1830	Coop	CtS
Sood	James		1836	Carr	PrpPt
Sorrel	Josef		1791	StL	Span
Sorret	Pedro		1780	StL	Mil
Soulard	James	S	1820	StL	Prop
Soulard's Heirs	Antoine		1830	Ray	Prop
Southard	Daniel		1859	Reyn	DTL
Souval	Pierre		1805	Steg	Prop
Sox	William		1843	Audr	Prop
Sox	Thomas		1843	Audr	Prop
Sox	Samuel		1843	Audr	Prop
Sox	Jackson		1843	Audr	Prop
Sox, Jr	William		1843	Audr	Prop
Spain	John		1836	StC	Prop
Spain	Mark	D	1844	Osag	Real
Spalding	Thomas		1836	StC	Prop
Spanhouse	Phillip		1836	StC	Prop
Spanhouse	Charles		1836	StC	Prop
Sparks	John		1840	Call	Poll
Sparks	Samuel		1840	Call	Poll
Sparks	John		1840	Call	Poll
Sparks	Samuel		1840	Call	Poll
Sparks	Joseph		1834	Call	DTL
Sparks	George		1834	Call	DTL
Spawn	Mayberry		1821	Ray	Prop
Spear	E	A	1867	Reyn	DTL
Spear's Heirs	Timothy		1836	Carr	Prop
Spear's Heirs	Timothy		1836	Carr	PrpPt
Sped	Henry	J	1840	Call	Poll
Sped	Henry	J	1840	Call	Poll
Spencer	Joseph	D	1843	Audr	Prop
Spencer	George	R	1821	StC	Ct
Spencer	George	S	1836	StC	Prop
Spencer	Sarah		1836	StC	Prop
Spencer	William		1836	StC	Prop
Spencer	Joseph		1836	StC	Prop
Spencer	Robert		1836	StC	Prop
Spencer	Wilson		1822	Clay	Poll
Spencer's Heirs	George		1836	StC	Prop
Spencer, Jr	Robert	A	1836	StC	Prop

Last Name	First Name	Int	Year	County	Type
Spencer, Sr	Robert		1836	StC	Prop
Spera	James		1838	Audr	DTL
Sperry	Jas		1843	Audr	Prop
Spires	George		1836	StC	Prop
Sprig	Wm		1826	Coop	DTL
Sprig	Wm		1827	Coop	DTL
Sprig	William		1827	Coop	DTL
Sprig	William		1826	Coop	DTL
Springer	Charles		1839	Wash	Lisc
Spud	Henry	J	1840	Call	Poll
Spurtmarys	Hugh		1843	Char	DTL
Srimble	Peter		1836	Carr	PrpPt
Sryer	John		1836	Carr	PrpPt
St Aubin	Louis		1830	How	DTL
St August	Andre		1821	StC	CtS
St Jean	????		1820	StL	Prop
St. Germain	????		1844	Osag	Real
St. Louis	John	B	1836	StC	Prop
Staff	Benj		1830	How	DTL
Stakes	William		1837	Lew	DTL
Standley	Perry		1838	Ripl	DTL
Stanley	Page		1825	Clay	DTL
Stanley	Rubin		1840	Call	Poll
Stanley	William		1840	Call	Poll
Stanley	William		1821	Ray	Prop
Stanley	Larkin		1821	Ray	Prop
Stanley	Page		1822	Clay	Poll
Stap	Elijah		1827	Mari	Prop
Staple's Heirs	Joseph		1836	Carr	PrpPt
Staples	Samuel		1830	Wash	DTL
Staples	Thomas		1836	Carr	Prop
Staples	Thomas		1836	Carr	PrpPt
Stapp	Elijah		1827	Mari	Prop
Stapp	Preston		1827	Mari	Prop
Stapp	Darwin		1827	Mari	Prop
Starks	Pnueman	B	1840	Call	Poll
Starle	R	Q	1837	Lew	DTL
Starnes	Abraham		1836	Carr	Prop
Starnes	Abraham		1836	Carr	PrpPt
Starr	Peter		1839	John	DTL
Starr	Peter		1839	John	DTL
Staton	Baton		1818	Lawr	DTL

Last Name	First Name	Int	Year	County	Type
Steel	Robert		1817	How	Prop
Steelsmith	Anthony		1836	StC	Prop
Steen	John		1844	Osag	Real
Steiner	John		1867	Reyn	DTL
Step	Michael		1843	Audr	Prop
Step	Stephen		1836	Carr	Prop
Step	Stephen		1836	Carr	PrpPt
Step	Stephen		1830	Ray	Prop
Stephen	Addam		1836	StC	Prop
Stephens	J William		1836	Bent	DTL
Stephens	W	E	1840	Call	Poll
Stephens	W	E	1840	Call	Poll
Stephens	William		1840	Call	Poll
Stephens	Alfred	K	1830	Coop	CtS
Stephens	Peter		1830	Coop	CtS
Stephens	A	S	1867	Reyn	DTL
Stephens	Calvin		1821	Ray	Prop
Stephens	Isreal		1837	Lew	DTL
Stephens	Christopher		1839	Lew	DTL
Stephens	William		1837	Bent	DTL
Stephenson	John		1836	Carr	PrtPt
Stephenson	J	C	1867	Reyn	DTL
Stephenson	Thomas	D	1836	StC	Prop
Stephenson	Nancy		1817	How	Prop
Stephenson, dec	Marquis		1817	How	Prop
Sterer	Francis		1836	StC	Prop
Sterne	W	J	1867	Reyn	DTL
Sterret	N	M	1836	Carr	Prop
Sterret	N	M	1836	Carr	PrpPt
Stevens	Thomas		1836	Carr	Prop
Stevens	Thomas		1836	Carr	PrpPt
Stevens	John		1823	How	DTL
Stevenson	Augustus		1828	Boon	Lisc
Steward	James		1836	Perr	Poll
Steward	William		1836	Perr	Poll
Steward	William		1838	Steg	DTL
Steward	Samuel		1836	Carr	Prop
Steward	Samuel		1836	Carr	PrpPt
Steward	John		1840	Call	Poll
Steward	William		1818	StL	Real
Steward	John		1839	Lew	DTL
Steward	Hamilton	C	1844	Osag	Real

Last Name	First Name	Int	Year	County	Type
Stewart	John		1843	Audr	Prop
Stewart	Thomas		1838	Perr	Lisc
Stewart	Thomas		1838	Perr	Adv
Stewart	Charles	W	1836	Perr	Poll
Stewart	John		1836	Carr	Prop
Stewart	John		1836	Carr	PrpPt
Stewart	William		1840	Call	Poll
Stewart	Garret	N	1840	Call	Poll
Stewart	James		1840	Call	Poll
Stewart	Rueben		1840	Call	Poll
Stewart	Charles		1867	Reyn	DTL
Stewart	Joseph		1839	John	DTL
Stewart	John		1830	Ray	Prop
Stibb's Heirs	John		1836	Carr	Prop
Stibb's Heirs	John		1836	Carr	PrpPt
Stickney	William		1830	Ray	Prop
Stickney	Silvester		1830	Ray	Prop
Stiles	Chas		1867	Reyn	DTL
Still	Will		1843	Audr	Prop
Still	John		1838	Audr	DTL
Still	Andrew		1838	Audr	DTL
Still	Meredith		1838	Audr	DTL
Still	William		1838	Audr	DTL
Stillwell	Joseph		1810	Ark	Prop
Stillwell	Harold		1810	Ark	Prop
Stillwell	Joseph		1815	Ark	Prop
Stillwell	John		1815	Ark	Prop
Stillwell	Harold		1815	Ark	Prop
Stimpson	????		1820	StL	Prop
Stinemiller	Addam		1836	StC	Prop
Stipe	Mathew	L	1867	Reyn	DTL
Stird	John		1836	StC	Prop
Stith	David	B	1823	Call	NRP
Stockslager	P	A	1836	StC	Prop
Stockwell	Abel		1836	Carr	Prop
Stockwell	Abel		1836	Carr	PrpPt
Stoddard	Nathan		1830	Ray	Prop
Stoddard's Heirs	Amos		1823	Call	NRP
Stokes	Nimrod		1837	Cass	DTL
Stokes	Henry	W	1840	Call	Poll
Stokes	????		1820	StL	Prop
Stokey	Benjamin		1844	Osag	Real

Last Name	First Name	Int	Year	County	Type
Stollings	Hardy		1836	Carr	Prop
Stollings	Hardy		1836	Carr	PrpPt
Stone	Thomas	T	1843	Audr	Prop
Stone	Thomas		1859	Reyn	DTL
Stone	Nathaniel		1836	Carr	PrpPt
Stone	Thomas		1836	Carr	PrpPt
Stone	W	B	1840	Call	Poll
Stone	W	B	1840	Call	Poll
Stone	James		1840	Call	Poll
Stone	Oran		1829	Char	DTL
Stone	William	T	1838	Audr	DTL
Stone	Christopher		1821	Ray	Prop
Stookey	Benjamin		1840	Call	Poll
Stoplet	David		1840	Call	Poll
Storrs	Asahel		1829	Char	DTL
Story	Johnson		1838	Ripl	DTL
Stratton	Gabriel		1838	Cass	DTL
Straube	Kitty		1843	Audr	Prop
Straube	Jas		1843	Audr	Prop
Straube	Christian		1843	Audr	Prop
Strickland	Thos		1843	Audr	Prop
Strickland	T		1843	Audr	Prop
Strickland	Peter		1805	Steg	Prop
Strickland	James		1838	Steg	DTL
Stricklen	John		1840	Call	Poll
Stricklin	Thomas		1838	Audr	DTL
Stringer	Daniel		1830	How	DTL
Strode	????		1845	Sali	Lisc
Strong	Joseph		1829	Char	DTL
Strong	William		1810	Ark	Prop
Strong	John		1810	Ark	Prop
Strong	John		1815	Ark	Prop
Stroops	Jacob		1810	Ark	Prop
Strope	John		1836	Carr	Prop
Strope	John		1836	Carr	PrpPt
Strother	George	F	1830	Wash	DTL
Strother	F		1839	Wash	Lisc
Strother	George		1836	StC	Prop
Stroud	Thomas		1859	Reyn	DTL
Stroukhoff	Herman		1836	StC	Prop
Stroup	Andrew		1863	Jeff	Ass
Stroup	John		1844	Osag	Real

Last Name	First Name	Int	Year	County	Type
Stuard	William		1836	StC	Prop
Stuart	Charles		1836	Perr	Poll
Stubblefield	Jeremiah		1837	Mill	DTL
Stultsmith	Andrew		1836	StC	Prop
Stump	George		1836	StC	Prop
Stump	Curthbert		1836	StC	Prop
Stump	John		1836	StC	Prop
Stump	Miles		1836	StC	Prop
Stupp	Andrew		1836	StC	Prop
Sturd	John		1836	StC	Prop
Sturd	Francis		1836	StC	Prop
Sturd	Elias	C	1836	StC	Prop
Suber	Joseph		1843	Audr	Prop
Subus	Juan Bapt		1780	StL	Mil
Suet	Nelson		1836	Carr	Prop
Suet	Nelson		1836	Carr	PrpPt
Sugett	Benjamin	D	1840	Call	Poll
Sugg	Joseph		1836	Carr	PrpPt
Sugg	Josiah		1836	Carr	Prop
Sugg	Josiah		1836	Carr	PrpPt
Sugg	Josiah		1836	Carr	PrpPt
Suggett	John		1840	Call	Poll
Suggett	Minte		1840	Call	Poll
Suggett	Volney		1840	Call	Poll
Suggett	Henry	H	1840	Call	Poll
Suggett	Joseph	R	1840	Call	Poll
Suggett	Thomas		1840	Call	Poll
Suggett, Jr	James		1840	Call	Poll
Suggett, Sr	James		1840	Call	Poll
Suliven	Jeremia		1836	StC	Prop
Suliven	David		1836	StC	Prop
Sullen	Jesse		1844	Osag	Real
Sullen	Benjamin	C	1844	Osag	Real
Sullens	W	H	1863	Jeff	Ass
Sullivan	Wm		1859	Reyn	DTL
Sullivan	Dennis		1859	Reyn	DTL
Sullivan	Michael		1859	Reyn	DTL
Sullivan	James		1836	Carr	Prop
Sullivan	James		1836	Carr	PrpPt
Sullivan	Edward		1867	Reyn	DTL
Sullivan	Thomas		1867	Reyn	DTL
Sullivan	J	C	1829	Char	DTL

Last Name	First Name	Int	Year	County	Type
Sullivan	William		1818	StL	Real
Sullivan	William		1820	StL	Prop
Sullivan	L		1839	Lew	DTL
Sullivant	Daniel		1839	Wash	Lisc
Sulten, Sr	John		1844	Osag	Real
Sumande	Esteban		1780	StL	Mil
Sumande	Joseph		1780	StL	Mil
Sumner	Jonathan		1837	Cass	DTL
Sumner	Francis		1836	StC	Prop
Sumner	Joseph		1836	StC	Prop
Sutee	Elen		1836	StC	Prop
Sutile	Simon		1830	Call	DTL
Sutterwell	Boswell		1867	Reyn	DTL
Suttle	John	W	1839	Lew	DTL
Sutton	William M		1839	Plat	Prop
Sutton	John	C	1836	Perr	Poll
Sutton	John	L	1829	Char	DTL
Swan	Henry		1859	Reyn	DTL
Swan	Richard		1836	Perr	Poll
Swathercup	Joseph		1836	StC	Prop
Swearingen	Thomas		1840	Call	Poll
Sweeney	David		1836	Carr	Prop
Sweeney	David		1836	Carr	PrpPt
Sweet	Nelson		1836	Carr	PrpPt
Swenderman	George		1836	StC	Prop
Swenderman	Madden		1836	StC	Prop
Swezy	Peter		1831	Cole	DTL
Swindle	John	G	1843	Audr	Prop
Swindle	John	G	1838	Audr	DTL
Swinny	Edmond		1825	Char	DTL
Swiss	John		1837	Cass	DTL
Swope	Jesse		1834	Pett	Prop
Swope	Jesse		1834	Pett	PrpPt
Sylva	James		1836	StC	Prop
Sylva	Dennis		1836	StC	Prop
Synder	Jacob		1867	Reyn	DTL
Synder	Jacob		1867	Reyn	DTL
Tabeau	Uberto		1791	StL	Span
Tabeau	Santiago		1791	StL	Span
Tabo	Jacobo		1780	StL	Mil
Taffrey	John		1836	Carr	PrpPt
Tagart	Andrew		1836	StC	Prop

Last Name	First Name	Int	Year	County	Type
Tagart	James		1836	StC	Prop
Tagart	R	A	1836	StC	Prop
Tagart	Richard		1836	StC	Prop
Taggart	Archibald		1825	Char	DTL
Tailor	Robt		1838	Audr	DTL
Take	Edward		1867	Reyn	DTL
Tallon	Josepf		1791	StL	Span
Tallon	Carlos		1791	StL	Span
Tallon (son)	Josef		1791	StL	Span
Tally	Wiley		1843	Audr	Prop
Tally	Daniel		1843	Audr	Prop
Tally	George		1843	Audr	Prop
Tally	Jas	M	1843	Audr	Prop
Tally	Berry		1843	Audr	Prop
Tally	Judah		1843	Audr	Prop
Tally	Wm		1843	Audr	Prop
Tally	John		1843	Audr	Prop
Tally	Danl		1843	Audr	Prop
Tally	Daniel	W	1838	Audr	DTL
Tally	George		1838	Audr	DTL
Tally	William		1838	Audr	DTL
Talmadge	T	W	1867	Reyn	DTL
Tamau	Nicholas		1805	Steg	Prop
Tamu	Jn Baptist		1805	Steg	Prop
Tanfield	Jacob		1836	Carr	PrpPt
Tarin	Daniel		1839	John	DTL
Tarley	James	N	1828	Boon	Lisc
Tarter	Robert		1840	Call	Poll
Tate	Allen		1836	Bent	DTL
Tate	Calet	W	1840	Call	Poll
Tate	John	G	1840	Call	Poll
Tate	Nathaniel	N	1840	Call	Poll
Tate	Polly		1818	StL	Real
Tate	Sally		1820	StL	Prop
Tate	Allen		1837	Bent	DTL
Tator	H	M	1867	Reyn	DTL
Tator	H	M	1867	Reyn	DTL
Tatum	Wily	G	1840	Call	Poll
Tatum	Ira	E	1836	StC	Prop
Taylor	Robert		1843	Audr	Prop
Taylor	Felix		1818	Lawr	DTL
Taylor	William		1837	Perr	Lisc

Last Name	First Name	Int	Year	County	Type
Taylor	William		1836	Perr	Poll
Taylor	Warren		1836	Carr	Prop
Taylor	Jesse		1836	Carr	Prop
Taylor	Richard		1836	Carr	Prop
Taylor	Warren		1836	Carr	PrpPt
Taylor	Jesse		1836	Carr	PrpPt
Taylor	Richard		1836	Carr	PrpPt
Taylor	Thomas		1840	Call	Poll
Taylor	James		1840	Call	Poll
Taylor	Benj	B	1840	Call	Poll
Taylor	J	T	1863	Jeff	Ass
Taylor	Peter		1867	Reyn	DTL
Taylor	John		1823	Call	NRP
Taylor	R	E	1836	StC	Prop
Taylor	Samuel		1836	StC	Prop
Taylor	Nancy		1836	StC	Prop
Taylor	Washington		1836	StC	Prop
Taylor	William		1836	StC	Prop
Taylor	Sarah		1836	StC	Prop
Taylor	????		1820	StL	Prop
Taylor	William		1817	How	Prop
Taylor	William		1830	Ray	Prop
Taylor	John		1839	Lew	DTL
Taylor	George		1839	Lew	DTL
Taylor	Thomas		1844	Osag	Real
Taylor's Heirs	John	M	1836	StC	Prop
Taylor's Heirs	Francis		1836	StC	Prop
Tayon	Joseph		1780	StL	Mil
Tayon	Carlos		1780	StL	Mil
Tayon	Joseph		1836	StC	Prop
Tayon	Pier		1836	StC	Prop
Teabo	Antwine		1836	StC	Prop
Teage	James		1844	Osag	Real
Teage	Joab		1844	Osag	Real
Teakle	Horace		1839	Lew	DTL
Teaque	Pearson		1837	Cass	DTL
Teaque	Parson		1831	Jack	DTL
Tease	Joel		1834	Craw	DTL
Teater	John		1836	StC	Prop
Teater, Sr	Benj		1836	StC	Prop
Tegard	Richard		1823	Call	NRP
Telleson	Aug		1863	Jeff	Ass

Last Name	First Name	Int	Year	County	Type
Telton	James	I	1827	Boon	Lisc
Tembal	Juan Pablo		1780	StL	Mil
Teneroso	Joseph		1780	StL	Mil
Tengeldene	Adam		1836	StC	Prop
Tennison	John	R	1838	Audr	DTL
Terrence	Daniel		1867	Reyn	DTL
Tesen	Albert		1830	Linc	DTL
Tesero	Jn		1805	Steg	Prop
Tesier	Joseph		1780	StL	Mil
Tesson	H Louis		1818	StL	Real
Tesson	M		1820	StL	Prop
Tesson	Jos Honore Louis		1820	StL	Prop
Tesson	Michel		1820	StL	Prop
Thacker	Ransom		1830	Howa	DTL
Thackston	James	M	1840	Call	Poll
Thackum	Jonathan		1818	Lawr	DTL
Tharp	Lewis		1836	Perr	Poll
Tharp	William		1818	StL	Real
Tharp	Dodson	H	1823	How	DTL
Thatcher	Charles		1836	Carr	Prop
Thatcher	Charles		1836	Carr	PrpPt
Thaxton	Robert		1838	John	DTL
TherreseTurnely	Joseph		1836	StC	Prop
Thilmony	P		1867	Reyn	DTL
Tholozan	John	C	1818	StL	Real
Thomas	Peter		1838	Cass	DTL
Thomas	John		1836	Carr	Prop
Thomas	John		1836	Carr	PrpPt
Thomas	Hiram	S	1840	Call	Poll
Thomas	James		1840	Call	Poll
Thomas	William		1867	Reyn	DTL
Thomas	Jesse		1836	StC	Prop
Thomas	James	P	1836	StC	Prop
Thomas	Jonathan		1836	StC	Prop
Thomas	James		1827	Mari	Prop
Thomas	John		1830	Ray	Prop
Thomas	Robinson		1844	Osag	Real
Thomas, Jr	John		1829	Mari	DTL
Thompon	William		1859	Reyn	DTL
Thompson	R	L	1843	Audr	Prop
Thompson	Williams		1859	Reyn	DTL
Thompson	William	R	1836	Perr	Poll

Last Name	First Name	Int	Year	County	Type
Thompson	William		1836	Carr	PrpPt
Thompson	George		1836	Carr	PrpPt
Thompson	Henry	I	1836	Carr	Prop
Thompson	Henry	I	1836	Carr	PrpPt
Thompson	James		1836	Carr	PrpPt
Thompson	Thomas		1828	Boon	Lisc
Thompson	Phillip	W	1830	Coop	CtS
Thompson	John		1830	Howa	DTL
Thompson	Geo		1830	Howa	DTL
Thompson	George	W	1863	Jeff	Ass
Thompson	Jos		1863	Jeff	Ass
Thompson	Danl		1867	Reyn	DTL
Thompson	James		1823	Call	NRP
Thompson	Waddy		1836	StC	Prop
Thompson	Wylie		1810	Ark	Prop
Thompson	Hypolite		1818	StL	Real
Thompson	William		1837	Lew	DTL
Thompson	Robert		1817	How	Prop
Thompson	John		1822	Clay	Poll
Thompson	William		1844	Osag	Real
Thompson	Saml		1837	Bent	DTL
Thompson	Solomon		1838	Ripl	DTL
Thompson	Ahab		1838	Ripl	DTL
Thompson	Jos	D N	1834	Call	DTL
Thomson	William		1818	Lawr	DTL
Thomson	John		1815	Ark	Prop
Thomson	Joseph		1815	Ark	Prop
Thornhill	John		1836	StC	Prop
Thornhill	Mary		1836	StC	Prop
Thornhill's Heirs	Reuben		1836	StC	Prop
Thornton	Bernard	F	1821	StC	Ct
Thornton	James		1844	Osag	Real
Thorp	James		1817	How	Prop
Thorton	Samuel		1823	How	DTL
Thrasher	Stephen		1829	Mari	DTL
Thrasher	John	F	1827	Mari	Prop
Thrasher	Stephen	F	1827	Mari	Prop
Throckmorton	Henry		1843	Audr	Prop
Throckmorton	Robert		1843	Audr	Prop
Thruett	Osborn		1821	StC	CtS
Thubeault	Alexis		1820	StL	Prop
Thumbell	????		1818	StL	Real

Last Name	First Name	Int	Year	County	Type
Thurman	Archibald		1836	Perr	Poll
Thurman	Jeptha		1827	Mari	Prop
Thurmure	Jn Baptiste		1805	Steg	Prop
Thurston	J	M	1829	Char	DTL
Tibo	Joseph		1780	StL	Mil
Tidwell	John		1818	Lawr	DTL
Tift	Solomon		1859	Reyn	DTL
Tigert	Hugh		1831	Craw	DTL
Tillson	John		1863	Jeff	Ass
Tilman	????		1837	Lew	DTL
Tilmon	Daniel		1817	How	Prop
Timberlake	Benjamin		1836	StC	Prop
Timsley	Abraham	B	1838	Audr	DTL
Tindel	M		1840	Call	Poll
Tingley	Daniel		1830	Ray	Prop
Tinker	John		1831	Craw	DTL
Tinkler	William		1838	Ripl	DTL
Tinsley	Abraham	B	1843	Audr	Prop
Tinsley	Caleb		1843	Audr	Prop
Tiohall	Michael		1825	Clay	DTL
Tipcer	Henry		1836	StC	Prop
Tippett	Jas	A	1836	Char	DTL
Tipplett	Jos		1843	Char	DTL
Tipton	Joel		1840	Call	Poll
Tiron	Juan Bapt		1791	StL	Span
Tisdale	Joseph		1836	StC	Prop
Tisscart	Henry		1836	StC	Prop
Tobbe	George		1836	StC	Prop
Todd	Hugh		1843	Audr	Prop
Todd	John		1843	Audr	Prop
Todd	R	N	1824	Boon	Deed
Todd	Roger	N	1828	Boon	Lisc
Todd	David		1830	Coop	CtS
Todd	Roger	N	1823	Call	NRP
Todd	Thomas		1817	How	Prop
Todd	Elisha		1817	How	Prop
Todson	Dr George	W	1820	StL	Prop
Tolbert	Joseph		1834	Craw	DTL
Tolmadge	T	W	1867	Reyn	DTL
Tolmadge	T	W	1867	Reyn	DTL
Tomlinson	William		1840	Call	Poll
Tong	H	N	1867	Reyn	DTL

Last Name	First Name	Int	Year	County	Type
Tongate	Achilles		1834	Craw	DTL
Toniech	Widow		1805	Steg	Prop
Tooms	John		1831	Cole	DTL
Toon	Lorceco	H	1863	Jeff	Ass
Toplenure	John		1822	Clay	Poll
Topliff	George	W	1837	Boon	PM
Topscot's Heirs	James		1836	Carr	Prop
Topscot's Heirs	James		1836	Carr	PrpPt
Tousant	Cerre		1830	Linc	DTL
Towers	Roger		1836	StC	Prop
Town	Ephraim		1820	StL	Prop
Townley	John	M	1844	Osag	Real
Townsend	Jesse		1829	Char	DTL
Townsend	William	S	1839	Lew	DTL
Trammell	Philip		1817	How	Prop
Travel	John		1867	Reyn	DTL
Travis	Thomas	J	1836	StC	Prop
Travis	Francis		1817	How	Prop
Treat	Stephen		1834	Craw	DTL
Tredeau	Louis		1805	Steg	Prop
Trent	Alexander		1825	Char	DTL
Trevilion	John		1823	Call	NRP
Trickey	Asa		1836	Perr	Poll
Trigg	Thomas	J	1840	Call	Poll
Trimble	Jas		1830	Call	DTL
Trince	Abasalom		1810	Ark	Prop
Tritley	Peter		1836	StC	Prop
Tritley	John		1836	StC	Prop
Tritley	John	P	1836	StC	Prop
Trobridge	Richard		1867	Reyn	DTL
Tros	Isaac		1780	StL	Mil
Troth	Isaac		1834	Craw	DTL
Trotter	Robert		1836	Perr	Poll
Trotter	David		1817	How	Prop
Trotter	John		1822	Clay	Poll
Troutman	Harvey		1867	Reyn	DTL
Trudeau	Juan		1791	StL	Span
Trudeau	Louis		1818	StL	Real
Trudeau	Widow		1815	Ark	Prop
Trudeau's Heirs	Jos		1810	Ark	Prop
Trudo	Baptista		1780	StL	Mil
Truedales	William		1867	Reyn	DTL

Last Name	First Name	Int	Year	County	Type
Truett	John	W	1843	Audr	Prop
Truett	Thomas		1840	Call	Poll
Trusdale	Waltman		1867	Reyn	DTL
Tucker	William		1818	Lawr	DTL
Tucker	James	F	1837	Perr	Lisc
Tucker	James		1837	Perr	Adv
Tucker	William	A	1859	Reyn	DTL
Tucker	John	P	1836	Perr	Poll
Tucker	Francis		1836	Perr	Poll
Tucker	James	F	1836	Perr	Poll
Tucker	John	T	1836	Perr	Poll
Tucker	Joseph		1836	Perr	Poll
Tucker	Nicholas		1836	Perr	Poll
Tucker	Thomas		1836	Perr	Poll
Tucker	William	T	1836	Perr	Poll
Tucker	John		1838	Cass	DTL
Tucker	Benjamin		1836	Carr	Prop
Tucker	Benjamin		1836	Carr	PrpPt
Tucker	Alexander		1840	Call	Poll
Tucker	Zachariah		1840	Call	Poll
Tucker	D	M	1840	Call	Poll
Tucker	Henry	H	1835	Barr	DTL
Tucker	George		1844	Osag	Real
Tucker, dec	William		1844	Osag	Real
Tully	??eiville		1859	Reyn	DTL
Tumbo	Joseph		1834	Craw	DTL
Tunley	James		1837	Cass	DTL
Turell	Rosewell		1836	Carr	Prop
Turell	Rosewell		1836	Carr	PrpPt
Turk's Heirs	Elias		1836	Carr	Prop
Turk's Heirs	Elias		1836	Carr	PrpPt
Turley	George	W	1843	Audr	Prop
Turley	Jas	E	1840	Call	Poll
Turley	Samuel		1817	How	Prop
Turley	Stephen		1817	How	Prop
Turman	Benidict		1840	Call	Poll
Turnbeau	Therese		1836	StC	Prop
Turner	Andrew		1843	Audr	Prop
Turner	Jackson		1843	Audr	Prop
Turner	John		1843	Audr	Prop
Turner	Thos		1843	Audr	Prop
Turner	D	D	1843	Audr	Prop

Last Name	First Name	Int	Year	County	Type
Turner	Smith		1824	Boon	Deed
Turner	John		1859	Reyn	DTL
Turner	Nathan		1837	Cass	DTL
Turner	Ezekiel		1836	Carr	Prop
Turner	Edward		1836	Carr	Prop
Turner	Ezekiel		1836	Carr	PrpPt
Turner	Edward		1836	Carr	PrpPt
Turner	Ezekial		1836	Carr	PrpPt
Turner	Jas		1840	Call	Poll
Turner	Martin	G	1840	Call	Poll
Turner	????		1845	Sali	Lisc
Turner	Joseph		1867	Reyn	DTL
Turner	T		1829	Char	DTL
Turner	William		1836	StC	Prop
Turner	Edward		1838	Audr	DTL
Turner	John		1838	Audr	DTL
Turner	Enich		1817	How	Prop
Turner	Phillip		1817	How	Prop
Turner	Smith		1817	How	Prop
Turner	Edward		1817	How	Prop
Turner	Charles	L	1827	Mari	Prop
Turner	Gabriel		1827	Mari	Prop
Turner (1)	James		1817	How	Prop
Turner (2)	James		1817	How	Prop
Turner (2)	John		1817	How	Prop
Turner (2)	James		1817	How	Prop
Turnham	Frederick		1836	Carr	Prop
Turnham	Frederick		1836	Carr	PrpPt
Turnley	Paul		1836	StC	Prop
Tusley	G	W	1838	Audr	DTL
Tussay	Jonathan		1834	Pett	Prop
Tutt	Henry		1840	Call	Poll
Tutt	John	H	1840	Call	Poll
Tuttle	Thomas	S	1840	Call	Poll
Twyman	Thomas		1836	Perr	Poll
Twyman	Leo		1836	StC	Prop
Ublady	Tomas		1780	StL	Mil
Umbrazio	Nora		1859	Reyn	DTL
Underhill	Andrew		1867	Reyn	DTL
Underwood	William		1840	Call	Poll
Upshaw	George	A	1836	StC	Prop
Uptergrod	George		1830	Ray	Prop

Last Name	First Name	Int	Year	County	Type
Uptergrove	George		1836	Carr	PrpPt
Uptingrove	George		1836	Carr	Prop
Uptingrove	George		1836	Carr	PrpPt
Ureuges, Jr	A		1844	Osag	Real
Vachard	Joseph		1818	StL	Real
Vachard	Joseph		1820	StL	Prop
Vaillant	Antoine		1818	StL	Real
Valentine	Jas		1867	Reyn	DTL
Valle	Widow		1805	Steg	Prop
Valle	Jn Baptiste		1805	Steg	Prop
Valois	Francois		1820	StL	Prop
Van Carop	Richard		1827	Mari	Prop
Van Cleave	Jesse		1840	Call	Poll
Van's Heirs	Cornelius		1836	Carr	PrpPt
Vanaman	Levi		1859	Reyn	DTL
Vanburkeler	Samuel		1836	StC	Prop
Vanburkeler	William		1836	StC	Prop
Vancamp	R		1837	Lew	DTL
Vance	John	P	1843	Audr	Prop
Vanderpool	John		1834	Call	DTL
Vanlandingham	Lewis		1827	Mari	Prop
Vanlandingham	Meshak		1827	Mari	Prop
Vanlaningham	Wilm		1837	Lew	DTL
Vanneter	John		1836	Carr	Prop
Vanneter	John		1836	Carr	PrpPt
Vanphal	H		1829	Char	DTL
Vanquinbuin	Charles	H	1836	StC	Prop
Vansant	Joshua		1836	Carr	Prop
Vansant	Joshua		1836	Carr	PrpPt
Vansperker	Charles		1836	StC	Prop
Vantricht	Abram		1840	Call	Poll
Vardiman	Jeremiah		1843	Audr	Prop
Varner	Henry		1836	Carr	Prop
Varner	Henry		1836	Carr	PrpPt
Varner	Henry		1830	Ray	Prop
Vasor	Regis		1791	StL	Span
Vasques	Wid Julie		1820	StL	Prop
Vasquez	Joseph		1818	StL	Real
Vasquez	J W Joseph		1818	StL	Real
Vasquez	Antoine		1818	StL	Real
Vasquez	Hypolete		1820	StL	Prop
Vasquez	Joseph		1820	StL	Prop

Last Name	First Name	Int	Year	County	Type
Vasquez	Antoine		1820	StL	Prop
Vasseur	Regis		1818	StL	Real
Vasseur	Regis		1820	StL	Prop
Vasseur	Joseph		1815	Ark	Prop
Vassuer	Victor		1810	Ark	Prop
Vaughn	Martin		1843	Audr	Prop
Vaughn	S		1837	Sali	DTL
Vaughn	Thomas		1830	How	DTL
Vaughn	Thomas		1817	How	Prop
Vaughn	Alexander		1844	Osag	Real
Vaughn	Enoch		1834	Call	DTL
Vaughn	Sterling		1829	NMad	DTL
Vaugin	Francis		1810	Ark	Prop
Vaugine	Francis		1815	Ark	Prop
Vawel	John		1839	John	DTL
Vazquez	Benito		1791	StL	Span
Veach	Joseph		1844	Osag	Real
Velmyer	Henry		1836	StC	Prop
Venable	Lewis	R	1843	Audr	Prop
Venables	John		1821	StC	Ct
Venables	Jno		1821	StC	CtS
Venibb	Lewis	R	1838	Audr	DTL
Vennibb	Lewis	R	1838	Audr	DTL
Venzan	Ant		1780	StL	Mil
Verdon	Joseph		1780	StL	Mil
Verdon	Josef		1791	StL	Span
Verdon	Madam		1791	StL	Span
Verdun	Nicolas		1818	StL	Real
Verille	Nathaniel		1830	Ray	Prop
Verio	Francisco		1780	StL	Mil
Vermyer	John		1836	StC	Prop
Vermyer	Stephen		1836	StC	Prop
Vessels	George	W	1836	Perr	Poll
Vessels	George		1836	Perr	Poll
Vesser	John		1822	Clay	Poll
Vesser	Samuel		1822	Clay	Poll
Vest	Jas		1843	Audr	Prop
Vest	Asbury		1840	Call	Poll
Vest	Little	B	1834	Craw	DTL
Vieman	Nicholas		1805	Steg	Prop
Vier	Garland	A	1840	Call	Poll
Vige	Josef		1791	StL	Span

Last Name	First Name	Int	Year	County	Type
Vigo	Francisco		1780	StL	Mil
Vilemont	Charles		1810	Ark	Prop
Villars	Francisco		1780	StL	Mil
Vincan	Joseph		1840	Call	Poll
Vincent	Frances		1838	Steg	DTL
Vincent	Antonio		1791	StL	Span
Vincent	George	S	1836	StC	Prop
Vincent	Jesse		1810	Ark	Prop
Vinzente	Charles		1838	Perr	Lisc
Vinzente	Charles		1838	Perr	Adv
Viont	Francis		1836	StC	Prop
Vior	Luis		1780	StL	Mil
Vivion	John		1840	Call	Poll
Vizonete	Andre		1780	StL	Mil
Vizonete	Pedro		1780	StL	Mil
Vizonete	Francisco		1780	StL	Mil
Vizonete	Baptiste		1780	StL	Mil
Voisard	John		1836	StC	Prop
Voisard	Joseph		1836	StC	Prop
Vonphul	Henry		1820	StL	Prop
Vosburg	John		1836	Carr	Prop
Vosburg	John		1836	Carr	PrpPt
Wack	Jno		1863	Jeff	Ass
Waddington	Josiah		1836	Carr	Prop
Waddington	Josiah		1836	Carr	PrpPt
Waddle	Henry		1820	StL	Prop
Wade's Heirs	John		1836	Carr	PrpPt
Wadley	John		1834	Call	DTL
Wadley	Francis		1834	Call	DTL
Wadly	John		1840	Call	Poll
Waggenor	J	H	1863	Jeff	Ass
Waggoner	Daniel		1840	Call	Poll
Waggoner	Stokeley		1840	Call	Poll
Wagner	Joseph		1867	Reyn	DTL
Wagoner	Thomas		1818	Lawr	DTL
Wahrendorff	Charles		1820	StL	Prop
Wainscot	Nathan		1840	Call	Poll
Walche	Augustus		1836	StC	Prop
Walkeep	R	D	1828	Boon	Lisc
Walker	Jesse	R	1836	Perr	Poll
Walker	William	A	1836	Perr	Poll
Walker	John	P	1838	Cass	DTL

Last Name	First Name	Int	Year	County	Type
Walker	Spencer		1836	Carr	Prop
Walker	Spencer		1836	Carr	PrpPt
Walker	Benjamin	F	1836	StC	Prop
Walker	Warren		1836	StC	Prop
Walker	Joel		1810	Ark	Prop
Walker	Dr		1820	StL	Prop
Walker	David	N	1820	StL	Prop
Walker	Jeremiah		1830	Ray	Prop
Walker	Joseph		1839	Lew	DTL
Walker	John	B	1829	NMad	DTL
Walker, Sr	Edward		1840	Call	Poll
Wallace	Robert		1826	Coop	DTL
Wallace	Robert		1827	Coop	DTL
Wallace	William		1840	Call	Poll
Wallace	Gordon	H	1836	StC	Prop
Wallace	Robert		1827	Coop	DTL
Wallace	Robert		1826	Coop	DTL
Wallace	John		1817	How	Prop
Wallace's Heirs	Joseph		1836	StC	Prop
Wallis	George		1828	Sali	DTL
Wallis	Perley		1815	Ark	Prop
Wallis	Martha		1837	Mill	DTL
Walls	Aaron		1836	Carr	PrpPt
Walsh	Esther		1820	StL	Prop
Walsh	Bart		1830	Ray	Prop
Walsinger	John		1836	Carr	Prop
Walsinger	John		1836	Carr	PrpPt
Walsinger	John		1836	Carr	PrpPt
Walter	Peter		1844	Osag	Real
Walter	John		1844	Osag	Real
Walter's Heirs	Edwards		1836	Carr	Prop
Walter's Heirs	Edwards		1836	Carr	PrpPt
Walton	Thompson		1834	Call	DTL
Wanrer	Jabez		1818	StL	Real
Wansly	John		1840	Call	Poll
Ward	Jacob		1836	Carr	Prop
Ward	Jacob		1836	Carr	PrpPt
Ward	Jas	R	1840	Call	Poll
Ward	John	M	1840	Call	Poll
Ward	Patrick		1840	Call	Poll
Ward	C	R	1838	Audr	DTL
Ward	Evan		1827	Mari	Prop

Last Name	First Name	Int	Year	County	Type
Ward	Patrick		1831	Cole	DTL
Ward	Seby		1838	Ripl	DTL
Warden	John		1817	How	Prop
Wardlaw	H	W	1836	StC	Prop
Wardlow	B		1836	StC	Prop
Wardlow	Lackham		1836	StC	Prop
Warner	Jude		1818	StL	Real
Warner	Jabez		1820	StL	Prop
Warnich	Charles		1838	John	DTL
Warnick	Bud		1838	John	DTL
Warnick (1)	Allen		1838	John	DTL
Warnick (2)	Allen		1838	John	DTL
Warren	William	W	1836	Carr	Prop
Warren	William	W	1836	Carr	PrpPt
Warren	Lot		1836	Carr	PrpPt
Warren's Heirs	Willaim		1830	Ray	Prop
Wash	Robert		1830	Howa	DTL
Wash	Robert		1830	Jeff	DTL
Wash	Robert		1830	Linc	DTL
Wash	Robert		1820	StL	Prop
Washington	William	H	1867	Reyn	DTL
Wasson	Thos	D	1859	Reyn	DTL
Wasson	????		1859	Reyn	DTL
Wat??n, Jr	Leandon		1859	Reyn	DTL
Waterman	Samuel		1836	Carr	Prop
Waterman	Luke		1836	Carr	Prop
Waterman	Samuel		1836	Carr	PrpPt
Waterman	Luke		1836	Carr	PrpPt
Waters	John		1836	Perr	Poll
Waters	David		1836	Perr	Poll
Waters	B		1827	Boon	Lisc
Wathen	R	M	1867	Reyn	DTL
Wather	Spencer		1836	Carr	PrpPt
Watkins	David		1836	Perr	Poll
Watkins	Thomas		1836	Carr	Prop
Watkins	Thomas		1836	Carr	PrpPt
Watkins	John		1830	Jeff	DTL
Watson	Robert	G	1822	NMad	Lisc
Watson	Thomas		1834	Pett	Prop
Watson	Mary		1836	StC	Prop
Watson	Samuel	S	1836	StC	Prop
Watson	James		1836	StC	Prop

Last Name	First Name	Int	Year	County	Type
Watson	A	D	1836	StC	Prop
Watson	Edward		1838	Ripl	DTL
Watson's Heirs	Archibald		1836	StC	Prop
Wattes	George	W	1836	StC	Prop
Wattes	Anthony	B	1836	StC	Prop
Watts	Littlebury		1843	Audr	Prop
Watts	John		1843	Audr	Prop
Watts	Stanford		1843	Audr	Prop
Watts	Joseph		1843	Audr	Prop
Watts	Roland	H	1843	Audr	Prop
Watts	Roland		1843	Audr	Prop
Watts	Standord		1843	Audr	Prop
Watts	Joseph		1843	Audr	Prop
Watts	Roling		1838	Audr	DTL
Watts	Littlebury		1838	Audr	DTL
Watts	Joseph		1838	Audr	DTL
Watts	Alexander		1838	Ripl	DTL
Way	Charles		1836	Carr	Prop
Way	Charles		1836	Carr	PrpPt
Way	Charles		1830	Ray	Prop
Wayn	A	H	1843	Audr	Prop
Wayne	Temple		1843	Audr	Prop
Wayne	William	L	1843	Audr	Prop
Wayne	William	L	1838	Audr	DTL
Wayne	A	H	1838	Audr	DTL
Wayne	Temple		1838	Audr	DTL
Wayner	John	W	1840	Call	Poll
Wear	D	H	1867	Reyn	DTL
Weare	John		1810	Ark	Prop
Wears	Phil	D	1863	Jeff	Ass
Wease	Jno		1863	Jeff	Ass
Weatherington	Alfred	G	1833	Lew	DTL
Weaver	John	J	1843	Audr	Prop
Weaver	Benjamin		1817	How	Prop
Webb	Townsend		1815	Ark	Prop
Webster	????		1820	StL	Prop
Weeden	Benjamin		1817	How	Prop
Weeden	Henry		1817	How	Prop
Weis	Elizabeth		1867	Reyn	DTL
Welch	Richard		1836	Perr	Poll
Welch	Edward		1836	Carr	Prop
Welch	David		1836	Carr	Prop

Last Name	First Name	Int	Year	County	Type
Welch	Edward		1836	Carr	PrpPt
Welch	David		1836	Carr	PrpPt
Welch	William		1867	Reyn	DTL
Welch	William		1867	Reyn	DTL
Welch	James	E	1823	Call	NRP
Welch	Margaret		1810	Ark	Prop
Welch	William	W	1838	Audr	DTL
Welch	James	E	1818	StL	Real
Welch	William		1817	How	Prop
Welde	Charles		1836	StC	Prop
Weldon	Benedict		1822	Clay	Poll
Wellborne	Curtis		1810	Ark	Prop
Wellborne	Elisha		1810	Ark	Prop
Welle's Heirs	Samuel		1836	StC	Prop
Welles	Samuel		1836	StC	Prop
Welles	Hiram		1836	StC	Prop
Wells	Peter	P	1831	Jack	DTL
Wells	Robert		1836	Carr	Prop
Wells	Robert		1836	Carr	PrpPt
Wells	Joseph	C	1840	Call	Poll
Wells	Robert	M	1840	Call	Poll
Wells	Samuel		1830	Linc	DTL
Wells	John		1810	Ark	Prop
Wells	Jacob		1810	Ark	Prop
Wells' Heirs	Samuel		1836	StC	Prop
Welot	Conrad		1836	StC	Prop
Welsy	Isarel	S	1867	Reyn	DTL
Welton	Lewis		1840	Call	Poll
Welton	Moses		1840	Call	Poll
Welton	Moses		1844	Osag	Real
Wensenvickles	Henry		1836	StC	Prop
Wenzel	Peter		1836	StC	Prop
Werick	Valentine		1867	Reyn	DTL
West	William	C	1843	Audr	Prop
West	Jeremiah		1843	Audr	Prop
West	W	C	1843	Audr	Prop
West	Nimrod	S	1836	Carr	Prop
West	Nimrod	S	1836	Carr	PrpPt
West	Branford		1827	Boon	Lisc
West	John		1840	Call	Poll
West	William	C	1838	Audr	DTL
West	James	H	1838	Audr	DTL

Last Name	First Name	Int	Year	County	Type
West	James	M	1839	Lew	DTL
West	Samuel		1844	Osag	Real
West	Hardin		1837	Mill	DTL
Westbanks	Levi		1836	Carr	PrpPt
Westman	Saml		1830	Coop	Ct
Westman	Saml		1830	Coop	CtS
Weston	Joel		1839	Lew	DTL
Westover	Isaac		1836	Perr	Poll
Westrick	John		1844	Osag	Real
Wetmore	John		1836	StC	Prop
Wetmore	Lorrence		1836	StC	Prop
Whaley	David	L	1840	Call	Poll
Whaley	William		1827	Mari	Prop
Whaley	Edward		1827	Mari	Prop
Whaley	James		1827	Mari	Prop
Wharton	S		1828	Boon	Lisc
Wheate	Martin		1829	NMad	DTL
Wheeler	Asa		1818	StL	Real
Wheeler	????		1820	StL	Prop
Wheeler	Solomon	B	1831	Craw	DTL
Whelenburger	Trenius		1836	Perr	Poll
Whelston	John		1867	Reyn	DTL
Wheredon	Thomas		1867	Reyn	DTL
Wheredon	Thomas		1867	Reyn	DTL
Wheredon	Thomas		1867	Reyn	DTL
Wherry	A	E	1843	Audr	Prop
Wherry	Macky		1820	StL	Prop
Wherry	D	B	1844	Osag	Real
Whetstone	Peter		1810	Ark	Prop
While	Joseph		1810	Ark	Prop
Whipple	William		1867	Reyn	DTL
Whipple	William		1867	Reyn	DTL
White	William		1843	Audr	Prop
White	Benedict		1818	Lawr	DTL
White	William		1836	Perr	Poll
White	I	M	1839	Wash	Lisc
White	David		1828	Boon	Lisc
White	Lewis		1840	Call	Poll
White	Daniel		1840	Call	Poll
White	John		1821	StC	CtS
White	James		1830	Howa	DTL
White	James		1867	Reyn	DTL

Last Name	First Name	Int	Year	County	Type
White	James		1867	Reyn	DTL
White	Jacob		1836	StC	Prop
White	William		1838	Audr	DTL
White	Isaac	W	1820	StL	Prop
White	John	B	1827	Mari	Prop
White	Edward		1827	Mari	Prop
White	Clement		1827	Mari	Prop
White	John		1827	Mari	Prop
White	Elisha		1815	Ark	Prop
White	Hezekiah		1836	Char	DTL
White (1)	Augustus		1836	Char	DTL
White (2)	Augustus		1836	Char	DTL
Whitehead	Armstead		1836	Carr	Prop
Whitehead	Armstead		1836	Carr	PrpPt
Whiteman	Martin	C	1836	Carr	Prop
Whiteman	Jonathan		1836	Carr	Prop
Whiteman	Martin	C	1836	Carr	PrpPt
Whiteman	Jonathan		1836	Carr	PrpPt
Whiteman	William		1839	Lew	DTL
Whitesides	James		1823	Call	NRP
Whitesides	James		1829	Char	DTL
Whiting	Jason		1826	Coop	DTL
Whiting	Jason		1826	Coop	DTL
Whitledge	John		1836	Perr	Poll
Whitley	Solomon		1821	StC	CtS
Whitlock	Tarlton		1817	How	Prop
Whitney	Abijah		1830	Ray	Prop
Whitney's Heirs	Abijah		1836	Carr	Prop
Whitney's Heirs	Abijah		1836	Carr	PrpPt
Whittle	John	S	1836	StC	Prop
Whittlesey	Joseph		1836	Carr	Prop
Whittlesey	Joseph		1836	Carr	PrpPt
Wickham	Robert		1836	Carr	Prop
Wickham	Robert		1836	Carr	PrpPt
Wicks	Samuel		1840	Call	Poll
Wideman	Thomas	H	1863	Jeff	Ass
Wideman	????		1863	Jeff	Ass
Wideman, Jr	J	L	1863	Jeff	Ass
Widhite	Fielding		1827	Boon	Lisc
Widow Juana	Free Negro		1791	StL	Span
Wiegle	Peter		1867	Reyn	DTL
Wiett	Reuben	C	1836	StC	Prop

231

Last Name	First Name	Int	Year	County	Type
Wiggins	Stephen	R	1823	Call	NRP
Wikey	George		1830	Ray	Prop
Wilbar	Charles		1830	Ray	Prop
Wilber	Charles		1836	Carr	PrtPt
Wilcox	Daniel		1836	Carr	Prop
Wilcox	Daniel		1836	Carr	PrpPt
Wilcox	Daniel	P	1828	Boon	Lisc
Wildes	Michael		1836	Carr	Prop
Wildes	Michael		1836	Carr	PrpPt
Wileby	John		1836	Carr	PrpPt
Wiley	Jno	J	1863	Jeff	Ass
Wilfrey	Joseph		1843	Audr	Prop
Wilfrey	Jas		1843	Audr	Prop
Wilhite	F		1828	Boon	Lisc
Wilhors	Drury	C	1836	Carr	PrpPt
Wilkait	Milton		1844	Osag	Real
Wilkerson	Thomas		1836	Perr	Poll
Wilkerson	James		1867	Reyn	DTL
Wilkey	George		1836	Carr	Prop
Wilkey	George		1836	Carr	PrpPt
Wilkins	Fannihile		1828	Sali	DTL
Wilkinson	Joseph		1836	Perr	Poll
Wilkinson	B	B	1838	Audr	DTL
Wilks	Atha		1836	Carr	PrpPt
Willbram	August		1844	Osag	Real
William	Anderson		1836	Carr	Prop
William	Anderson		1836	Carr	PrpPt
William	David		1836	Carr	PrpPt
William	William	S	1840	Call	Poll
William	Richards		1840	Call	Poll
William	Joseph		1840	Call	Poll
William	L		1867	Reyn	DTL
Williams	Grand		1843	Audr	Prop
Williams	Gideon	P	1843	Audr	Prop
Williams	Calup	V	1843	Audr	Prop
Williams	Benjamin		1836	Perr	Poll
Williams	John		1836	Carr	PrpPt
Williams	John		1836	Carr	Prop
Williams	William		1836	Carr	Prop
Williams	James		1836	Carr	Prop
Williams	George		1836	Carr	Prop
Williams	John		1836	Carr	PrpPt

Last Name	First Name	Int	Year	County	Type
Williams	William		1836	Carr	PrpPt
Williams	James		1836	Carr	PrpPt
Williams	George		1836	Carr	PrpPt
Williams	Permenios		1836	Carr	PrpPt
Williams	John		1827	Boon	Lisc
Williams	A		1828	Boon	Lisc
Williams	Saml		1840	Call	Poll
Williams	Bird		1840	Call	Poll
Williams	Daniel		1840	Call	Poll
Williams	John		1840	Call	Poll
Williams	George		1840	Call	Poll
Williams	Wm		1840	Call	Poll
Williams	Peyton		1840	Call	Poll
Williams	Richard		1840	Call	Poll
Williams	Marcus		1830	Coop	Ct
Williams	Justainian		1830	Coop	Ct
Williams	Ezekiel		1830	Coop	Ct
Williams	John		1830	Coop	Ct
Williams	Marcus		1830	Coop	CtS
Williams	Henry	T	1830	Howa	DTL
Williams	Miles		1838	John	DTL
Williams	Wilson		1863	Jeff	Ass
Williams	A	S	1863	Jeff	Ass
Williams	Dudley		1867	Reyn	DTL
Williams	E	A	1867	Reyn	DTL
Williams	Henry	T	1829	Char	DTL
Williams	Parker		1829	Char	DTL
Williams	Thomas	S	1836	StC	Prop
Williams	I	H	1838	Audr	DTL
Williams	Colet	V	1838	Audr	DTL
Williams	Caleb		1838	Audr	DTL
Williams	G	P	1838	Audr	DTL
Williams	W	L	1838	Audr	DTL
Williams	F		1818	StL	Real
Williams	John	B	1837	Lew	DTL
Williams	Francis		1820	StL	Prop
Williams	Ezekiel		1817	How	Prop
Williams	Coledon		1817	How	Prop
Williams	Henry	T	1830	Ray	Prop
Williams	John		1830	Ray	Prop
Williams	John		1815	Ark	Prop
Williams	John	P	1839	Lew	DTL

Last Name	First Name	Int	Year	County	Type
Williams	J	W	1839	Lew	DTL
Williams	James		1822	Clay	Poll
Williams	William	D	1822	Clay	Poll
Williams	James		1835	Barr	DTL
Williams	Hiram		1835	Barr	DTL
Williams	James	H	1844	Osag	Real
Williams	Joseph		1844	Osag	Real
Williams	Richard		1834	Lew	DTL
Williams' Heors	Jacob	D	1836	StC	Prop
Williams. Sr	John		1830	Jeff	DTL
Willingham	Wm		1843	Audr	Prop
Willingham	Isham	I	1843	Audr	Prop
Willingham	Delony		1843	Audr	Prop
Willingham	John		1843	Audr	Prop
Willingham	George		1843	Audr	Prop
Willingham	John		1843	Audr	Prop
Willingham	John		1827	Boon	Lisc
Willingham	Isam		1838	Audr	DTL
Willingham	William		1838	Audr	DTL
Willingham	John		1838	Audr	DTL
Willingham, Sr	Isham		1843	Audr	Prop
Willis	William		1836	Carr	Prop
Willis	William		1836	Carr	PrpPt
Willis	Durret		1828	Boon	Lisc
Willis	Robert		1867	Reyn	DTL
Willis	Joseph		1830	Ray	Prop
Willis	Hawkins		1834	Call	DTL
Wills	Joseph		1836	Carr	Prop
Wills	Joseph		1836	Carr	PrpPt
Wills	Benoni		1830	Call	DTL
Willson	Nicholas		1836	StC	Prop
Willson	Andrew	A	1836	StC	Prop
Wilson	Rueben		1843	Audr	Prop
Wilson	John	H	1843	Audr	Prop
Wilson	John		1843	Audr	Prop
Wilson	David		1843	Audr	Prop
Wilson	George	W	1843	Audr	Prop
Wilson	Ann		1819	Steg	Lic
Wilson	Thomas		1859	Reyn	DTL
Wilson	Robert		1836	Perr	Poll
Wilson	Moses		1836	Carr	PrpPt
Wilson	William		1836	Carr	Prop

Last Name	First Name	Int	Year	County	Type
Wilson	Giles		1836	Carr	Prop
Wilson	Giles		1836	Carr	PrpPt
Wilson	William		1836	Carr	PrpPt
Wilson	Eli	B	1840	Call	Poll
Wilson	Andrew		1821	StC	CtS
Wilson	William	D	1830	Coop	Ct
Wilson	William	D	1830	Coop	CtS
Wilson	William	D	1830	Coop	CtS
Wilson	Samuel		1838	John	DTL
Wilson	Robt		1863	Jeff	Ass
Wilson	Aquilla		1863	Jeff	Ass
Wilson	Jno		1863	Jeff	Ass
Wilson	Allen		1863	Jeff	Ass
Wilson	Hugh	B	1867	Reyn	DTL
Wilson	Hugh	B	1867	Reyn	DTL
Wilson	Hugh	B	1867	Reyn	DTL
Wilson	C		1867	Reyn	DTL
Wilson	W	A	1867	Reyn	DTL
Wilson	J	F	1867	Reyn	DTL
Wilson	Philip		1867	Reyn	DTL
Wilson	John		1867	Reyn	DTL
Wilson	Charles		1867	Reyn	DTL
Wilson	David		1838	Audr	DTL
Wilson	Robert		1820	StL	Prop
Wilson	Joseph	H	1839	Lew	DTL
Wilson	John		1822	Clay	Poll
Wilson	James		1835	Barr	DTL
Wilson	Josiah		1838	Ripl	DTL
Winacot	Richard		1817	How	Prop
Winfield	William		1836	Perr	Poll
Winkle	Edward		1867	Reyn	DTL
Winkler	????		1859	Reyn	DTL
Winn	Thomas	R	1840	Call	Poll
Winsor	A	S P	1840	Call	Poll
Winthrop	????		1810	Ark	Prop
Winul	Douglas	J	1840	Call	Poll
Wirt	William		1836	Carr	Prop
Wirt	William		1836	Carr	PrpPt
Wisdom	Francis		1843	Audr	Prop
Wisdom	Jas	M	1843	Audr	Prop
Wisdom	Brenaby		1827	Boon	Lisc
Wise	Jonathan		1863	Jeff	Ass

Last Name	First Name	Int	Year	County	Type
Wise	Joseph		1836	StC	Prop
Wiseman	Nancy		1844	Osag	Real
Wiseman	T		1844	Osag	Real
Wisley	Joel		1840	Call	Poll
Woff	John	T	1834	Lew	DTL
Wolcup	Robert		1817	How	Prop
Wolf	John		1836	StC	Prop
Wolfskill	William		1817	How	Prop
Wolfskill	Joseph		1817	How	Prop
Wood	John	L	1836	Carr	Prop
Wood	John	L	1836	Carr	PrpPt
Wood	James		1827	Boon	Lisc
Wood	Anna		1828	Boon	Lisc
Wood	M		1828	Boon	Lisc
Wood	Thomas	E	1840	Call	Poll
Wood	William		1867	Reyn	DTL
Wood	O	J	1867	Reyn	DTL
Wood	Caleb		1829	Mari	DTL
Wood	Alexander		1817	How	Prop
Wood	Jesse		1817	How	Prop
Wood	Jonathan		1830	Ray	Prop
Wood	Jesse		1843	Char	DTL
Wood	Jas		1834	Craw	DTL
Wood's Heirs	Thomas	L	1836	StC	Prop
Woodes	Sydney	S	1836	StC	Prop
Wooding	Timothy		1843	Audr	Prop
Woodle	Jonathan		1836	Carr	Prop
Woodle	Jonathan		1836	Carr	PrpPt
Woods	William		1843	Audr	Prop
Woods	David	H	1843	Audr	Prop
Woods	Michael		1824	Boon	Deed
Woods	Jas		1840	Call	Poll
Woods	Zadoc		1821	StC	Ct
Woods	James		1821	StC	CtS
Woods	Simon		1830	Jeff	DTL
Woods	John	P	1867	Reyn	DTL
Woods	William		1838	Audr	DTL
Woods	P	H	1838	Audr	DTL
Woods	Archibald		1817	How	Prop
Woods	Adam		1817	How	Prop
Woods	Anderson		1817	How	Prop
Woods	Patrick		1817	How	Prop

Last Name	First Name	Int	Year	County	Type
Woods	T J	L G	1837	Mill	DTL
Woodson	David		1843	Audr	Prop
Woodson	George		1839	Lew	DTL
Woody	Davis	S	1844	Osag	Real
Woody	John		1844	Osag	Real
Woolbass' Heirs	Lewis		1836	Carr	PrpPt
Wooley	C	S	1859	Reyn	DTL
Woolf	Christian		1836	StC	Prop
Woolf	Anthony		1815	Ark	Prop
Woolfolk	Z	T	1836	StC	Prop
Woolfolk	R	A	1836	StC	Prop
Woolford	Wid Ann		1820	StL	Prop
Woolfork	Robert	B	1836	StC	Prop
Woolsey	Park	H	1867	Reyn	DTL
Woolsey	Thomas		1810	Ark	Prop
Woolton's Heirs	William		1836	StC	Prop
Wooten	William		1821	StC	Ct
Word	Joseph		1836	StC	Prop
World	Robert		1839	Lew	DTL
Wray	B		1836	StC	Prop
Wray	John	C	1836	StC	Prop
Wright	John		1836	Carr	PrpPt
Wright	John	E	1836	Carr	Prop
Wright	Martin		1836	Carr	Prop
Wright	John	E	1836	Carr	PrpPt
Wright	Martin		1836	Carr	PrpPt
Wright	John		1836	Carr	PrpPt
Wright	James		1836	Carr	PrpPt
Wright	Oliver		1840	Call	Poll
Wright	Ignatius		1840	Call	Poll
Wright	Alexander		1840	Call	Poll
Wright	Libourn		1830	Coop	CtS
Wright	H		1838	Audr	DTL
Wright	M	D	1839	Lew	DTL
Writesman	Peter		1822	Clay	Poll
Wyatt	William		1836	Carr	Prop
Wyatt	William		1836	Carr	PrpPt
Wyatt	John	S	1836	StC	Prop
Yager	????		1836	StC	Prop
Yancy	Thomas		1840	Call	Poll
Yarberry	????		1810	Ark	Prop
Yardley	George		1836	StC	Prop

Last Name	First Name	Int	Year	County	Type
Yardley	Joseph		1836	StC	Prop
Yardley	William		1836	StC	Prop
Yardley	Frederick		1836	StC	Prop
Yarger	Jacob		1867	Reyn	DTL
Yarlington	H		1867	Reyn	DTL
Yarnel	Stephen		1836	StC	Prop
Yarnel	Elizabeth		1836	StC	Prop
Yarnel's Heirs	John		1836	StC	Prop
Yarnold	Amos		1836	StC	Prop
Yates	Elias		1863	Jeff	Ass
Yates	W	V S	1867	Reyn	DTL
Yeager	Jacob		1867	Reyn	DTL
Yews	John	D	1810	Ark	Prop
Yoakum	Barnet		1844	Osag	Real
Yoisti	Wid Theotiste		1820	StL	Prop
Yokum	Riley		1836	StC	Prop
Yong	Joseph	H	1867	Reyn	DTL
Yosty	Emilian		1791	StL	Span
Young	Mary		1843	Audr	Prop
Young	Thomas		1843	Audr	Prop
Young	William		1843	Audr	Prop
Young	John		1843	Audr	Prop
Young	B		1843	Audr	Prop
Young	Rufus		1837	Cass	DTL
Young	Levi		1836	Carr	Prop
Young	George		1836	Carr	Prop
Young	George		1836	Carr	PrpPt
Young	J	P	1840	Call	Poll
Young	William		1830	Coop	Ct
Young	Clinton		1834	Pett	Prop
Young	Hiram		1836	StC	Prop
Young	Benjamin		1836	StC	Prop
Young	Oglesbe		1836	StC	Prop
Young	Emilie		1836	StC	Prop
Young	John		1838	Audr	DTL
Young	George		1820	StL	Prop
Young	Benjamin		1817	How	Prop
Young	George		1838	Ripl	DTL
Young	John		1838	Ripl	DTL
Young	John		1838	Ripl	DTL
Young	William		1834	Call	DTL
Young	Louis		1834	Call	DTL

Last Name	First Name	Int	Year	County	Type
Young	Levi		1836	Carr	PrpPt
Yount	James		1859	Reyn	DTL
Yount	David		1840	Call	Poll
Yount	Joseph		1840	Call	Poll
Yows	John		1817	How	Prop
Zaneyain	Henry		1844	Osag	Real
Zarlington	H		1867	Reyn	DTL
Zeddies	William		1836	StC	Prop
Zedediah (?)			1867	Reyn	DTL
Zeigler	Sebastian		1859	Reyn	DTL
Zeigler	John		1863	Jeff	Ass
Zieglas	C	C	1859	Reyn	DTL
Zumalt	Andrew		1836	StC	Prop
Zumalt	Samuel		1836	StC	Prop
Zumalt	Jonathan		1836	StC	Prop
Zumalt	Solomon		1836	StC	Prop
Zumalt	Gabriel		1836	StC	Prop
Zumalt	John		1836	StC	Prop
Zumalt	Jacob		1836	StC	Prop
Zumalt	William		1836	StC	Prop
Zumalt's Heirs	George		1836	StC	Prop
Zumwalt	Abraham		1840	Call	Poll
Zumwalt	Anthony		1840	Call	Poll
Zumwalt	Frederick		1840	Call	Poll
Zumwalt	David		1840	Call	Poll
Zumwalt	Isaac		1840	Call	Poll
Zumwalt	David		1823	Call	NRP
Zumwalt	Abram		1834	Call	DTL